END-USER LICENSE AGREEMENT FOR OFFICIAL MICROSO

**PLEASE READ THIS END-USER LICENSE AGREEMENT ("EUI
USING OR INSTALLING THE SOFTWARE THAT ACCOMPAN
CONTENT"), YOU AGREE TO THE TERMS OF THIS EULA. IF ⌐ ᴜᴊᴇ ᴛʜᴇ LICENSED
CONTENT.**

---

1.   **GENERAL.** This EULA is a legal agreement between you (either an individual or a single entity) and Microsoft Corporation ("Microsoft"). This EULA governs the Licensed Content, which includes computer software (including online and electronic documentation), training materials, and any other associated media and printed materials. This EULA applies to updates, supplements, add-on components, and Internet-based services components of the Licensed Content that Microsoft may provide or make available to you unless Microsoft provides other terms with the update, supplement, add-on component, or Internet-based services component. Microsoft reserves the right to discontinue any Internet-based services provided to you or made available to you through the use of the Licensed Content. This EULA also governs any product support services relating to the Licensed Content except as may be included in another agreement between you and Microsoft. An amendment or addendum to this EULA may accompany the Licensed Content.

2.   **GENERAL GRANT OF LICENSE.** Microsoft grants you the following rights, conditioned on your compliance with all the terms and conditions of this EULA. Microsoft grants you a limited, non-exclusive, royalty-free license to install and use the Licensed Content solely in conjunction with your participation as a student in an Authorized Training Session (as defined below). You may install and use one copy of the software on a single computer, device, workstation, terminal, or other digital electronic or analog device ("Device"). You may make a second copy of the software and install it on a portable Device for the exclusive use of the person who is the primary user of the first copy of the software. A license for the software may not be shared for use by multiple end users. An "Authorized Training Session" means a training session conducted at a Microsoft Certified Technical Education Center, an IT Academy, via a Microsoft Certified Partner, or such other entity as Microsoft may designate from time to time in writing, by a Microsoft Certified Trainer (for more information on these entities, please visit www.microsoft.com). WITHOUT LIMITING THE FOREGOING, COPYING OR REPRODUCTION OF THE LICENSED CONTENT TO ANY SERVER OR LOCATION FOR FURTHER REPRODUCTION OR REDISTRIBUTION IS EXPRESSLY PROHIBITED.

3.   **DESCRIPTION OF OTHER RIGHTS AND LICENSE LIMITATIONS**

    3.1   *Use of Documentation and Printed Training Materials.*

        3.1.1   The documents and related graphics included in the Licensed Content may include technical inaccuracies or typographical errors. Changes are periodically made to the content. Microsoft may make improvements and/or changes in any of the components of the Licensed Content at any time without notice. The names of companies, products, people, characters and/or data mentioned in the Licensed Content may be fictitious and are in no way intended to represent any real individual, company, product or event, unless otherwise noted.

        3.1.2   Microsoft grants you the right to reproduce portions of documents (such as student workbooks, white papers, press releases, datasheets and FAQs) (the "Documents") provided with the Licensed Content. You may not print any book (either electronic or print version) in its entirety. If you choose to reproduce Documents, you agree that: (a) use of such printed Documents will be solely in conjunction with your personal training use; (b) the Documents will not republished or posted on any network computer or broadcast in any media; (c) any reproduction will include either the Document's original copyright notice or a copyright notice to Microsoft's benefit substantially in the format provided below; and (d) to comply with all terms and conditions of this EULA. In addition, no modifications may made to any Document.

        Form of Notice:

        Copyright undefined.

        © 2004. Reprinted with permission by Microsoft Corporation. All rights reserved.

        Microsoft and Windows are either registered trademarks or trademarks of Microsoft Corporation in the US and/or other countries. Other product and company names mentioned herein may be the trademarks of their respective owners.

    3.2   *Use of Media Elements.* The Licensed Content may include certain photographs, clip art, animations, sounds, music, and video clips (together "Media Elements"). You may not modify these Media Elements.

    3.3   *Use of Sample Code.* In the event that the Licensed Content include sample source code ("Sample Code"), Microsoft grants you a limited, non-exclusive, royalty-free license to use, copy and modify the Sample Code; if you elect to exercise the foregoing rights, you agree to comply with all other terms and conditions of this EULA, including without limitation Sections 3.4, 3.5, and 6.

    3.4   *Permitted Modifications.* In the event that you exercise any rights provided under this EULA to create modifications of the Licensed Content, you agree that any such modifications: (a) will not be used for providing training where a fee is charged in public or private classes; (b) indemnify, hold harmless, and defend Microsoft from and against any claims or lawsuits, including attorneys' fees, which arise from or result from your use of any modified version of the Licensed Content; and (c) not to transfer or assign any rights to any modified version of the Licensed Content to any third party without the express written permission of Microsoft.

3.5   *Reproduction/Redistribution Licensed Content.* Except as expressly provided in this EULA, you may not reproduce or distribute the Licensed Content or any portion thereof (including any permitted modifications) to any third parties without the express written permission of Microsoft.

4.   **RESERVATION OF RIGHTS AND OWNERSHIP.** Microsoft reserves all rights not expressly granted to you in this EULA. The Licensed Content is protected by copyright and other intellectual property laws and treaties. Microsoft or its suppliers own the title, copyright, and other intellectual property rights in the Licensed Content. You may not remove or obscure any copyright, trademark or patent notices that appear on the Licensed Content, or any components thereof, as delivered to you. **The Licensed Content is licensed, not sold.**

5.   **LIMITATIONS ON REVERSE ENGINEERING, DECOMPILATION, AND DISASSEMBLY.** You may not reverse engineer, decompile, or disassemble the Software or Media Elements, except and only to the extent that such activity is expressly permitted by applicable law notwithstanding this limitation.

6.   **LIMITATIONS ON SALE, RENTAL, ETC. AND CERTAIN ASSIGNMENTS.** You may not provide commercial hosting services with, sell, rent, lease, lend, sublicense, or assign copies of the Licensed Content, or any portion thereof (including any permitted modifications thereof) on a stand-alone basis or as part of any collection, product or service.

7.   **CONSENT TO USE OF DATA.** You agree that Microsoft and its affiliates may collect and use technical information gathered as part of the product support services provided to you, if any, related to the Licensed Content. Microsoft may use this information solely to improve our products or to provide customized services or technologies to you and will not disclose this information in a form that personally identifies you.

8.   **LINKS TO THIRD PARTY SITES.** You may link to third party sites through the use of the Licensed Content. The third party sites are not under the control of Microsoft, and Microsoft is not responsible for the contents of any third party sites, any links contained in third party sites, or any changes or updates to third party sites. Microsoft is not responsible for webcasting or any other form of transmission received from any third party sites. Microsoft is providing these links to third party sites to you only as a convenience, and the inclusion of any link does not imply an endorsement by Microsoft of the third party site.

9.   **ADDITIONAL LICENSED CONTENT/SERVICES.** This EULA applies to updates, supplements, add-on components, or Internet-based services components, of the Licensed Content that Microsoft may provide to you or make available to you after the date you obtain your initial copy of the Licensed Content, unless we provide other terms along with the update, supplement, add-on component, or Internet-based services component. Microsoft reserves the right to discontinue any Internet-based services provided to you or made available to you through the use of the Licensed Content.

10.   **U.S. GOVERNMENT LICENSE RIGHTS**. All software provided to the U.S. Government pursuant to solicitations issued on or after December 1, 1995 is provided with the commercial license rights and restrictions described elsewhere herein. All software provided to the U.S. Government pursuant to solicitations issued prior to December 1, 1995 is provided with "Restricted Rights" as provided for in FAR, 48 CFR 52.227-14 (JUNE 1987) or DFAR, 48 CFR 252.227-7013 (OCT 1988), as applicable.

11.   **EXPORT RESTRICTIONS**. You acknowledge that the Licensed Content is subject to U.S. export jurisdiction. You agree to comply with all applicable international and national laws that apply to the Licensed Content, including the U.S. Export Administration Regulations, as well as end-user, end-use, and destination restrictions issued by U.S. and other governments. For additional information see <http://www.microsoft.com/exporting/>.

12.   **TRANSFER.** The initial user of the Licensed Content may make a one-time permanent transfer of this EULA and Licensed Content to another end user, provided the initial user retains no copies of the Licensed Content. The transfer may not be an indirect transfer, such as a consignment. Prior to the transfer, the end user receiving the Licensed Content must agree to all the EULA terms.

13.   **"NOT FOR RESALE" LICENSED CONTENT.** Licensed Content identified as "Not For Resale" or "NFR," may not be sold or otherwise transferred for value, or used for any purpose other than demonstration, test or evaluation.

14.   **TERMINATION.** Without prejudice to any other rights, Microsoft may terminate this EULA if you fail to comply with the terms and conditions of this EULA. In such event, you must destroy all copies of the Licensed Content and all of its component parts.

15.   **DISCLAIMER OF WARRANTIES.** **TO THE MAXIMUM EXTENT PERMITTED BY APPLICABLE LAW, MICROSOFT AND ITS SUPPLIERS PROVIDE THE LICENSED CONTENT AND SUPPORT SERVICES (IF ANY) *AS IS AND WITH ALL FAULTS,* AND MICROSOFT AND ITS SUPPLIERS HEREBY DISCLAIM ALL OTHER WARRANTIES AND CONDITIONS, WHETHER EXPRESS, IMPLIED OR STATUTORY, INCLUDING, BUT NOT LIMITED TO, ANY (IF ANY) IMPLIED WARRANTIES, DUTIES OR CONDITIONS OF MERCHANTABILITY, OF FITNESS FOR A PARTICULAR PURPOSE, OF RELIABILITY OR AVAILABILITY, OF ACCURACY OR COMPLETENESS OF RESPONSES, OF RESULTS, OF WORKMANLIKE EFFORT, OF LACK OF VIRUSES, AND OF LACK OF NEGLIGENCE, ALL WITH REGARD TO THE LICENSED CONTENT, AND THE PROVISION OF OR FAILURE TO PROVIDE SUPPORT OR OTHER SERVICES, INFORMATION, SOFTWARE, AND RELATED CONTENT THROUGH THE LICENSED CONTENT, OR OTHERWISE ARISING OUT OF THE USE OF THE LICENSED CONTENT. ALSO, THERE IS NO WARRANTY OR CONDITION OF TITLE, QUIET ENJOYMENT, QUIET POSSESSION, CORRESPONDENCE TO DESCRIPTION OR NON-INFRINGEMENT WITH REGARD TO THE LICENSED CONTENT. THE ENTIRE RISK AS TO THE QUALITY, OR ARISING OUT OF THE USE OR PERFORMANCE OF THE LICENSED CONTENT, AND ANY SUPPORT SERVICES, REMAINS WITH YOU.**

16.   **EXCLUSION OF INCIDENTAL, CONSEQUENTIAL AND CERTAIN OTHER DAMAGES.** **TO THE MAXIMUM EXTENT PERMITTED BY APPLICABLE LAW, IN NO EVENT SHALL MICROSOFT OR ITS SUPPLIERS BE LIABLE FOR ANY SPECIAL, INCIDENTAL, PUNITIVE, INDIRECT, OR CONSEQUENTIAL DAMAGES WHATSOEVER (INCLUDING, BUT NOT**

LIMITED TO, DAMAGES FOR LOSS OF PROFITS OR CONFIDENTIAL OR OTHER INFORMATION, FOR BUSINESS INTERRUPTION, FOR PERSONAL INJURY, FOR LOSS OF PRIVACY, FOR FAILURE TO MEET ANY DUTY INCLUDING OF GOOD FAITH OR OF REASONABLE CARE, FOR NEGLIGENCE, AND FOR ANY OTHER PECUNIARY OR OTHER LOSS WHATSOEVER) ARISING OUT OF OR IN ANY WAY RELATED TO THE USE OF OR INABILITY TO USE THE LICENSED CONTENT, THE PROVISION OF OR FAILURE TO PROVIDE SUPPORT OR OTHER SERVICES, INFORMATION, SOFTWARE, AND RELATED CONTENT THROUGH THE LICENSED CONTENT, OR OTHERWISE ARISING OUT OF THE USE OF THE LICENSED CONTENT, OR OTHERWISE UNDER OR IN CONNECTION WITH ANY PROVISION OF THIS EULA, EVEN IN THE EVENT OF THE FAULT, TORT (INCLUDING NEGLIGENCE), MISREPRESENTATION, STRICT LIABILITY, BREACH OF CONTRACT OR BREACH OF WARRANTY OF MICROSOFT OR ANY SUPPLIER, AND EVEN IF MICROSOFT OR ANY SUPPLIER HAS BEEN ADVISED OF THE POSSIBILITY OF SUCH DAMAGES. BECAUSE SOME STATES/JURISDICTIONS DO NOT ALLOW THE EXCLUSION OR LIMITATION OF LIABILITY FOR CONSEQUENTIAL OR INCIDENTAL DAMAGES, THE ABOVE LIMITATION MAY NOT APPLY TO YOU.

17. <u>LIMITATION OF LIABILITY AND REMEDIES</u>. NOTWITHSTANDING ANY DAMAGES THAT YOU MIGHT INCUR FOR ANY REASON WHATSOEVER (INCLUDING, WITHOUT LIMITATION, ALL DAMAGES REFERENCED HEREIN AND ALL DIRECT OR GENERAL DAMAGES IN CONTRACT OR ANYTHING ELSE), THE ENTIRE LIABILITY OF MICROSOFT AND ANY OF ITS SUPPLIERS UNDER ANY PROVISION OF THIS EULA AND YOUR EXCLUSIVE REMEDY HEREUNDER SHALL BE LIMITED TO THE GREATER OF THE ACTUAL DAMAGES YOU INCUR IN REASONABLE RELIANCE ON THE LICENSED CONTENT UP TO THE AMOUNT ACTUALLY PAID BY YOU FOR THE LICENSED CONTENT OR US$5.00. THE FOREGOING LIMITATIONS, EXCLUSIONS AND DISCLAIMERS SHALL APPLY TO THE MAXIMUM EXTENT PERMITTED BY APPLICABLE LAW, EVEN IF ANY REMEDY FAILS ITS ESSENTIAL PURPOSE.

18. **APPLICABLE LAW.** If you acquired this Licensed Content in the United States, this EULA is governed by the laws of the State of Washington. If you acquired this Licensed Content in Canada, unless expressly prohibited by local law, this EULA is governed by the laws in force in the Province of Ontario, Canada; and, in respect of any dispute which may arise hereunder, you consent to the jurisdiction of the federal and provincial courts sitting in Toronto, Ontario. If you acquired this Licensed Content in the European Union, Iceland, Norway, or Switzerland, then local law applies. If you acquired this Licensed Content in any other country, then local law may apply.

19. **ENTIRE AGREEMENT; SEVERABILITY.** This EULA (including any addendum or amendment to this EULA which is included with the Licensed Content) are the entire agreement between you and Microsoft relating to the Licensed Content and the support services (if any) and they supersede all prior or contemporaneous oral or written communications, proposals and representations with respect to the Licensed Content or any other subject matter covered by this EULA. To the extent the terms of any Microsoft policies or programs for support services conflict with the terms of this EULA, the terms of this EULA shall control. If any provision of this EULA is held to be void, invalid, unenforceable or illegal, the other provisions shall continue in full force and effect.

Should you have any questions concerning this EULA, or if you desire to contact Microsoft for any reason, please use the address information enclosed in this Licensed Content to contact the Microsoft subsidiary serving your country or visit Microsoft on the World Wide Web at http://www.microsoft.com.

Si vous avez acquis votre Contenu Sous Licence Microsoft au CANADA :

DÉNI DE GARANTIES. Dans la mesure maximale permise par les lois applicables, le Contenu Sous Licence et les services de soutien technique (le cas échéant) sont fournis *TELS QUELS ET AVEC TOUS LES DÉFAUTS* par Microsoft et ses fournisseurs, lesquels par les présentes dénient toutes autres garanties et conditions expresses, implicites ou en vertu de la loi, notamment, mais sans limitation, (le cas échéant) les garanties, devoirs ou conditions implicites de qualité marchande, d'adaptation à une fin usage particulière, de fiabilité ou de disponibilité, d'exactitude ou d'exhaustivité des réponses, des résultats, des efforts déployés selon les règles de l'art, d'absence de virus et d'absence de négligence, le tout à l'égard du Contenu Sous Licence et de la prestation des services de soutien technique ou de l'omission de la 'une telle prestation des services de soutien technique ou à l'égard de la fourniture ou de l'omission de la fourniture de tous autres services, renseignements, Contenus Sous Licence, et contenu qui s'y rapporte grâce au Contenu Sous Licence ou provenant autrement de l'utilisation du Contenu Sous Licence. PAR AILLEURS, IL N'Y A AUCUNE GARANTIE OU CONDITION QUANT AU TITRE DE PROPRIÉTÉ, À LA JOUISSANCE OU LA POSSESSION PAISIBLE, À LA CONCORDANCE À UNE DESCRIPTION NI QUANT À UNE ABSENCE DE CONTREFAÇON CONCERNANT LE CONTENU SOUS LICENCE.

<u>EXCLUSION DES DOMMAGES ACCESSOIRES, INDIRECTS ET DE CERTAINS AUTRES DOMMAGES.</u> DANS LA MESURE MAXIMALE PERMISE PAR LES LOIS APPLICABLES, EN AUCUN CAS MICROSOFT OU SES FOURNISSEURS NE SERONT RESPONSABLES DES DOMMAGES SPÉCIAUX, CONSÉCUTIFS, ACCESSOIRES OU INDIRECTS DE QUELQUE NATURE QUE CE SOIT (NOTAMMENT, LES DOMMAGES À L'ÉGARD DU MANQUE À GAGNER OU DE LA DIVULGATION DE RENSEIGNEMENTS CONFIDENTIELS OU AUTRES, DE LA PERTE D'EXPLOITATION, DE BLESSURES CORPORELLES, DE LA VIOLATION DE LA VIE PRIVÉE, DE L'OMISSION DE REMPLIR TOUT DEVOIR, Y COMPRIS D'AGIR DE BONNE FOI OU D'EXERCER UN SOIN RAISONNABLE, DE LA NÉGLIGENCE ET DE TOUTE AUTRE PERTE PÉCUNIAIRE OU AUTRE PERTE

DE QUELQUE NATURE QUE CE SOIT) SE RAPPORTANT DE QUELQUE MANIÈRE QUE CE SOIT À L'UTILISATION DU CONTENU SOUS LICENCE OU À L'INCAPACITÉ DE S'EN SERVIR, À LA PRESTATION OU À L'OMISSION DE LA 'UNE TELLE PRESTATION DE SERVICES DE SOUTIEN TECHNIQUE OU À LA FOURNITURE OU À L'OMISSION DE LA FOURNITURE DE TOUS AUTRES SERVICES, RENSEIGNEMENTS, CONTENUS SOUS LICENCE, ET CONTENU QUI S'Y RAPPORTE GRÂCE AU CONTENU SOUS LICENCE OU PROVENANT AUTREMENT DE L'UTILISATION DU CONTENU SOUS LICENCE OU AUTREMENT AUX TERMES DE TOUTE DISPOSITION DE LA U PRÉSENTE CONVENTION EULA OU RELATIVEMENT À UNE TELLE DISPOSITION, MÊME EN CAS DE FAUTE, DE DÉLIT CIVIL (Y COMPRIS LA NÉGLIGENCE), DE RESPONSABILITÉ STRICTE, DE VIOLATION DE CONTRAT OU DE VIOLATION DE GARANTIE DE MICROSOFT OU DE TOUT FOURNISSEUR ET MÊME SI MICROSOFT OU TOUT FOURNISSEUR A ÉTÉ AVISÉ DE LA POSSIBILITÉ DE TELS DOMMAGES.

LIMITATION DE RESPONSABILITÉ ET RECOURS. MALGRÉ LES DOMMAGES QUE VOUS PUISSIEZ SUBIR POUR QUELQUE MOTIF QUE CE SOIT (NOTAMMENT, MAIS SANS LIMITATION, TOUS LES DOMMAGES SUSMENTIONNÉS ET TOUS LES DOMMAGES DIRECTS OU GÉNÉRAUX OU AUTRES), LA SEULE RESPONSABILITÉ 'OBLIGATION INTÉGRALE DE MICROSOFT ET DE L'UN OU L'AUTRE DE SES FOURNISSEURS AUX TERMES DE TOUTE DISPOSITION DEU LA PRÉSENTE CONVENTION EULA ET VOTRE RECOURS EXCLUSIF À L'ÉGARD DE TOUT CE QUI PRÉCÈDE SE LIMITE AU PLUS ÉLEVÉ ENTRE LES MONTANTS SUIVANTS : LE MONTANT QUE VOUS AVEZ RÉELLEMENT PAYÉ POUR LE CONTENU SOUS LICENCE OU 5,00 $US. LES LIMITES, EXCLUSIONS ET DÉNIS QUI PRÉCÈDENT (Y COMPRIS LES CLAUSES CI-DESSUS), S'APPLIQUENT DANS LA MESURE MAXIMALE PERMISE PAR LES LOIS APPLICABLES, MÊME SI TOUT RECOURS N'ATTEINT PAS SON BUT ESSENTIEL.

À moins que cela ne soit prohibé par le droit local applicable, la présente Convention est régie par les lois de la province d'Ontario, Canada. Vous consentez Chacune des parties à la présente reconnaît irrévocablement à la compétence des tribunaux fédéraux et provinciaux siégeant à Toronto, dans de la province d'Ontario et consent à instituer tout litige qui pourrait découler de la présente auprès des tribunaux situés dans le district judiciaire de York, province d'Ontario.

Au cas où vous auriez des questions concernant cette licence ou que vous désiriez vous mettre en rapport avec Microsoft pour quelque raison que ce soit, veuillez utiliser l'information contenue dans le Contenu Sous Licence pour contacter la filiale de succursale Microsoft desservant votre pays, dont l'adresse est fournie dans ce produit, ou visitez écrivez à : Microsoft sur le World Wide Web à http://www.microsoft.com

Contents

About This Course

This section provides you with a brief description of the course, audience, suggested prerequisites, and course objectives.

Description

This course provides content on reacting to incident requests from users by troubleshooting and escalating or repairing problems with Microsoft® Windows® desktop operating systems. It also provides the basic knowledge of system architecture and security needed to provide students with the skills required to support users.

Audience

This course is primarily intended for people who have little or no job experience in the information technology (IT) industry. Students must have experience working with Windows desktop operating systems and the appropriate prerequisite knowledge. Target students are:

- New entrants to the IT field
- Career changers entering the IT field
- Academic students

The secondary audience for this course consists of people who are currently working in the Tier 1 job role and want to obtain a Microsoft Certified Desktop Support Technician (MCDST) credential. They will likely have most of the skills that are covered in this course, but will not have the formal education that might be required to pass the exams.

Student prerequisites

This course requires that students meet the following prerequisites:

- Basic experience using a Microsoft Windows operating system such as Microsoft Windows XP
- Basic understanding of Microsoft Office applications and Microsoft Windows accessories, including Internet Explorer
- Basic understanding of core operating system technologies, including installation and configuration
- Basic understanding of hardware components and their functions
- Basic understanding of the major desktop components and interfaces and their functions
- Basic understanding of Transmission Control Protocol/Internet Protocol (TCP/IP) settings
- How to use command-line utilities to manage the operating system
- Basic understanding of technologies that are available for establishing Internet connectivity

Course objectives

After completing this course, the student will be able to:

- Customize the desktop, Start menu, and taskbar, and switch views in Control Panel.
- Support users in a desktop support environment.
- Identify and resolve desktop management issues.
- Identify and resolve network connectivity issues.
- Identify and resolve hardware issues.
- Identify and resolve file and folder issues.
- Identify and resolve printer issues.
- Identify and resolve installation issues.

Student Materials Compact Disc Contents

The Student Materials compact disc (CD) contains the following files and folders:

- *Addread*. This folder contains the additional reading pertaining to this course.

- *Autorun.exe*. When the compact disc is inserted into the CD-ROM drive, or when you double-click the **Autorun.exe** file, this file opens the CD and allows you to browse the Student Materials CD.

- *Autorun.inf*. When the compact disc is inserted into the CD drive, this file opens Autorun.exe.

- *Default.htm*. This file opens the Student Materials Web page. It provides you with resources pertaining to this course, including additional reading, review and lab answers, lab files, multimedia presentations, and course-related Web sites.

- *Readme.txt*. This file explains how to install the software for viewing the Student Materials compact disc and its contents and how to open the Student Materials Web page.

- *Flash*. This folder contains the installer for the Macromedia Flash 5.0 browser plug-in.

- *Fonts*. This folder contains fonts that may be required to view the Microsoft Word documents that are included with this course.

- *Labfiles*. This folder contains files that are used in the hands-on labs. These files may be used to prepare the student computers for the hands-on labs.

- *Media*. This folder contains files that are used in multimedia presentations for this course.

- *Mplayer*. This folder contains the setup file to install Microsoft Windows Media® Player.

- *Practices*. This folder contains files that are used in the hands-on practices.

- *Webfiles*. This folder contains the files that are required to view the course Web page. To open the Web page, open Windows Explorer, and in the root directory of the CD, double-click **Default.htm** or **Autorun.exe**.

- *Wordview*. This folder contains the Word Viewer that is used to view any Word document (.doc) files that are included on the CD.

Document Conventions

The following conventions are used in course materials to distinguish elements of the text.

Convention	Use
Bold	Represents commands, command options, and syntax that must be typed exactly as shown. It also indicates commands on menus and buttons, dialog box titles and options, and icon and menu names.
Italic	In syntax statements or descriptive text, indicates argument names or placeholders for variable information. Italic is also used for introducing new terms, for book titles, and for emphasis in the text.
Title Capitals	Indicate domain names, user names, computer names, directory names, and folder and file names, except when specifically referring to case-sensitive names. Unless otherwise indicated, you can use lowercase letters when you type a directory name or file name in a dialog box or at a command prompt.
ALL CAPITALS	Indicate the names of keys, key sequences, and key combinations—for example, ALT+SPACEBAR.
►	Indicates a procedure with sequential steps.

Introduction

Contents

Introduction

- Name
- Company affiliation
- Title / function
- Job responsibility
- Windows version experience
- Expectations for the course

Course Materials

- **Name card**
- **Student workbook**
- **Student Materials compact disc**

The following materials are included with your kit:

- *Name card*. Write your name on both sides of the name card.

- *Student workbook*. The student workbook contains the material covered in class, in addition to the hands-on lab exercises.

- *Student Materials compact disc (CD)*. The Student Materials CD contains the Web page that provides you with links to resources pertaining to this course, including additional readings, review and lab answers, lab files, multimedia presentations, and course-related Web sites.

Note To open the Web page, insert the Student Materials CD into the CD-ROM drive, and then in the root directory of the CD, double-click **Autorun.exe** or **Default.htm**.

- *Course evaluation*. Near the end of the course, you will have the opportunity to provide feedback on the course, training facility, and instructor by completing an online evaluation.

- *Evaluation software*. If evaluation software is included in the product, please remove it.

To provide additional comments or feedback on the course, send e-mail to support@mscourseware.com. To inquire about the Microsoft Certified Professional program, send e-mail to mcphelp@microsoft.com.

Prerequisites

- Basic experience using a Microsoft Windows operating system such as Microsoft Windows XP
- Basic understanding of Microsoft Office applications and Microsoft Windows accessories, including Internet Explorer
- Basic understanding of core operating system technologies, including installation and configuration
- Basic understanding of hardware components and their functions

This course requires that you meet the following prerequisites:

- Basic experience using a Microsoft® Windows® operating system such as Microsoft Windows XP
- Basic understanding of Microsoft Office applications and Microsoft Windows accessories, including Internet Explorer
- Basic understanding of core operating system technologies, including installation and configuration
- Basic understanding of hardware components and their functions

Prerequisites (*continued*)

- Basic understanding of the major desktop components and interfaces, and their functions
- Basic understanding of TCP/IP settings
- Basic experience using command-line utilities to manage the operating system
- Basic understanding of technologies that are available for establishing Internet connectivity

---

- Basic understanding of the major desktop components and interfaces and their functions
- Basic understanding of Transmission Control Protocol/Internet Protocol (TCP/IP) settings
- Basic experience using command-line utilities to manage the operating system
- Basic understanding of technologies that are available for establishing Internet connectivity

Course Outline

- Module 1: Introduction to the Desktop Support Technician Role and Environment
- Module 2: Exploring and Configuring the Windows XP User Interface
- Module 3: Resolving Desktop Management Issues
- Module 4: Resolving Network Connectivity Issues

Module 1, "Introduction to the Desktop Support Technician Role and Environment," describes the role and key skills of a desktop support technician (DST), as well as the role of a DST within Microsoft Operations Framework (MOF). It discusses the end-user support environment and the corporate support environment in which DSTs work, and the skills required to successfully interact with users.

Module 2, "Exploring and Configuring the Windows XP User Interface," introduces Microsoft Windows XP Professional and Microsoft Windows XP Home Edition, and explains how to configure various aspects of the desktop. This module also explains the importance of using Control Panel when troubleshooting end-user issues, and how to examine Control Panel in Category View and Classic View. After completing this module, you will be able to customize the desktop, Start menu and taskbar, and switch views in Control Panel.

Module 3, "Resolving Desktop Management Issues," provides information about domain and workgroup environments, user rights and profiles, user logon, file and folder migration, accessibility and multilingual configurations, security policies, and system performance. After completing this module, you will be able to troubleshoot these areas of desktop management.

Module 4, "Resolving Network Connectivity Issues," discusses how to help users manage computer addressing and name resolution, and how to assist customers in properly configuring remote connections. After completing this module, you will be able to troubleshoot problems with network connections, networking protocols, and the way in which computers are addressed.

Course Outline (*continued*)

- **Module 5: Resolving Hardware Issues**
- **Module 6: Resolving File and Folder Issues**
- **Module 7: Resolving Printer Issues**
- **Module 8: Resolving Installation Issues**

Module 5, "Resolving Hardware Issues," discusses issues that occur with different hardware components and configurations, and with device drivers. After completing this module, you will be able to troubleshoot storage devices, display devices, input/output (I/O) devices, and power configurations.

Module 6, "Resolving File and Folder Issues," describes how to support users who are attempting to perform file and folder management tasks, such as compressing files, enabling and disabling encryption, verifying permissions, or specifying access to files and folders. After completing this module, you will be able to troubleshoot file and folder issues whether they occur locally or across a network.

Module 7, "Resolving Printer Issues," explains how to troubleshoot printer installations, printer drivers, and issues that are related to print jobs. After completing this module, you will be able to troubleshoot print issues.

Module 8, "Resolving Installation Issues," discusses how to perform both an attended and unattended installations of Windows 2000 Professional, Windows XP Professional, and Windows XP Home Edition. This module also explains how to perform upgrades to these operating systems. After completing this module, you will be able to troubleshoot these installation processes and the boot process.

Demonstration: How to Use Virtual PC

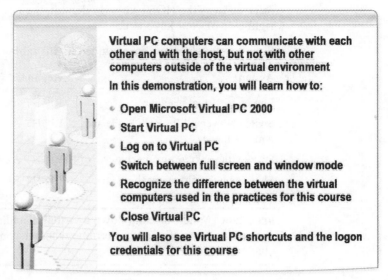

Virtual PC computers can communicate with each other and with the host, but not with other computers outside of the virtual environment

In this demonstration, you will learn how to:

- **Open Microsoft Virtual PC 2000**
- **Start Virtual PC**
- **Log on to Virtual PC**
- **Switch between full screen and window mode**
- **Recognize the difference between the virtual computers used in the practices for this course**
- **Close Virtual PC**

You will also see Virtual PC shortcuts and the logon credentials for this course

Virtual computers can communicate with each other and with the host, but they cannot communicate with other computers that are outside of the virtual environment. (For example, no Internet access is available from the virtual environment.) In this demonstration, your instructor will help familiarize you with the Microsoft Virtual PC 2000 environment, in which you will work to complete the practices in this course. You will learn:

- How to open Virtual PC.
- How to start Virtual PC.
- How to log on to Virtual PC.
- How to switch between full screen and window modes.
- How to tell the difference between the virtual computers that are used in the practices for this course.
- How to close Virtual PC and save changes.
- How to close Virtual PC and discard changes.
- How to pause and resume a virtual machine.

Your instructor will also show you some Virtual PC keyboard shortcuts.

Note For more information about Virtual PC, see Microsoft Virtual PC Help.

Virtual PC keyboard shortcuts

While working in the virtual machine environment, you may find it useful to use keyboard shortcuts. All virtual machine shortcuts include a key that is referred to as the HOST key. By default, the HOST key is the ALT key on the right side of your keyboard.

Some useful shortcuts are included in this table.

Action	Keyboard shortcut
Log on to virtual machine.	RIGHT ALT+DELETE
Switch between full screen mode and window modes.	RIGHT ALT+ENTER
Display the next virtual machine.	RIGHT ALT+RIGHT ARROW
Shut down the virtual machine.	RIGHT ALT+F4

Important   When shutting down a virtual machine, pay close attention to the lab or practice instructions to determine whether you should save or discard changes.

Microsoft Learning

> 2261, *Supporting Users Running the Microsoft Windows XP Operating System*
>
> 2262, *Supporting Users Running Applications on a Microsoft Windows XP Operating System*
>
> http://www.microsoft.com/learning/   *Microsoft* | Learning

Introduction

Microsoft Learning develops Official Microsoft Learning Products for computer professionals who design, develop, support, implement, or manage solutions by using Microsoft products and technologies. These learning products provide comprehensive skills-based training in instructor-led and online formats.

Additional recommended courses

Each learning product relates in some way to another course. A related course may be a prerequisite, a follow-up course in a recommended series, or a course that offers additional training.

It is recommended that you take the following courses in this order:

- 2261: *Supporting Users Running the Microsoft Windows XP Operating System*
- 2262: *Supporting Users Running Applications on a Microsoft Windows XP Operating System*

Other related courses may become available in the future, so for up-to-date information about recommended courses, visit the Microsoft Learning Web site.

Microsoft Learning information

For more information, visit the Microsoft Learning Web site at http://www.microsoft.com/learning/.

Microsoft Certified Professional Program

Exam number and title	Core exam for the following track
70-271: *Supporting Users and Troubleshooting a Microsoft Windows XP Operating System*	MCDST

http://www.microsoft.com/learning/

Microsoft
C E R T I F I E D
Professional

Introduction

Microsoft Learning offers a variety of certification credentials for developers and information technology (IT) professionals. The Microsoft Certified Professional (MCP) program is the leading certification program for validating your experience and skills, keeping you competitive in today's changing business environment.

Related certification exam

This course helps students to prepare for Exam 70-271: *Supporting Users and Troubleshooting a Microsoft Windows XP Operating System.*

Exam 70-271: *Supporting Users and Troubleshooting a Microsoft Windows XP Operating System* is a core exam for the Microsoft Certified Desktop Support Technician (MCDST) on Microsoft Windows XP certification.

MCP certifications

The Microsoft Certified Professional program includes the following certifications:

- MCDST on Microsoft Windows XP

  The Microsoft Certified Desktop Support Technician (MCDST) certification is designed for professionals who successfully support and educate end users and troubleshoot operating system and application issues on desktop computers running the Microsoft Windows operating system.

- MCSA on Microsoft Windows Server™ 2003

  The Microsoft Certified Systems Administrator (MCSA) certification is designed for professionals who implement, manage, and troubleshoot existing network and system environments based on the Windows Server 2003 platform. Implementation responsibilities include installing and configuring parts of the systems. Management responsibilities include administering and supporting the systems.

- MCSE on Microsoft Windows Server 2003

  The Microsoft Certified Systems Engineer (MCSE) credential is the premier certification for professionals who analyze the business requirements and design and implement the infrastructure for business solutions based on the Windows Server 2003 platform. Implementation responsibilities include installing, configuring, and troubleshooting network systems.

- MCAD

  The Microsoft Certified Application Developer (MCAD) for Microsoft .NET credential is appropriate for professionals who use Microsoft technologies to develop and maintain department-level applications, components, Web or desktop clients, or back-end data services, or work in teams developing enterprise applications. The credential covers job tasks ranging from developing to deploying and maintaining these solutions.

- MCSD

  The Microsoft Certified Solution Developer (MCSD) credential is the premier certification for professionals who design and develop leading-edge business solutions with Microsoft development tools, technologies, platforms, and the Microsoft Windows DNA architecture. The types of applications MCSDs can develop include desktop applications and multiuser, Web-based, N-tier, and transaction-based applications. The credential covers job tasks ranging from analyzing business requirements to maintaining solutions.

- MCDBA on Microsoft SQL Server™ 2000

  The Microsoft Certified Database Administrator (MCDBA) credential is the premier certification for professionals who implement and administer Microsoft SQL (structured query language) Server databases. The certification is appropriate for individuals who derive physical database designs, develop logical data models, create physical databases, create data services by using Transact-SQL, manage and maintain databases, configure and manage security, monitor and optimize databases, and install and configure SQL Servers.

- MCP

  The Microsoft Certified Professional (MCP) credential is for individuals who have the skills to successfully implement a Microsoft product or technology as part of a business solution in an organization. Hands-on experience with the product is necessary to successfully achieve certification.

- MCT

  Microsoft Certified Trainers (MCTs) demonstrate the instructional and technical skills that qualify them to deliver Microsoft Learning through Microsoft Certified Technical Education Centers (Microsoft CTECs).

Certification requirements

The certification requirements differ for each certification category and are specific to the products and job functions addressed by the certification. To become a Microsoft Certified Professional, you must pass rigorous certification exams that provide a valid and reliable measure of technical proficiency and expertise.

For More Information   See the Microsoft Learning Web site at http://www.microsoft.com/learning/.

You can also send e-mail to mcphelp@microsoft.com if you have specific certification questions.

Acquiring the skills tested by an MCP exam

Official Microsoft Learning Products can help you develop the skills that you need to do your job. They also complement the experience that you gain while working with Microsoft products and technologies. However, no one-to-one correlation exists between Microsoft Learning courses and MCP exams. Microsoft does not expect or intend for the courses to be the sole preparation method for passing MCP exams. Practical product knowledge and experience is also necessary to pass MCP exams.

To help prepare for MCP exams, use the preparation guides that are available for each exam. Each Exam Preparation Guide contains exam-specific information such as a list of the topics on which you will be tested. These guides are available on the Microsoft Learning Web site at http://www.microsoft.com/learning/.

Facilities

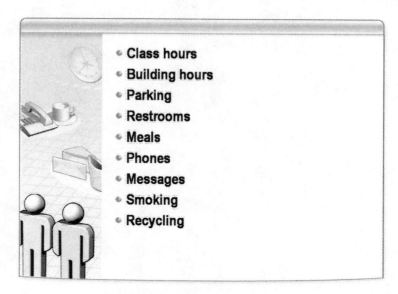

- Class hours
- Building hours
- Parking
- Restrooms
- Meals
- Phones
- Messages
- Smoking
- Recycling

Module 1: Introduction to the Desktop Support Technician Role and Environment

Contents

Overview

- Examining the Desktop Support Technician Role
- Examining the Desktop Support Environment
- Interacting with Users

Introduction

As a desktop support technician (DST), part of your job is to support end users and troubleshoot various types of tasks. The responsibilities of a DST, however, involve much more than simply resolving a problem. A DST must be able to listen to a user, gather information from that user, diagnose and resolve the problem (or escalate the problem to a senior technician or system administrator), and properly document the resolution of the problem in the manner dictated by company policy. The goal of this module is to introduce you to the role of the DST and to teach you how best to support the end users running Microsoft® Windows® XP Professional in a corporate environment or Microsoft Windows XP Home Edition in a home environment.

Objectives

After completing this module, you will be able to:

- Describe the role and general responsibilities of a DST.
- Describe Microsoft Operations Framework (MOF) and the role of the DST within MOF.
- Successfully interact with users.

Lesson: Examining the Desktop Support Technician Role

- **What Is a Desktop Support Technician?**
- **What Is the Role of a Desktop Support Technician?**

Introduction

As a DST, your job is to help users be productive by troubleshooting and trying to solve issues that arise. To do this, you must understand your role in the support environment. The goal of this lesson is to introduce you to the DST role and explain where DSTs fit within the technical support structure. Finally, this lesson describes the general responsibilities of the DST within an organization.

Lesson objectives

After completing this lesson, you will be able to:

- Describe the role of the DST within an organization.
- Describe the general responsibilities of the DST.

What Is a Desktop Support Technician?

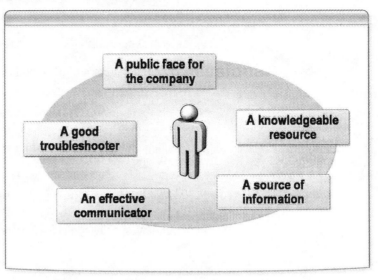

Introduction

A DST is expected to fulfill a number of roles in the support environment. A good DST must possess both technical skills and nontechnical skills, such as the interpersonal skills that are necessary for building rapport with the user to better troubleshoot and resolve the user's issues. Some of the primary roles of the DST include:

- A public face for the company—in most cases, the only human point of contact.

- A knowledgeable resource who is familiar with the product and able to perform hardware and software installation tasks and system monitoring and maintenance.

- A source of information, because even if you do not know the answer, you know where to get the answer or to redirect the end user.

- An effective communicator, because customers are not calling to be sociable—many of them are distressed or upset, and you will need to manage the interaction effectively.

- A good troubleshooter who is able to quickly isolate an issue by performing specific tasks.

What Is the Role of a Desktop Support Technician?

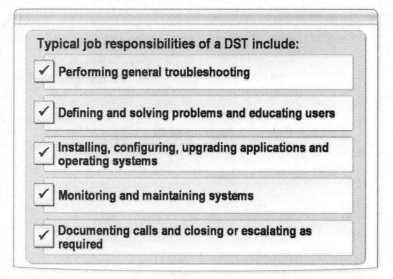

Typical job responsibilities of a DST include:

✓ Performing general troubleshooting

✓ Defining and solving problems and educating users

✓ Installing, configuring, upgrading applications and operating systems

✓ Monitoring and maintaining systems

✓ Documenting calls and closing or escalating as required

Introduction

It is important to understand where DSTs fit within the technical support structure. This section describes the tier structure that corporations often use to define technical support roles, where DSTs fit within this structure, and the standard job responsibilities and job titles of DSTs.

The position of DSTs within the technical support structure

Organizations frequently structure technical support into levels or tiers. This structure enables organizations to route requests based on the skill level of the DST and the complexity of the issue. Organizations usually employ a three- or four-level tier in which the lowest level handles end-user issues and the highest level handles the most complex issues. For example, new requests are assigned to tier 1, where the DST categorizes the problem and attempts to resolve the issue. If the tier 1 technician cannot resolve the request, the request is escalated to tier 2 personnel.

As a DST, your position is located in tier 1, the help desk. The following table provides an overview of the technical support structure.

Tier	Description
Tier 1, help desk	Support: Supports day-to-day client operating systems, applications, and hardware troubleshooting. Follows prescriptive guidelines and provides end user phone support.
Tier 2, administrator	Operational: Provides day-to-day server and software troubleshooting. Performs operating system management and support.
Tier 3, engineer	Tactical: Analyzes and designs within a single technology and implements the technology. Handles complex troubleshooting, including escalations from administrators.
Tier 4, architect	Strategic: Analyzes and designs enterprises.

Typical DST responsibilities

As a tier 1 entry-level technical support employee, your job is to provide end user support. At a high level, you should be prepared to perform the following tasks:

- Perform general troubleshooting of the operating system and installed applications.

- Provide customer service, including listening to the customer, defining and solving the problem, and educating the user on how to avoid the problem in the future.

- Install, configure, and upgrade software, including applications and operating systems.

- Monitor and maintain systems.

- Document calls and close them or escalate them as required by company policy and time limits set by Service Level Agreements (SLAs). An *SLA* defines the parameters of service provided by a company to a user. SLAs typically cover:

  - The amount of time that the DST has to resolve an issue before escalating the call

  - Services to be delivered

  - Fees and expenses

  - Customer responsibilities

  - Documentation requirements

  - Support policies

The scope of the DST role

As a DST, your first step is to identify the scope of the problem and determine whether the issue is within the scope of your job role. If it is outside the scope of your role, it should be escalated to a higher tier level. A DST is expected to troubleshoot and provide information about many aspects of the Windows XP operating system, such as resolving installation and connectivity issues; configuring and troubleshooting users' desktop environments; troubleshooting multiple boot or multiuser computers; and installing, configuring, and troubleshooting hardware. As a DST, you are expected to employ proper procedures to document the incident and to operate within the environment's SLAs. For example, you must resolve a problem in a particular amount of time or within a specified budget. In contrast, a DST is not expected to perform tasks that are typically performed by administrators such as complex server or software troubleshooting.

Typical DST job titles

There are various job titles and job roles for tier 1 DSTs. When you create a résumé, search for employment, or interview for a job, make sure that you are familiar with these titles. Each of the following job titles is a tier 1 entry-level job, and all are quite similar:

- Desktop support technician
- Call center support representative
- Customer service representative
- Help desk specialist (or technician)
- Product support specialist
- PC support specialist
- PC technician

Practice: Performing the Desktop Support Technician Role

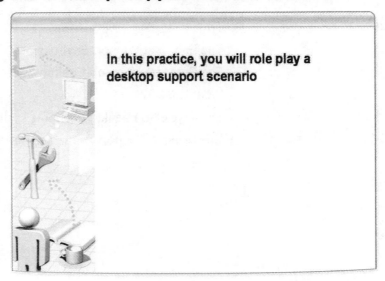

Objective

In this practice, you and a classmate will use the following information to role-play a desktop support scenario.

Instructions

Choose a partner for this practice. One of you will play the role of a DST while the other person plays the role of a user who is calling for assistance. Then you will change roles.

Scenario

You are a tier 1 DST and receive a call from Bob, a power user, who says that he cannot connect to the network. Bob is very angry and says this is the third time this week he has been unable to connect to the network.

Practice

Information for the person playing Bob:

- You have an important presentation to write, and vital information is located *only* on the network. You know of no other way to access the information other than to log on to the network yourself. None of your colleagues have access to the files you require.

- You become increasingly impatient until it seems that the DST is actually helping you.

Information for the person playing the DST:

- Through dialog with Bob and by performing some diagnostic steps on his computer (either remotely or with Bob's help), Bob determines that he is receiving an Internet Protocol (IP) address from the wrong Dynamic Host Configuration Protocol (DHCP) server. What are your next steps?

Lesson: Examining the Desktop Support Environment

* The End-User Support Environment
* The Corporate Support Environment
* What Is MOF?
* The Role of the Desktop Support Technician in MOF
* Key Desktop Support Terms and Definitions

Introduction

There are several types of desktop support environments in which you might be employed. Understanding these environments and your place in them is crucial to your success. This section provides an overview of the end-user support environment and the corporate support environment.

Lesson objectives

After completing this lesson, you will be able to:

* Describe the end-user support environment.
* Describe the corporate support environment.
* Explain the concept of MOF.
* Describe the role of DSTs within MOF.
* Understand and apply important DST and MOF terminology.

The End-User Support Environment

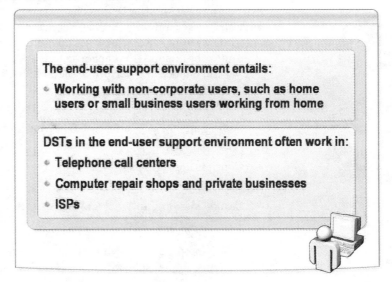

The end-user support environment entails:

- Working with non-corporate users, such as home users or small business users working from home

DSTs in the end-user support environment often work in:

- Telephone call centers
- Computer repair shops and private businesses
- ISPs

Introduction

End user support entails working with non-corporate users, such as home users or small business users working from home. DSTs who work with these users are often employed by telephone call centers, repair shops and private businesses, or Internet Service Providers (ISPs). The following list describes the DST role in these end-user support environments:

- *Telephone call centers*. Telephone call centers accept calls from end users and resolve problems over the telephone. These calls can be hardware- or software-related, depending on the company and its clients. A DST's place in this environment is defined by using a tier system similar to that in a corporate environment.

- *Computer repair shops and private businesses*. DSTs also work in small repair shops, large repair shop chains, computer sales chains, computer manufacturers, or hardware testing labs. If you intend to work as a DST in any of these settings, you should also be either A+ or Network+ certified. Unlike a DST, an employee at a repair shop, or one who owns his or her own business, has much more hands-on computer work than those who answer phones. These DSTs replace hardware, add memory, repair printers, and perform similar tasks in addition to the tasks required of a DST.

■ *ISPs*. ISPs are companies that provide Internet access to subscribers for a monthly fee. Subscribers can be individuals or entire corporations. Some ISPs do more than offer Internet access; they design Web pages, consult with businesses, provide feedback concerning Web page traffic, and send out virus warnings. Some also set up, secure, and maintain e-commerce Web sites for clients. If you choose to work for an ISP, you will most likely answer the phones and perform general help desk duties, as previously defined. The most common tasks required of a DST working for an ISP include:

- Setting up new accounts by using Microsoft Outlook® or Outlook Express and other e-mail clients.

- Configuring settings to filter spam by creating rules and blocking senders.

- Troubleshooting Internet and e-mail access.

- Troubleshooting servers and physical connections.

- Resolving problems with various connection types, including dial-up modems, digital subscriber line (DSL), cable, and wireless connections.

- Resolving and escalating calls when necessary.

DSTs working for an ISP must be familiar with Internet technologies, Domain Name System (DNS) name resolution, connection types, available modems, and other common ISP tools. ISPs, like other DST employers, generally use a tier system, and moving up the tier is dependent on experience, education, and training.

The Corporate Support Environment

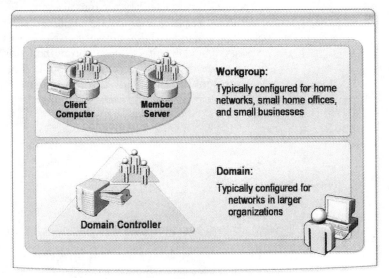

Introduction	There are two types of networks that you will encounter as a DST in a corporate support environment: workgroups and domains. In both environments, users can share common resources, such as files, folders, and printers. These environments also provide security measures to keep users' personal data, network resources, and company data secure and protected from outside forces. Despite their similarities, there are important differences between workgroups and domains and these differences are discussed in this section.
Workgroups	*Workgroups*, which are logical groupings of networked computers that share resources, are often referred to as *peer-to-peer networks*. The workgroup is the easiest network to set up and maintain, but it is the least secure. Each computer maintains its own local security database, which contains the valid user accounts for logging onto and using that computer. The user accounts secure data on the computer and protect the computer from unwanted access. Because no single computer provides centralized security of user accounts for all the computers on the network, the network is considered decentralized.
	Note Workgroups are typically configured for home networks, small home offices, and small businesses in which the computers are in close proximity to one another and can be connected using a hub, switch, or router. Because workgroups are not the most secure option for a network, they are not often used in larger corporations.
Domains	*Domains* are logical groupings of networked computers that share a common database of users and centrally managed security on a single server (or group of servers) called a *domain controller*. A single domain must have one or more domain controllers, and these computers provide Microsoft Active Directory® directory services, such as access to resources, security, and a single point of administration. Domains are logical groupings, so they are independent of the actual physical structure of the network. Domains can span a building, city, state, country, or even the globe; or they can be configured for a small office. The computers can be connected by dial-up, Ethernet, Integrated Services Digital Network (ISDN) lines, satellite, or even wireless connections.

Note Domains are typically configured for networks in larger companies and corporations because they are the most secure option for a network, offer centralized security and management, and are extensible. Smaller companies generally opt against domains because domains have more overhead, are more expensive, and require more attention than workgroups do. Workgroups and domains are discussed in detail in Module 3 of this course, "Resolving Desktop Management Issues."

What Is MOF?

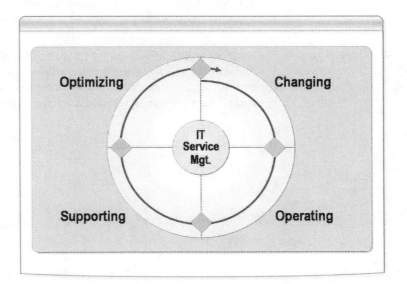

Introduction

DSTs in corporate support environments rely on an operational framework, such as Microsoft Operations Framework (MOF) to maintain day-to-day IT operations. MOF is guidance on how to effectively design, develop, deploy, operate, and support solutions that are built on Microsoft products and technologies. It is a collection of best practices, principles, and models that are delivered through white papers, operation guides, services, and courses.

The MOF Process Model

IT service management is the concept of applying a structured set of common functions and processes to service solutions to meet service-level requirements that are agreed to with the customer. In IT, models are used to establish order and structure for processes. The *MOF Process Model* is one of three core MOF models that focus on life cycle iteration in the context of an ongoing operations environment: the MOF Process Model, the MOF Team Model, and the MOF Risk Model. The MOF Process Model describes the Microsoft approach to the IT operations and service management life cycle.

MOF Process Model quadrants

Central to the MOF Process Model is its division into four quadrants of operational processes and procedures called service management functions (SMFs). *SMFs* are foundational-level best practices and prescriptive guidance for operating and maintaining an IT environment. The following four quadrants encompass virtually every activity within an operations environment:

- *Changing quadrant*. Includes the SMFs required to identify, review, approve, and incorporate change into a managed IT environment. This includes changes in software, hardware, documentation, roles and responsibilities, and so on, in addition to specific process and procedural changes.

- *Operating quadrant*. Includes the SMFs required to monitor, control, manage, and administer service solutions on a daily basis to achieve and maintain service levels within predetermined parameters.

- *Supporting quadrant.* Includes the SMFs required to identify, assign, diagnose, track, and resolve incidents, problems, and requests within the approved requirements contained in the service level agreements (SLAs).

- *Optimizing quadrant.* Includes the SMFs that contribute to maintaining business and IT alignment by focusing on decreasing IT costs while maintaining or improving service levels. This includes: review of outages and incidents; examination of cost structure; staff assessments; availability and performance analysis; and capacity forecasting.

The Role of the Desktop Support Technician in MOF

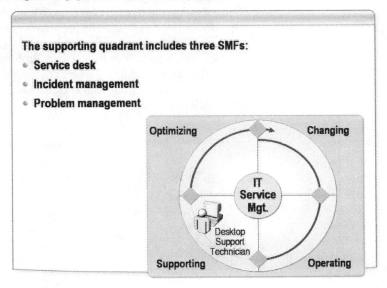

The supporting quadrant includes three SMFs:
- Service desk
- Incident management
- Problem management

Introduction

DST responsibilities are located within the supporting quadrant of the MOF Process Model. It is essential that you understand the purpose and function of this quadrant because it provides the framework for this course.

Supporting quadrant mission of service

The supporting quadrant mission of service is to quickly resolve incidents, problems, and inquiries. This quadrant incorporates the following key ideas:

- Service restoration is the first priority.

- Incidents, problems, and known errors must be clearly distinguished from one another.

- Service levels are governed by SLAs.

- Customers interact with the service desk for the resolution of problems.

- Electronic self-help does not make human representatives obsolete.

SMFs in the supporting quadrant

The following three SMFs comprise the supporting quadrant and help to accomplish its mission:

- *Service desk SMF.* The service desk coordinates all activities and customer communications regarding incidents, problems, and inquiries related to production systems. It is the single point of contact between service providers and end users on a day-to-day basis. Service desks receive requests for help with solving issues and problems across a vast array of applications, communication systems, desktop configurations, and facilities.

- *Incident management SMF.* Incident management, which is the primary activity of the service desk, is the process of managing and controlling faults and disruptions in the use or implementation of IT services as reported by users. The primary goal of incident management is to restore normal service operation as quickly as possible when it is disrupted and minimize any adverse impact on end-user or corporate operations.

- *Problem management SMF*. The goal of problem management is to identify and correct underlying problems in the IT infrastructure through both reactive and proactive means. *Reactive problem management* is initiated when the service desk reports problems, while *proactive problem management* involves continuously monitoring and evaluating data to identify problems before they occur. Problem management is responsible for escalation procedures, incident correlation, root cause analysis, problem resolution, and reporting, and is tightly coupled with incident management performed at the service desk level.

Key Desktop Support Terms and Definitions

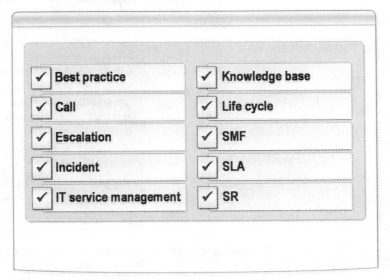

Introduction

Understanding the key terms and their definitions listed in the following table will enhance your performance as a DST.

Key term	Definition
Best practice	An optimal set of procedures and functional principles that, when followed, produce superior system reliability, availability, supportability, and manageability, resulting in effective IT service management.
Call	A call is any type of contact that a customer makes with desktop support, such as by telephone, voice mail, e-mail, or online support.
Escalation	When an issue cannot be resolved by a tier 1 DST, it must be referred to someone who has more time or knowledge to address the problem. This referral is an escalation.
Incident	An incident is any occurrence that is not part of normal hardware or software performance and that diminishes or stops that performance.
IT service management	An approach that IT organizations can utilize to plan, develop, deliver, and maintain quality IT services that are customer focused and process driven, and that meet both cost and performance targets as defined by the service level agreement or operating level agreement.

(continued)

Key term	Definition
Knowledge Base (KB)	A knowledge base is a database of past incidents and solutions that is created and added to by gathering information from service requests. Microsoft maintains a database of support articles at http://support.microsoft.com /default.aspx?scid=fh;EN-US;KBHOWTO. The Microsoft Knowledge Base should be one of the first places that a DST searches to find an answer to an issue involving a Microsoft product. It reflects the accumulated experience and wisdom of many generations of Microsoft support professionals from around the world.
Life cycle	The phases that an IT component goes through from the time it is conceived to the time it is retired from service. The life cycle represents an approval process for configuration items, problem reports, and change documents.
Service management function (SMF)	Foundational-level best practices and prescriptive guidance that are the core of the MOF Process Model. Although no SMF is exclusive to a given quadrant in MOF, each SMF has a primary planning and execution quadrant.
Service level agreement (SLA)	The SLA is the document that identifies the type of support the customer has purchased from your company, in addition to the support functions your company is obligated to perform.
	From a desktop support standpoint, it is very important that you understand a customer's SLA. If the issue is not covered in the SLA, it is not the DST's responsibility to fix. This does not mean that the issue can be rejected; instead, it means that you have a clear set of limits as to how far you can go to support the customer.
Service request (SR)	A service request is a customer contact (see *Call*) that has been logged in a company's help desk system.

Practice: Supporting Users in End-User and Corporate Support Environments

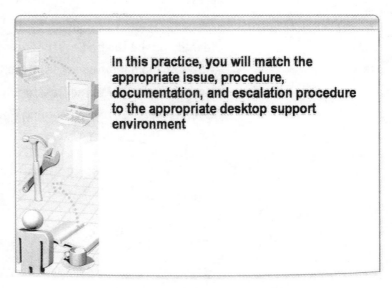

In this practice, you will match the appropriate issue, procedure, documentation, and escalation procedure to the appropriate desktop support environment

Objective

In this practice, you will use concepts that you learned in this lesson to match issues and procedures to the appropriate environment.

The following table is a list of user issues that are often found in a corporate environment running Windows XP Professional and issues found in an end-user environment, such as a home computing environment running Windows XP Home Edition.

Determine whether the issues and procedures are applicable to the corporate environment, the end-user environment, or both.

Issues and procedures	Environment
Unable to print to a local printer	
Unable to print to a network printer	
A DOS-based game does not function properly	
Unable to connect to Microsoft Exchange Server	
Loss of Internet connectivity (cable or DSL)	
A virus is detected	
Cannot log on to the local computer	
Cannot log on to the domain	

Lesson: Interacting with Users

- Desktop Support Technician Skills
- Identifying the User's Level of Expertise
- How to Obtain Information from the User
- User Expectations of the Desktop Support Technician
- Overview of the Troubleshooting Process

Introduction

The ability to effectively interact with users is vital to a DST's success. You must also know how to talk to users with various levels of experience—how to ask questions, how to interpret what users say, and how to suggest changes. You must know where to search for answers to problems and how to apply and document the solutions to those problems. The end user must be satisfied with the solution and believe that he or she was treated fairly and with respect. This lesson describes how to effectively interact with users and introduces you to basic troubleshooting techniques, including how to gather information about a problem, research and implement solutions, and document your activities.

Lesson objectives

After completing this lesson, you will be able to:

- Describe the core skills of a DST.
- Identify a user's level of experience.
- Obtain information from a user.
- Explain what users expect from DSTs.
- Explain the troubleshooting process.

Desktop Support Technician Skills

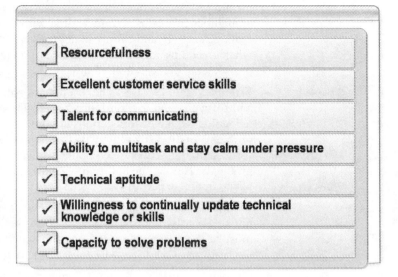

Introduction

Companies and clients want to hire and keep the best DSTs that they can find, and they look for several specific traits and qualities. It does not matter whether you work in a corporate environment or offer in-home computer repair services; the traits and skills are the same. To be the best DST you can be, work to demonstrate as many of the following qualities as possible:

- *Resourcefulness*. The primary skill of successful DSTs is the ability to quickly determine whether they have the answer for the customer and, if not, where to find the answer. This includes determining whether they should research the issue using all resources available or escalate the issue to someone who knows the answer.

- *Excellent customer service skills*. Successful DSTs have the ability and emotional intelligence to teach highly technical content to users with any level of experience. They can speak to any user about any problem and define that problem in terms the user can understand (without making the user feel inadequate). They have skills that any successful customer service employee has: They are polite, are concerned for the customer, and have a sincere desire to service the customer's needs. Beyond emotional intelligence, they also have social intelligence, which is the ability to handle their (or others') anxieties, anger, and sadness; to be self-motivated; and to have empathy for others.

- *Talent for communicating*. Qualified DSTs can communicate with end users of any level of experience, any personality, and any level of the corporate ladder. They can communicate technical information to nontechnical users and can acquire technical information from those who cannot explain the problem clearly. Qualified DSTs also take the time to explain in simple terms why the problem occurred, how it can be avoided in the future, and how and where to get help when no DST is available. Qualified DSTs document the problems, their communications with users, and the solutions they try so that they can communicate even better with users the next time around.

- *Ability to multitask and stay calm under pressure.* DSTs must deal with ongoing problems, multiple open troubleshooting tickets, deadlines for meeting SLAs, accountability to upper management and end users, and ambiguous problems. While dealing with these issues, DSTs must be able to work effectively and calmly under pressure. DSTs must also respond calmly when an end user becomes frustrated or angry, and must maintain a professional demeanor at all times.

- *Technical aptitude.* DSTs have a natural aptitude for computers, hardware, and software, and for configuring each. They enjoy working with the technologies; have workstations at home at which they troubleshoot problems in their spare time; welcome new technologies; and show a talent for visualizing networks, components, shared files and folders, and problems. Having the ability to visualize an issue is the first step to becoming an expert in your field.

- *Willingness to continually update technical knowledge or skills.* DSTs are not necessarily required to have in-depth knowledge of a product, but they must have a basic understanding of the concepts involved with the pieces of the software, how they work together, and common issues.

- *Capacity to solve problems.* Talented DSTs have the capacity to solve problems quickly. They are good at solving logic problems, operating mentally within the abstract, uncovering hidden clues, chasing leads, and discovering and attempting solutions without complicating the problem further. Communication and linear and logical troubleshooting abilities are skills employers look for. Technical skills can be taught much more easily than these skills, which have more to do with overall intelligence, personality, and social abilities than technical skills do. You must strive to develop critical thinking and problem-solving skills for dealing with a problem. The capacity to solve problems can be improved through training, experience, trial and error, observation, and working with higher-level DSTs.

Identifying the User's Level of Expertise

Skill level	Description
Highly experienced	These users are extremely experienced. Their problems generally need to be escalated quickly
Generally experienced	These users can use e-mail and the Internet, configure simple networks, and do minor troubleshooting
Targeted experience	These users have experience in one or two applications but almost no other computing skills
No experience	These users are completely new to computing and have little or no experience with using e-mail or applications

Introduction

There are many types of end users. Each user has expertise in different areas, and each user has varying degrees of expertise. Some end users have no computer experience at all and barely understand basic computer terms; some have targeted experience; still others have many years of experience. The following table lists and describes the different types of users you are likely to encounter.

Skill level	Description
Highly experienced	These users are extremely experienced and most likely know more than you do concerning the problem at hand. Their problems generally need to be escalated quickly.
Generally experienced	These users can use e-mail and the Internet, download and install programs, follow wizards, install and configure programs, set up simple networks, and do minor troubleshooting. Tier 1 or tier 2 support personnel can generally assist these users.
Targeted experience	These users have experience in one or two applications that they use daily to do their jobs. Other than this experience, they have almost no computing skills. Depending on the application in question, tier 1 or tier 2 support personnel can generally assist these users.
No experience	These users are completely new to computing and have little or no experience with using e-mail, accessing the Internet, or installing or using applications. Tier 1 personnel should be able to handle most of these calls.

After you gain some experience as a DST, you will be able to determine how experienced the user is after speaking with him or her for only a few minutes. In the interim, you will learn how to work with and assist the various types of end users by communicating with them through written scripts and by following specific (and proven) troubleshooting guidelines.

Note Always keep in mind that you will be assisting all levels of users. Never assume that the user knows less than you.

How to Obtain Information from the User

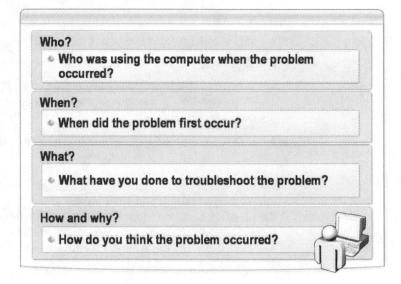

Who?
- Who was using the computer when the problem occurred?

When?
- When did the problem first occur?

What?
- What have you done to troubleshoot the problem?

How and why?
- How do you think the problem occurred?

Introduction

Often users are unable to provide a detailed description of their issue or they may be reluctant to explain the circumstances that caused the problem. Just as a reporter or police officer asks questions to obtain the information to perform his or her job, you must ask questions in your role as a DST. The information that you acquire will help you determine why the problem occurred. Then, with that knowledge, you can often resolve the problem. The following section lists common who-, when-, what-, why-, and how-type questions and provides possible answers.

Ask who-type questions

The following questions will help you identify the person affected by a problem:

- Who was using the computer when the problem first occurred?
- Who else has been using the computer, and have they experienced similar problems?
- Who has worked on this problem previously (if it has happened before)?
- Who has the same problem on another computer (that you know of)?

The answers to these questions tell you who has firsthand knowledge of the problem and whether other users who access the same computer (under a different account) also encounter the problem. If multiple users have access, but only one user encounters the problem, you have already narrowed the issue. You will also learn from these questions who has worked on the problem before (you might find out that the user has) and whether other users on the network are having the same problem on their computers. If the latter is true, the problem could be a network-wide problem, such as a security policy issue, a virus, or some other problem with the entire system.

Ask when-type questions

The following questions will help you determine when a problem occurred and establish a timeline of activities that might relate to the problem:

- When did this problem first occur, and has it occurred since?
- When was the last time you downloaded or installed an application?
- When was the last time you installed new hardware?
- When did you last clean your hard drive with Disk Cleanup or Disk Defragmenter, delete temporary files or cookies, or perform similar deletions of data?
- When was the last time you uninstalled any applications?

The answers to these questions tell you how long the user has had this problem, whether the problem occurred after the user installed a new piece of hardware or a new application, and whether the user routinely maintains the computer. If the problem occurred after installing or uninstalling hardware or software, you have a good lead. Asking pointed questions about maintenance can also be helpful for finding out whether the user has recently cleaned out program or system folders, or has inadvertently deleted any necessary files.

Ask what-type questions

The following questions will help you find information about what the user thinks may be the cause of the problem and any solutions the user has already attempted:

- What are your thoughts on what caused the problem?
- What have you tried doing to troubleshoot the problem yourself?
- What do you think can be done to solve the problem?

The answers to these questions tell you what the user believes happened and give you an opportunity to involve him or her in the solution. Asking the user what he or she thinks can be done to solve the problem could also reveal a very simple solution. If the user recently reconfigured settings for a program or uninstalled a necessary file or program, you know where to begin. If the user has already tried to troubleshoot the problem, you need to know what changes he or she has made. Finally, if the user thinks that reconfiguring the e-mail account will solve the problem, he or she might have been doing something to that account earlier but does not want to admit it.

Ask how- and why-type questions

The following questions can often identify a solution quickly:

- Why do you think the problem occurred?
- How do you think the problem occurred?

If the user says, "The problem occurred because I spilled coffee on the keyboard," or "The problem occurred because I opened an attachment in an e-mail," you know exactly where to start. Keep in mind, however, that these answers will not always be useful; they might sometimes even be misleading (for instance, a user might have opened an attachment but might tell you that he or she did not). Remember, you are the expert.

As you work through these questions with an end user, document the answers carefully, listen to everything he or she has to say, be polite and professional, and make notes of possible solutions as you think of them. If you need to, leave the situation for a few minutes to digest the information and then check company documentation, online support, or other resources for answers.

User Expectations of the Desktop Support Technician

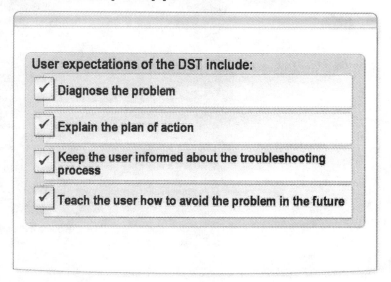

Introduction

It is likely that the end user with whom you work has spoken to a DST before. If the user's expectations were not met, the user may have lost trust in the desktop support process. As a DST, you are in a unique position to determine if there is a value gap between what the user expects and what the user receives and to ensure that users' needs are met. In general, however, users expect the DST to:

- *Diagnose the problem.* A user expects a DST to quickly grasp the nature of the problem based on the information that the user provides, regardless of the user's experience level.

- *Explain the plan of action.* After a DST has diagnosed the problem, users expect the DST to have a plan of action that entails a logical sequence of steps that either the DST or the user can quickly implement.

- *Keep the user informed about the troubleshooting process.* Users want to know what the DST is doing to troubleshoot the problem, if the plan of action is working, and how close the DST is to solving the problem.

- *Teach the user how to solve the problem and how to avoid it in the future.* Users want to understand how the problem occurred and how they can solve the problem without desktop support if it occurs in the future.

Overview of the Troubleshooting Process

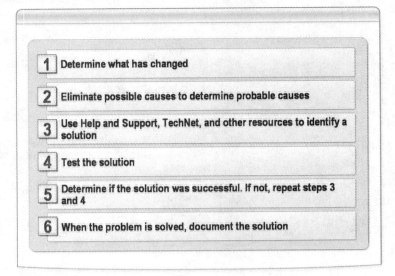

1	Determine what has changed
2	Eliminate possible causes to determine probable causes
3	Use Help and Support, TechNet, and other resources to identify a solution
4	Test the solution
5	Determine if the solution was successful. If not, repeat steps 3 and 4
6	When the problem is solved, document the solution

Introduction

Most frequently, customer calls for support are going to involve one of two types of issues:

1. "I have a problem."

   – or –

2. "I don't know how to…"

The latter is usually a simple matter of explaining to the customer how to perform a specific task or configure a feature within the operating system. The former requires troubleshooting, which is the topic of this section.

The troubleshooting process

When an end user has a problem, it may be necessary to troubleshoot the problem to determine its cause. The troubleshooting process must be logical to be successful. It is essentially the art of elimination. A good DST is able to quickly eliminate invalid issues. The pattern generally applied to the troubleshooting process is as follows:

1. Determine what has changed.

2. Eliminate possible causes to determine probable causes. Use your general knowledge of the operating system and the information in the Knowledge Base to determine the potential cause, and then compile a short list of potential solutions.

3. Identify a solution.

4. Test the solution.

5. Determine if the solution was successful. If not, repeat steps 3 and 4 or escalate the call.

6. When the problem is solved, document the solution.

Additional information on troubleshooting tools and techniques

The tools and techniques that are available to the DST are far too numerous to discuss in detail in this course. For more information about troubleshooting tools and techniques, refer to Chapter 26 of the Windows XP Professional Resource Kit at http://www.microsoft.com/technet/treeview /default.asp?url=/technet/prodtechnol/winxppro/reskit/prma_trb_ersf.asp.

How to locate information to solve an issue

No person can possibly know everything there is to know about computers. Therefore, a DST must know where and how to look for pertinent information when attempting to resolve an issue. There are three main sources that can assist you in providing a solution to the customer:

- *Help and Support.* An excellent resource, often overlooked, is the Help system packaged with the operating system. This resource can be accessed from the **Start** menu by clicking **Help and Support**. In Help and Support, you can accomplish the following:

  - Connect to another user's computer by using Remote Assistance.

  - Coordinate the download and installation of the latest updates by using Windows Update.

  - Research which hardware and software are compatible with the customer's Windows operating system.

  - Direct the customer to get help online from a support professional by using Microsoft Online Assistant.

  - Access System Restore.

  - Use tools such as System Information to manage and maintain the computer.

  - Gain access to a wide range of system Help files, public Knowledge Base articles, and other useful information.

- *The Microsoft Knowledge Base.* The Microsoft Knowledge Base (KB) contains thousands of articles detailing resolutions to issues for nearly every Microsoft product. It is the single most useful source for retrieving information pertinent to an issue and should be the DST's primary source of information. If the KB does not contain information regarding a specific issue, it is either a new issue or the DST's perceived notion of the problem is not the actual problem and the DST may need to reevaluate the situation.

Note   The KB can be accessed at http://support.microsoft.com. A link to the Knowledge Base is located under Internet Links on the Web page on the Student Materials compact disc.

- *Microsoft TechNet.* TechNet can be accessed at http://www.microsoft.com/technet/default.mspx. It offers comprehensive help on applications, operating systems, and components, such as Active Directory, Microsoft Internet Explorer, and Windows XP Professional— including planning, deployment, maintenance, and support. You can also access information security, get downloads, read how-to articles, read columns, and access troubleshooting and support pages.

- *Other online resources.* Another useful resource is the Internet. You can use public search engines to search for other online resources, such as manufacturers' sites, driver sites, and newsgroups discussing information specific to a case.

Practice: Interacting With Users

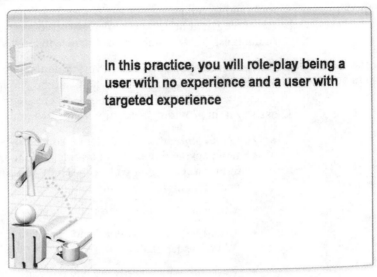

In this practice, you will role-play being a user with no experience and a user with targeted experience

Objective

In this practice, you will work with a partner to practice interacting with users.

Choose a partner for this practice. One of you will play the role of a user in two different scenarios. First, you will be a novice user with a computer-related issue that you cannot articulate clearly, and then you will be an expert user who is impatient and does not agree with what you perceive as the DST's solution. Your partner (the DST) will have a list that includes the following information: DST skills (build rapport, resourcefulness, and positive attitude), identify user experience level, obtain information, expectations of DSTs, and the troubleshooting process (determine what has changed, eliminate causes, determine probable causes, identify a solution, and test the solution).

Scenario 1

The DST receives a call from a novice user who says the Internet is down.

Scenario 2

The DST receives a call from an experienced user who says that he cannot connect to the Internet after he installed a Microsoft update. He insists that he is not using a third-party proxy product.

Note For more information on connecting to the Internet after installing Microsoft updates, see article 312176 in the Microsoft Knowledge Base.

Microsoft®

Module 2: Exploring and Configuring the Windows XP User Interface

Contents

Overview

- **Exploring and Configuring the Windows XP Desktop Environment**
- **Examining Control Panel Organizational Views**

Introduction

Before you can support end users running Microsoft® Windows® XP Professional and Microsoft Windows XP Home Edition, you must be familiar with the Windows XP user interface (UI). This module introduces these two Windows XP UIs and describes how to configure and customize common desktop settings so that you can quickly resolve end-user issues. For example, the troubleshooting process typically starts in Control Panel, yet there are two distinct ways users can view items in Control Panel: Category View and Classic View. Because tasks are performed slightly differently in each view, it is essential that you understand the differences between these two views.

Objectives

After completing this module, you will be able to:

- Describe the major features and functions of Windows XP Professional and Windows XP Home Edition and customize various settings on the Windows XP desktop, such as the Start menu and taskbar.

- Describe the differences between Category View and Classic View and how to switch between the two views in Control Panel.

Lesson: Exploring and Configuring the Windows XP Desktop Environment

- Introduction to the Windows XP Desktop Operating Systems
- How to Customize the Desktop
- How to Customize the Start Menu and Taskbar

Introduction

You receive a call from a user who says, "I just logged on to Windows and my taskbar is gone. The computer started normally and I didn't get an error message or any indication of a problem. How can I get my taskbar back?"

How would you approach this problem?

Lesson objectives

After completing this lesson, you will be able to:

- Explain the differences between Windows XP Professional and Windows XP Home Edition.
- Configure and customize the desktop.
- Configure and customize the Start menu and taskbar.

Introduction to the Windows XP Desktop Operating Systems

- **Windows desktop operating systems:**

  Windows XP Professional
  The advanced desktop operating system that lets you do more

  Windows XP Home Edition
  The reliable desktop operating system for home computing

- **Functional differences between Windows desktop operating systems:**
  - Remote access
  - Manageability
  - Security
  - Multi-lingual features
  - Performance

Introduction

As a desktop support technician (DST), you will assist users who run Windows XP Professional and Windows XP Home Edition. This section describes these two Windows desktop operating systems and explains their differences.

Windows XP desktop operating systems

In this course, you will become familiar with the following operating systems:

- Windows XP Professional. Windows XP Professional is generally used in a corporate environment, although it is commonly used in home environments also. Windows XP Professional includes all the features of Windows XP Home Edition, plus additional remote access, security, performance, manageability, and multi-lingual features.

- Windows XP Home Edition. Windows XP Home Edition is designed for the home environment. The core functionality of Windows XP Home Edition is essentially identical to that of Windows XP Professional; however, some of the features that are available in Windows XP Professional are not available in Windows XP Home Edition.

Note   You can upgrade from Windows XP Home Edition to Windows XP Professional, but you cannot upgrade from Windows XP Professional to Windows Home Edition.

Differences between Windows XP Professional and Windows XP Home Edition

The following table lists the major features in Windows XP Home Edition and Windows XP Professional.

Feature	Windows XP Home Edition	Windows XP Professional
Network Setup Wizard	X	X
Windows Messenger	X	X
Help & Support Center	X	X
Advanced laptop support	X	X
Wireless connections	X	X
Remote Desktop		X
Offline files and folders		X
Fast startup and power management	X	X
Multitasking	X	X
Scalable processor support		X
Windows Firewall	X	X
Internet Explorer privacy support	X	X
Encrypting File System		X
Access Control		X
Centralized administration		X
Group Policy		X
Software installation and maintenance		X
Roaming User Profiles		X
Remote Installation Service (RIS)		X
Single Worldwide Binary	X	X
Multilingual User Interface (MUI) add-on		X

How to identify the Windows XP desktops

When a user contacts you with a problem, you must know which operating system is installed on the user's computer, the version of the operating system, and whether service packs (SPs) are installed. Occasionally, you must explain to the user how to locate this information.

To determine the version of the operating system:

1. Click **Start**, and then click **Run**.

2. In the **Run** dialog box, in the **Open** box, type **winver** and then click **OK**.

   The **About Windows** dialog box displays the version of the operating system and the current Windows XP build number along with any installed service packs.

3. Click **OK** to close the **About Windows** dialog box.

How to Customize the Desktop

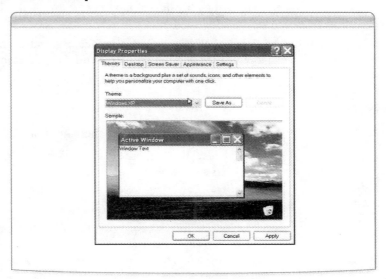

Introduction

The *desktop*, from which all user interactivity is launched, is the main user interface for Windows operating systems. All desktop content is stored within the user's profile in the Desktop folder.

The default desktop displays only the Recycling Bin shortcut. Some common shortcuts that are added to a desktop are My Computer, My Network Places, My Documents, Recycle Bin, and Internet Explorer.

How to customize Windows XP desktop settings

To customize general desktop settings for Windows XP Professional and Windows XP Home Edition:

1. Click **Start**, click **Control Panel**, click **Appearance and Themes**, and then click **Display**.

2. In the **Display Properties** dialog box, you can change desktop characteristics by using the following tabs:

    -   **Themes**. Sets a desktop theme, composed of desktop images, screen savers, specialized cursors, and sounds.

    -   **Desktop**. Changes the appearance of desktop items.

    -   **Screen Saver**. Sets the screen saver style.

    -   **Appearance**. Sets the Windows dialog box style, color, and font size.

    -   **Settings**. Sets the screen resolution and color quality.

Note **Appearance** and **Themes** are only available in Category View. To ensure that you are in Category View, in Control Panel, ensure that **Pick a Category** is displayed in the right pane. Control Panel views will be discussed in detail in the next lesson.

How to create desktop shortcuts

There are two ways to create a desktop shortcut in Windows XP:

- Right-click the desktop, point to **New**, click **Shortcut**, and then follow the Create Shortcut Wizard.

- Right-click **Start**, click **Explore**, right-click the file for which you want to create the shortcut, point to **Send To**, and then click **Desktop (create shortcut)**.

How to modify or delete shortcuts

To modify or to delete a shortcut:

- To modify a shortcut, right-click the shortcut, and then click **Properties**.

- To delete a shortcut, drag it to the Recycle Bin, or right-click the shortcut and then click **Delete**.

How to customize a shortcut

To customize a shortcut:

- Right-click the desktop, point to **Arrange Icons By**, and then choose from the options that are listed on the submenu. Some of the options include arranging icons by name, size, and type; automatically arranging; and aligning to grid.

How to update Web content on the desktop

To update Web content on the desktop:

1. Right-click the desktop, and then click **Properties**.

2. On the **Desktop** tab, click **Customize Desktop**.

3. On the **Web** tab, in the **Web pages** box, select one or more Web pages, click **Synchronize**, and then follow the New Desktop Item Wizard.

Note   In previous versions of Windows, Active Desktop® can be enabled or disabled. In Windows XP, Active Desktop is always enabled and cannot be disabled.

Practice: Customizing the Desktop

In this practice, you will:

- Change the desktop background
- Change the font size of the shortcut icons
- Remove unused shortcut icons from the desktop
- Align shortcut icons on the desktop

Objective

In this practice, you will customize the Windows XP desktop.

Scenario

You receive a call from a user who says, "A friend just upgraded my operating system to Windows XP Professional, and now my desktop is a mess. I lost my desktop background, the shortcut icons are too small to read, the desktop has shortcuts that I never use, and when I try to organize my shortcut icons, they bounce back to their original positions. How can I fix these problems?"

Practice

▶ **To change the desktop background**

1. Start Virtual PC.

2. On the Virtual PC Console window, click **2261_Bonn** and then click **Start**.

3. Using Bonn, log on locally as Administrator with a password of **P@ssw0rd**.

4. Click **Start**, click **Control Panel**, click **Appearance and Themes**, and then click **Display**.

5. Close the Appearance and Themes window.

6. In the **Display Properties** dialog box, on the **Desktop** tab, in the **Background:** box, click **Coffee Bean**, and then click **Apply**.

   The Windows XP default desktop changes to Coffee Bean.

7. Leave the **Display Properties** dialog box open.

▶ **To change the font size of shortcut icons**

1. In the **Display Properties** dialog box, on the **Appearance** tab, in the **Font size** box, select **Extra Large Fonts**, and then click **Apply**.

   The font size of the user's desktop and shortcut icons are larger.

2. In the **Font size** box, select **Normal**, and then click **Apply**.

3. Leave the **Display Properties** dialog box open.

▶ **To remove unused shortcut icons from the desktop**

1. In the **Display Properties** dialog box, on the **Desktop** tab, click **Customize Desktop**.

2. In the **Desktop Items** dialog box, click **Clean Desktop Now**, and then follow the instructions in the Desktop Cleanup Wizard.

   The user's unused shortcut icons are removed.

3. Close the **Desktop Items** and **Display Properties** dialog boxes.

▶ **To align shortcut icons in columns**

1. Drag the Recycle Bin to the center of the desktop.

2. Right-click the desktop, point to **Arrange Icons By**, and then click **Auto Arrange**.

   The Recycle Bin icon and other shortcut icons, if any, are arranged in columns on the left side of the screen.

3. Drag the Recycle Bin to the center of the desktop.

   The Recycle Bin is returned to the left side of the desktop.

4. Right-click the desktop, point to **Arrange Icons By**, and then click **Auto Arrange**.

5. On the 2261_Bonn – Microsoft Virtual PC 2004 window, on the **Action** menu, click **Pause**.

How to Customize the Start Menu and Taskbar

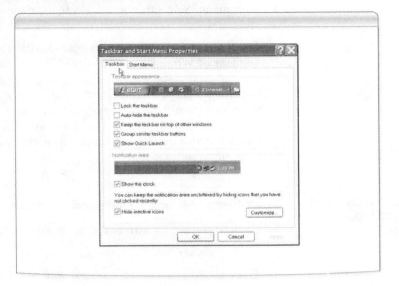

Introduction	The Start menu and taskbar are the primary tools with which users interact with the Windows XP operating systems. It is essential that you have a comprehensive knowledge of these tools and their settings to help you quickly resolve any issues users may have regarding these tools.
What is the Start menu?	The Start menu displays a menu that enables access to the most useful items on the computer. For example, All Programs lists the programs currently installed on the computer. The list of programs on the Start menu is divided into two parts:

- The programs displayed above the separator line (also known as the *pinned items list)*. The programs on this list are always available and require a click to start them. You can also add programs to the pinned items list.

- The programs displayed below the separator line (also known as the *most frequently used programs list*). Programs are added to this list as they are used. Windows XP has a default number of programs that are displayed on the most frequently used programs list. When the default number of programs is reached, the programs that have not been used recently are replaced by the programs that were used last.

What is the taskbar?	The taskbar contains the Start button and appears by default at the bottom of the desktop. You can click the taskbar buttons to switch between programs. You can also hide the taskbar, move it to the sides or top of the desktop, and customize it in other ways.
What is the notification area?	At the opposite end of the taskbar from the Start menu is the notification area. An application can place status or notification indicators here, even when the application is not active.

Start menu styles

Windows XP includes two Start menu styles:

- Start menu. Select this option to use the default Windows XP Start menu style.

- Classic Start menu. Select this option to use the menu style from earlier versions of Windows.

> **Important** The most important setting from a DST's perspective is the Start menu view that the user selects: Start menu or Classic Start menu. Each Start menu view dictates not only the layout and items that appear on the menu, but also the options that are available when a user clicks the Customize button.

How to configure Start menu and taskbar options

To configure both the Start menu and the taskbar options in Windows XP:

1. Click **Start**, click **Control Panel**, and then click **Appearance and Themes**.

2. Click **Taskbar and Start Menu**.

   There are two tabs in the **Taskbar and Start Menu Properties** dialog box:

   - *Taskbar*. Allows users to customize the actions of the taskbar. Some options for the taskbar include locking the taskbar, auto-hiding the taskbar, and hiding inactive icons.

   - *Start Menu*. Allows users to change icon size, specify the number of programs listed on the Start menu, and show Internet and e-mail icons on the Start menu.

How to resize and move the taskbar

You can drag the Windows taskbar to any side of the desktop. It can be resized by dragging the edge of the taskbar up or down, left or right.

How to show or hide the taskbar

To show or hide the taskbar:

- To show the taskbar, right-click the **Start** button, click **Properties**, and then on the **Taskbar** tab, clear the **Auto-hide the taskbar** check box.

- To hide the taskbar, right-click the **Start** button, click **Properties**, and then on the **Taskbar** tab, select the **Auto-hide the taskbar** check box.

How to customize the taskbar

To customize the taskbar:

1. Right-click the taskbar.

2. Click **Toolbars**, and then click one of the options on the submenu. Some options for the taskbar include adding a new toolbar and adding links.

> **Note** You can remove additional toolbar sections and place them anywhere on the desktop or attach them to the edges of the display area.

How to lock the taskbar

The Windows taskbar can be locked in Windows XP to prevent users from inadvertently changing it.

To lock the taskbar:

1. Click **Start**, click **Control Panel**, click **Appearance and Themes**, and then click **Taskbar and Start menu**.

2. In the **Taskbar and Start Menu Properties** dialog box, on the **Taskbar** tab, select the **Lock the taskbar** check box.

Practice: Customizing the Start Menu and Taskbar

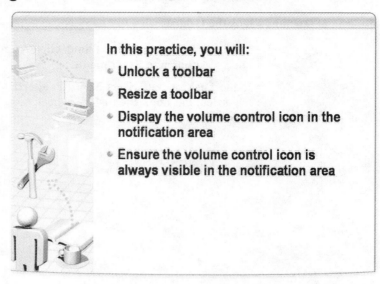

In this practice, you will:

- Unlock a toolbar
- Resize a toolbar
- Display the volume control icon in the notification area
- Ensure the volume control icon is always visible in the notification area

Objective

In this practice, you will customize the Start menu and taskbar.

Scenario

You receive a call from a user who says, "The taskbar at the bottom of my computer has become too wide and I cannot resize it like I used to. Also, the volume control recently disappeared from my taskbar, but even when it was there, it was often hidden. How do I add the volume control icon to the taskbar and keep it from hiding?"

Practice

▶ **To unlock a toolbar**

1. On the 2261_Bonn – Microsoft Virtual PC 2004 window, on the **Action** menu, click **Resume**.

2. Click **Start**, click **Control Panel**, click **Appearance and Themes**, and then click **Taskbar and Start menu**.

3. In the **Taskbar and Start Menu Properties** dialog box, on the **Taskbar** tab, clear the **Lock the taskbar** check box, and then click **OK**.

   The user's taskbar is no longer locked, and the user can now resize the taskbar.

4. Leave Control Panel open.

▶ **To resize a toolbar**

- To make a toolbar larger, place the mouse pointer at the top of the toolbar and then drag the toolbar up.

- To make a toolbar smaller, place the mouse pointer at the top of the toolbar and then drag the toolbar down.

▶ **To display the volume control icon in the notification area**

1. In the Appearance and Themes window, on the toolbar, click **Up**.

2. In Control Panel, click **Sounds, Speech, and Audio Devices**, and then click **Sounds and Audio Devices**.

3. In the **Sounds and Audio Devices Properties** dialog box, on the **Volume** tab, under **Device volume**, verify the **Place volume icon in the taskbar** check box is selected, and then click **OK**.

    The volume control icon appears in the notification area.

4. Leave Control Panel open.

Note   If the volume control icon is not visible in the notification area, click the left arrow icon to view the entire notification area.

▶ **To ensure the volume control icon is always visible in the notification area**

1. In the Sounds, Speech, and Audio Devices window, on the toolbar, click **Up**.

2. In Control Panel, click **Appearance and Themes**, and then click **Taskbar and Start Menu**.

3. In the **Taskbar and Start Menu Properties** dialog box, on the **Taskbar** tab, under **Notification area**, click **Customize**.

4. In the **Customize Notifications** dialog box, under **Current Items**, click **Volume**, and then in the Behavior column, select **Always show**.

5. To close the **Customize Notifications** dialog box, click **OK**.

6. To close the **Taskbar and Start Manu Properties** dialog box, click **OK** and then close the Appearance and Themes window.

    The volume control icon is always visible in the notification area.

7. Close all windows, log off, and pause Bonn.

Lesson: Examining Control Panel Organizational Views

- **Control Panel in Category View**
- **Control Panel in Classic View**

Introduction

You receive a call from a user who says, "I just inherited a computer that has Windows XP Professional installed. I had what I thought was a simple problem (changing the screen resolution), but the Windows XP Professional product documentation I have says to "Click Start, click Control Panel, and then click Appearance and Themes." However, Appearance and Themes is not listed in Control Panel. I'm confused."

How would you respond?

Lesson objectives

After completing this lesson, you will be able to:

- Describe Category View and how Control Panel is organized in this view.
- Describe Classic View and how Control Panel is organized in this view.

Control Panel in Category View

Introduction

You can switch the appearance of Control Panel by changing the view. In Windows XP, Control Panel includes two views: Category View that groups together similar items and Classic View that displays all items individually. It is important to understand the differences in these two views so that you can help users troubleshoot various Windows XP desktop issues.

What is Category View?

Category View is the default view in Windows XP. In Category View, Control Panel displays the most commonly used items organized by category. Control Panel displays nine categories of computer settings, such as Network and Internet connections. Each category includes a list of common and complex tasks, such as set up or change your Internet connection. You click the task you want to complete and then Windows XP opens the window you need to complete it. If you open Control Panel and do not see the item you want, switch to Classic View.

Note To find out more information about an item in Control Panel while in Category View, hold the mouse pointer over the icon or category name and read the text that appears.

How to set Control Panel to Category View

To set Control Panel to Category View:

1. Click **Start**, and then click **Control Panel**.

2. In Control Panel, in the Control Panel task pad, click Switch to Category View.

3. On the **General** tab, in the **Tasks** box, ensure that **Show common tasks in folders** is selected, and then click **OK**.

4. In Control Panel, in the right pane, ensure you are in Category View.

Control Panel in Classic View

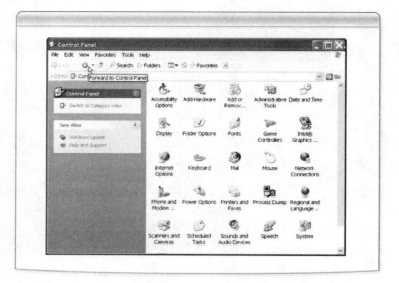

Introduction

Because Classic View is the view used in previous versions of Windows, some users prefer its familiarity. In contrast to Category View, which displays a list of categories that includes common tasks, Classic View displays a list of files and folders. This means that the user in this view must know which file or folder to open to perform a particular task.

How to set Control Panel to Classic View

1. Click **Start**, and then click **Control Panel**.

2. In Control Panel, on the **Tools** menu, click **Folder Options**.

3. On the **General** tab, in the **Tasks** box, ensure that **Show common tasks in folders** is selected, and then click **OK**.

4. In Control Panel, in the left pane, click **Switch to Classic View**.

Practice: Comparing Classic View and Category View

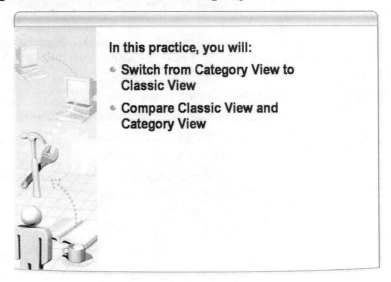

In this practice, you will:

- Switch from Category View to Classic View
- Compare Classic View and Category View

Objective

In this practice, you will change from the default view (Category View) in Control Panel to the view that is used in previous versions of Windows (Classic View). You will then compare these two views.

Scenario

You receive a call from a user who says, "I recently upgraded to Windows XP Professional, but I like the way items were displayed in Control Panel in Windows 2000 better. Is there any way to display the items in Control Panel like they were displayed in Windows 2000?"

Practice

▶ **To switch from Category View to Classic View**

1. Resume the 2261_Bonn virtual machine.

2. Using Bonn, log on locally as Administrator with a password of **P@ssw0rd**.

3. Click **Start**, click **Control Panel**, and then in the left pane, under Control Panel, click **Switch to Classic View**.

   Control Panel is now displayed in Classic View, the default view in previous versions of Windows. Notice the list of files and folders that is displayed and then hold the mouse over the file or folder names and read the tasks that can be performed.

▶ **To compare Classic View and Category View**

1. In Control Panel, in the Control Panel task pad, click **Switch to Category View**.

   Notice the ten categories that are displayed and then hold the mouse over the icons or category names and read the tasks that can be performed within each category.

2. Close Control Panel.

3. Click **Start**, and then click **Control Panel**.

   Notice that Control Panel maintained the Category View (the last view that was selected).

4. On the Virtual PC window, on the **Action** menu, click **Close**, select **Turn off and delete changes**, and then click **OK**.

Lab: Exploring and Configuring the Windows XP User Interface

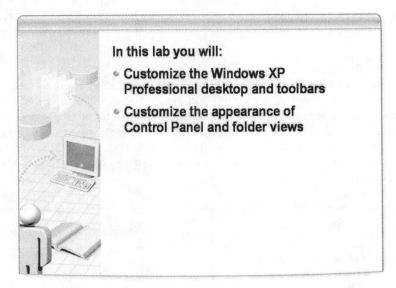

In this lab you will:

• Customize the Windows XP Professional desktop and toolbars

• Customize the appearance of Control Panel and folder views

Objectives

After completing this lab, you will be able to:

■ Customize the Windows XP Professional desktop and toolbars.

■ Customize the appearance of Control Panel and folder views.

Prerequisites

Before working on this lab, you must have an understanding of how to use Microsoft Virtual PC.

Scenario

You are a desktop support technician (DST) for Contoso, Ltd., a company whose workers use Windows XP Professional. Two users call with a number of desktop configuration and customization questions.

Estimated time to complete this lab: 60 minutes

Exercise 1
Customizing the Desktop and Toolbars

In this exercise, you will help a user customize his desktop and toolbars.

Scenario

The user would like to lock his desktop when he is away from his desk so that only he (or an administrator) can gain access to his computer. Also, the user prefers to use the toolbar to cut, copy, paste, and view Properties and would like help customizing his existing folder toolbar so he can use these functions. He states that there are times when she prefers his original toolbar, so he would like to learn how to reset the toolbar to its original setting. Finally, the user would like to learn how to display and customize the Quick Launch toolbar and create a new taskbar toolbar and add one or more applications to it.

Tasks	Guidance for completing the task
1. Start Bonn and log on as **Frank Lee** with a password of **P@ssw0rd**.	
2. Protect the desktop by using a screen saver password.	▪ Consider using the **Display** option in Control Panel.
3. Customize the default folder toolbar.	a. Consider adding a Separator to organize the buttons. b. Add the following buttons to the Windows Explorer toolbar: Cut, Copy, Paste, and Properties.
4. Reset the toolbar to the default toolbar.	▪ Consider the procedure in the previous task.
5. Display the Quick Launch toolbar.	▪ Right-click the taskbar background to access Toolbars.
6. Add a program icon to the Quick Launch toolbar.	▪ Select any program from the All Programs menu.
7. Create a new taskbar toolbar and add one or more programs to it.	▪ Right-click the taskbar background to access Toolbars.

Exercise 2
Customizing Control Panel and Folder View Appearance

In this exercise, you will help a user customize how items and folders are displayed in Control Panel.

Scenario

A user calls stating that her computer at work and her computer at home display items in Control Panel differently, and it is confusing. She explains that she double-clicks a folder to open it on her work computer, but she clicks a folder once to open it on her home computer. She would like the folder options on her work computer to match the options on her home computer. Finally, the user states the folders on both her home computer and work computer are displayed differently than when she installed Windows XP Professional--she doesn't like the task pad that shows up on the left side of the window.

Tasks	Guidance for completing the task
1. Using Bonn, determine the Control Panel organizational view.	*Control Panel View Classic or* (handwritten)
2. Switch Control Panel views.	
3. Change the number of mouse clicks required to open items.	■ Consider using Folder Options.
4. Reset all folders to the default Windows XP Professional settings.	■ Consider using Folder Options.
5. Close Bonn without saving changes.	a. On the **Action** menu, click **Close**. b. On the Close dialog box, select **Turn off and delete changes**, and then click **OK**.

Module 3: Resolving Desktop Management Issues

Contents

Overview

- ● Desktop Management Concepts
- ● Troubleshooting User Logon Issues
- ● Troubleshooting User Configuration Issues
- ● Troubleshooting Security Issues
- ● Troubleshooting System Performance

Introduction

As a desktop support technician (DST), you must ensure that you provide consistent, high-quality, and efficient desktop support for users that are running Microsoft® Windows® XP Professional and Microsoft Windows XP Home Edition. Resolving desktop management issues on Windows XP operating systems typically entails supporting end users who have software operation and application-related issues regarding the desktop.

Windows XP Professional allows you to centrally manage the privileges and permissions of users and client computers and to ensure that data, software, and settings are available to users. This module explains how to help users resolve common desktop management issues, such as user logon issues, user profiles, security policies, and system performance–related issues.

Objectives

After completing this module, you will be able to:

- ■ Understand the basic concepts necessary for resolving desktop management issues in the Windows XP Professional and Windows XP Home Edition environments.

- ■ Troubleshoot user logon issues.

- ■ Troubleshoot user configuration issues.

- ■ Troubleshoot security issues.

- ■ Troubleshoot system performance.

Lesson: Desktop Management Concepts

- **What Is a Domain Environment?**
- **What Is a Workgroup Environment?**
- **The Differences Between a Domain and a Workgroup**
- **How to Determine If a User is a Member of a Domain or a Workgroup**
- **What Are User Accounts?**
- **What Are User Profiles?**
- **What Are User Rights?**

Introduction

The troubleshooting options that are available are fundamentally different when a user is in a domain environment versus a workgroup environment. Therefore, one of your first tasks when you troubleshoot any desktop management issue is to determine the user's environment. This lesson describes the domain and workgroup environments and explains how user accounts establish the privileges that are assigned to each user.

Lesson objectives

After completing this lesson, you will be able to:

- Describe the domain environment and the considerations when troubleshooting in this environment.
- Describe the workgroup environment and the considerations when troubleshooting in this environment.
- Describe the differences in the Windows XP Professional functions that are available for a domain or a workgroup.
- Determine if a computer is a member of a domain or a workgroup.
- Describe the purpose and function of user accounts.
- Describe the purpose and function of user profiles.
- Describe the purpose and function of user rights.

What Is a Domain Environment?

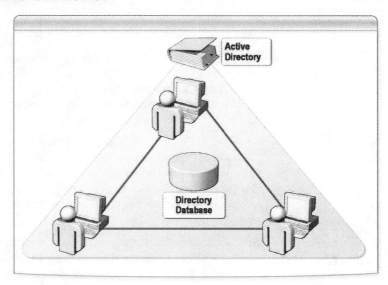

Introduction

One of the first tasks that you must perform before you troubleshoot any desktop management issue is to determine whether the user is in a domain or in a workgroup. This section describes the domain environment and the considerations to consider when you help users that are working in a domain environment.

What is Active Directory?

Microsoft Active Directory® directory service is used to store information and make information available to users and network administrators. A *network* is a group of two or more computers that are linked together. The Active Directory directory service stores information about *objects* (resources, such as files, folders, shared folders, or printers that have a distinct, named set of attributes) and then gives network users and administrators access to permitted resources anywhere on the network by using a single logon process.

What is a domain?

In a network running Active Directory, a *domain* is a collection of computers and users that share a common directory database, set of security policies, and set of security relationships with other domains. This means that the rights and permissions to access network resources are controlled from Active Directory.

Purpose of a domain

The purpose of a domain structure is to implement a logical, centralized security infrastructure on the network and to centralize the management of network users, their resources, and the policies applied to those users. Because all domain resources use Active Directory, the advantage to the user is that one logon enables access to all necessary network resources.

What is a domain controller?

Also, in a Windows domain environment, a *domain controller* is a computer running Active Directory that manages user access to network resources, including log on, *authentication* (the process of verifying that an entity or object is who or what it claims to be), and access to the directory and shared resources.

Considerations when troubleshooting in a domain environment

From a support standpoint, the implementation of a domain environment significantly changes the troubleshooting options that are available to the DST. Use the following considerations when you assist a user who logs on to a domain:

- *User rights*. A user may not have the necessary access rights on the local computer to perform desktop management tasks. Often, the DST is not the user's network administrator and therefore cannot log on to the domain to troubleshoot the user's issue. In these cases, the DST should direct the user to contact the network administrator to resolve the problem.

- *User profile settings*. Although a user may be able to log on to the computer with a local account instead of the domain account, the profile settings and the system environment will not be the same as when the user logs in to the domain. When the user logs in to a domain, the user is authenticated by a computer that uses an account over which the user will most likely have no control.

- *Startup scripts*. Domains can run startup scripts that initialize additional software or environmental settings on a user's local computer. Such additional features might have an impact on your ability to make assumptions about how the operating system should behave under certain conditions, and you will most likely be unable to isolate the user's computer in a non-domain state to perform troubleshooting effectively.

- *Domain resources*. Determine the degree to which the user interacts with and uses domain resources. Shared folders, applications, printers, and other resources that are located on the network may be protected, which means that the DST and user might not be able to troubleshoot issues involving these resources.

What Is a Workgroup Environment?

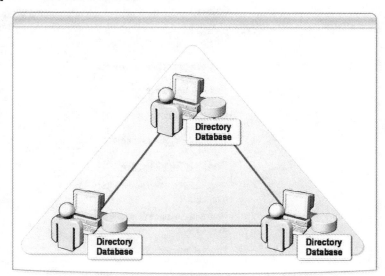

Introduction

Workgroups in a Windows XP environment do not offer the centralized management that is offered by domains. This section describes the workgroup environment and the considerations when troubleshooting users working in this environment.

What is a workgroup?

In many cases, most commonly in the home environment, the user's computer is *not* in an Active Directory domain, but instead in an environment that is known as a *peer-to-peer network* or a Windows *workgroup*. In a workgroup, users are authenticated by logging on to their local computer rather than by logging on to the domain.

Workgroups are intended for small groups of users who want to share local resources with each other without the need for a centralized server and the security, user account management tasks, and overhead associated with the domain model.

Considerations when troubleshooting in a workgroup environment

Use the following considerations when you assist a user who logs on in a workgroup:

- *User accounts*. Users in a workgroup environment can share resources; however, because computers in this environment do not share a user accounts database, each user must have a user account on each computer that contains resources that the user must access. That is, the logon rights granted to a specific resource are managed in each resource's accounts database.

- *Resource sharing*. Generally, working with a computer in a workgroup is similar to working with a standalone computer. Networking issues generally occur only with regard to connectivity, user accounts, and file sharing, and most networking issues can be resolved by working directly with the user.

The Differences Between a Domain and a Workgroup

Windows XP Professional Function	Domain	Workgroup
Part of a peer-to-peer network	No	Yes
Part of a home network	No	Yes
Computer account required	Yes	No
Welcome screen available	No	Yes
Fast User Switching available	No	Yes
Password Backup and Restore Wizard available	No	Yes
New and Classic Windows desktops available	Yes	Yes
Internet and e-mail access	Yes	Yes

Introduction

Windows XP Professional operates and looks differently depending on whether the user is a member of a domain or in a workgroup. The following table lists various Windows XP Professional functions and whether the function is available on a domain, in a workgroup, or both.

Functions in Windows XP Professional	Domain	Workgroup
Part of a peer-to-peer network	No	Yes
Part of a home network	No	Yes
Computer account required	Yes	No
Welcome screen available	No	Yes
Fast User Switching available	No	Yes
Password Backup and Restore Wizard available	No	Yes
New and Classic Windows desktops available	Yes	Yes
Internet and e-mail access	Yes	Yes

How to Determine If a User Is a Member of a Domain or Workgroup

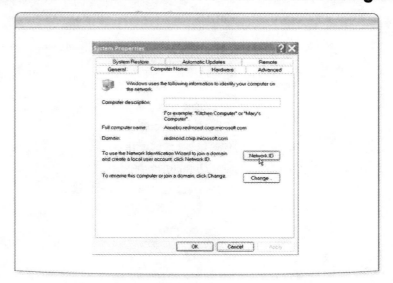

Introduction

Now that you understand what domain and workgroup environments are and the differences between these two environments, you are ready to learn how to determine what environment a user is in when a user calls requesting help with a desktop management issue.

How to determine the user environment

To determine if a computer is a member of a domain or a workgroup:

1. Click **Start**, and then click **Control Panel**.

2. In Control Panel, click **Performance and Maintenance**.

3. In Performance and Maintenance, click **System**.

4. In the **System Properties** dialog box, on the **Computer Name** tab, read the name for the workgroup or domain, as applicable.

What Are User Accounts?

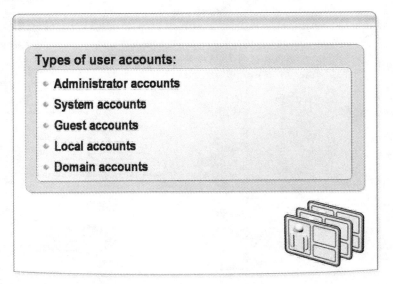

Types of user accounts:
- Administrator accounts
- System accounts
- Guest accounts
- Local accounts
- Domain accounts

Introduction

A *user account* is created by an administrator and defines the actions that a user can perform in Windows XP, such as logging on, changing a password, the groups to which the user has membership, the rights and permissions that the user has for using the computer and for accessing resources.

The user account is identified by a user name and a password that uniquely identify a user on a computer. Windows then controls access to computer resources based on the permissions and rights that are associated with each user account. In Windows XP, you can make security settings different for each user account.

Types of user accounts

There are several types of user accounts in Windows:

- *Administrator accounts*. Allow users to log on as administrators. Installed on every computer running Windows XP Professional.

- *System accounts*. Allow the operating system to access resources.

- *Guest accounts*. Allow users to temporarily log on to the computer in an extremely limited capacity. For increased security, consider disabling the Guest account.

- *Local accounts*. Each computer running Windows XP maintains its own set of accounts called local accounts, which allow users to log on to the computer rather than the domain. Default local accounts include a local Administrator account, a local Guest account, and the System account.

- *Domain accounts*. Allow users to log on to the domain where account management can be centrally administered. In an Active Directory domain, user accounts are centrally located and stored in the Active Directory directory service and are therefore considered domain accounts. Domain accounts should not be confused with an individual computer's local account.

What is a SID?

Every user account on a domain is given a unique *security identifier* (SID) when the account is created. A SID is similar to a user account in that it defines the actions that a user or group can perform in Windows XP. However, a SID is a numerical value that internal processes in Windows XP use to refer to a user account, rather than a user or group name. For security purposes, if a user account is deleted, the SID is discarded and never used again. If a user account is recreated, a new SID is generated.

How SIDs enable users to access resources

When a user logs on to a computer that is running Windows XP, either over a network or in a workgroup, the user is issued an *access token* that contains the SIDs of their user account, and of all the security groups of which the user account is a member. When the user attempts to access a resource, Windows checks the SIDs in the user's access token against those in the resource's *access control list* (ACL). If the SIDs match, the user is granted access to the resource that is specified in the ACL. If the SIDs do not match, the user is denied access.

When to use a local account versus a domain account

All computers running Windows XP maintain local accounts in a local database called a Security Accounts Manager (SAM). This means that if a computer is in a workgroup, to log on, a user must create a separate user account on each computer in the workgroup. This arrangement is manageable when a workgroup contains fewer than 10 computers; however, when a workgroup contains more than 10 computers, it is difficult for a network administrator to manage all the user accounts on each computer. One way to alleviate this problem is to create an Active Directory domain in which user accounts are considered domain accounts. This enables users to log on to any computer in the domain using one user account. This approach is scalable to millions of user accounts.

When to use both a local account and a domain account

From a troubleshooting perspective, the ability to log on to a local computer instead of a domain can be useful because it bypasses the network's security infrastructure that is provided by Active Directory. This can sometimes enable a DST to interact with resources that are otherwise protected, such as a printer that is not operating correctly. However, remember that users in a workgroup environment who log on by using a local account do not have access to domain resources because the Active Directory is not used and therefore cannot authenticate users.

One common way that organizations combine local accounts and domain accounts is to provide the user a local Administrator account and a domain account. In other words, the user has administrative rights on the local computer and is a member of a domain on the network.

Combining local accounts and domain accounts can also create problems. For example, if a user has a domain account and a local account but the local account is not a local Administrator account, the user will be unable to perform advanced management tasks, such as installing software or updating drivers. This can severely limit the DST's ability to troubleshoot a problem. In such cases, an information technology (IT) professional with local administrative rights must log on to the computer to resolve the issue.

What Are User Profiles?

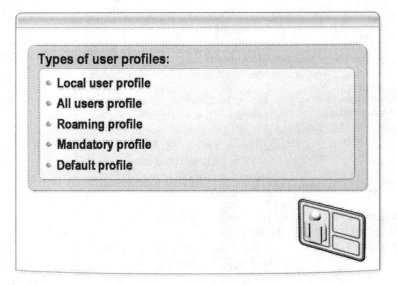

Types of user profiles:
- Local user profile
- All users profile
- Roaming profile
- Mandatory profile
- Default profile

Introduction

Every user account that is created, either locally or in a domain, has a unique user profile that is associated with it. A *user profile* contains settings and files that are specific to a user account, such as a user's personal registry settings, files that are specific to the user such as cookies, documents in the My Documents folder, Web browser favorites, and shortcuts to network places.

User profiles and logon

When a user logs on to a computer, that user profile loads the personalized user environment. By default, each user profile is stored on the local computer in the Documents and Settings folder.

Note   If a user profile is damaged, the computer experiences problems when it restarts, such as the inability to access the Windows desktop.

Types of user profiles

As a DST, you must be familiar with the following types of user profiles:

- *Local user profile*. By default, all user accounts that log on to a computer use a *local user profile* that is unique to the account and that is stored on that computer. This means that if a user normally logs on to one computer and then logs on to a different computer, the second computer will contain a different user profile.

- *All users profile*. The all users profile applies to all users that log on to the local computer. For example, some applications store their application settings within the All Users profile so that applications are available to everyone that logs on to the computer.

- *Roaming profile*. It can be very confusing to have the user profile change every time a user logs on to a different computer. Therefore, some domain administrators implement roaming profiles. A roaming profile is a profile that is stored elsewhere on the network and copied to the local computer when the user logs on. Regardless of which computer the user logs on to, her roaming profile is used. When the user logs off, any changes made to her profile are saved to the network copy.

- *Mandatory profile*. A mandatory profile works like a roaming profile except that changes made to a user profile are not saved when the user logs off. This maintains a homogeneous, unchanging user environment regardless of where the user logs on in the domain and regardless of what the user does to his profile during his logon session. Although this restricts the user's ability to make changes to his desktop environment, using a mandatory profile reduces costs related to profile support issues.

- *Default profile*. The first time a user logs on to a specific computer, a new user profile known as the default profile is created from a master copy inside Windows. This default profile can be the one shipped with Windows or a custom profile set up by an administrator. If this profile is corrupt, new user accounts will experience issues during logon.

Advantages of user profiles

User profiles provide the following advantages:

- When the user logs on to a computer, the computer uses the same settings that were in use when the user last logged off.

- When sharing a computer with other users, each user receives their customized desktop after logging on.

- Settings in the user profile are unique to each user. The settings cannot be accessed by other users.

How to copy a user profile

If a user profile becomes corrupt or if you want to present users with identical user profiles at their initial log on, you will need to copy user profiles. It is not a good practice to copy the files that are in one user profile folder directly into another user profile folder. For example, copying the Ntuser.dat file directly into another user profile can cause some features of the desktop environment to cease functioning. Instead, the preferred method for copying a user's profile is to use the **User Profile** tab in the **System Properties** dialog box in Control Panel.

Note You must be logged on as an administrator or a member of the Administrators group to copy a user profile. If the computer is connected to a network, network policy settings may prevent you from completing this process.

To copy a user profile from one user's account to another user's account:

1. In Control Panel, click **Performance and Maintenance**, and then click **System**.

2. On the **Advanced** tab, under **User Profiles**, click **Settings**.

3. Under **Profiles stored on this computer:**, click the user profile that you want to copy, and then click **Copy To**.

4. In the **Copy To** dialog box, click **Browse**, and then select the location to which you want to copy the user profile.

Note   In most instances, the user profile is copied into the second user's profile folder, which is located in the Documents and Settings folder.

By default, the first user uses the new copy of the user profile unless otherwise specified.

5. To set the second user as the user account for the copied profile, in the **Copy To** dialog box, under **Permitted to use**, click **Change**.

6. In the **Enter the object name to select (examples):** box, type the name of the user that will use this profile and then click **OK**.

7. To close the **Copy To** dialog box, click **OK**.

Important   When you select a destination folder to which to copy the user profile, the original content of the destination folder is deleted before the user profile is copied into it. For example, if the destination user profile contains files in the My Documents folder, these files are deleted.

What Are User Rights?

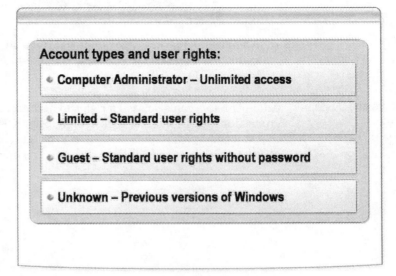

Account types and user rights:

- Computer Administrator – Unlimited access
- Limited – Standard user rights
- Guest – Standard user rights without password
- Unknown – Previous versions of Windows

Introduction

User rights are the tasks that a user is permitted to perform on a computer or domain, such as the right to back up files and folders. User rights are assigned by administrators to individual users or groups as part of the security settings for the computer.

Account types and user rights

Account types apply to both local and domain user accounts and determine the default rights that are assigned to each user account. A user account is one of four types:

- *Computer Administrator*. Has the most rights of the four types and has virtually unlimited access rights to the computer.

- *Limited*. Contains members of the Users group. By default, limited accounts can:

  - Change the password, picture, and Microsoft .NET Passport for the user accounts.

  - Use programs that have been installed on the computer.

  - View permissions if Simple File Sharing is disabled.

  - Create, change, and delete files in their My Documents folders.

  - View files in Shared Documents folders.

- *Guest*. Has the same rights as Limited account types but cannot create a password for the account. Disable the guest account when it is not in use.

- *Unknown.* Controls any accounts that are not represented by the other account types. Typically, these accounts were created in an earlier version of Windows that was upgraded to Windows 2000 Professional or Windows XP.

- Administrators can assign additional rights to specific user accounts from within the Users and Groups and Policy Editor tools in Computer Management.

User rights and custom user groups

Administrators can also assign rights to user accounts by creating custom user groups for specific tasks or logical organization. Because user groups provide or restrict additional rights to the user accounts contained within them, user accounts inherit these additional rights and restrictions.

Practice: Identifying and Changing the User Environment

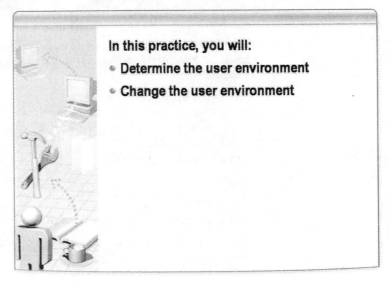

In this practice, you will:
- Determine the user environment
- Change the user environment

Objective

In this practice, you will change your computer name and environment from a workgroup environment to a domain environment.

Scenario

You receive a call from a user who says, "My computer is broken, so I am using my husband's computer. When I try to print a document, I receive an error message that says that I am not authorized to access the printer. I do not understand why I am getting this message. Can you tell me what I need to do to be able to use this printer?" You ask the caller whether the computer that she is using is in a workgroup or a domain, and she states that she doesn't know. First you determine whether the user is in a domain or workgroup environment, and then you instruct her to log off the domain, and then log on using a local user account.

▶ **To determine the user environment**

1. Start the 2261_London virtual machine.

2. After 2261_London displays the Windows logon screen, start 2261_Bonn.

3. Log on to Bonn as **Samantha Smith** with a password of **P@ssw0rd**.

4. In Control Panel, click **Performance and Maintenance**, and then click **System**.

5. In the **System Properties** dialog box, on the **Computer Name** tab, read the name for the workgroup or domain, as applicable.

6. Is Bonn in a domain or workgroup?

_____

_____

7. Close all windows.

▶ **To reproduce the issue**

1. On Bonn, click **Start**, click **Run**, type **notepad** in the **Open** box, and then click **OK**.

2. In the **Untitled – Notepad** window, type **This is a test print**. On the **File** menu, click **Print**, then click **HP LaserJet 5 on london**, and then click **Print**.

   A **Notepad** dialog box appears stating either that the RPC server is unavailable, or that access is denied.

3. Why are you unable to connect to the printer?

    Not on domain
   _____

   _____

4. On the **Notepad** dialog box, click **OK**.

5. Close Notepad without saving changes to the document, and then log off Bonn.

▶ **To join the NWTRADERS domain**

1. Log on to Bonn as Administrator with a password of **P@ssw0rd**

2. In Control Panel, click **Performance and Maintenance**, and then click **System**.

3. On the System Properties page, on the **Computer Name** tab, click **Change**.

4. On the **Computer Name Changes** dialog box, click **Domain**, and in the **Domain** box type **nwtraders** and then click **OK**.

5. In the **User name** box type **administrator**, and in the **Password** box, type **P@ssword**, and then click **OK**.

6. To close the **Welcome to the nwtraders domain** dialog box, click **OK**.

7. To close the restart notification, click **OK**.

8. To close the **System Properties** dialog box, click **OK**.

9. On the **System Settings Change** dialog box, click **Yes**.

   Bonn restarts.

► **To resolve the issue by logging on the NWTRADERS domain**

1. On the **Welcome to Windows dialog** box, press right-ALT+DEL.

2. On Bonn, in the **Log On to Windows** dialog box, if the **Log on to** box is not displayed, click **Options**.

3. In the Log on to box select NWTRADERS.

4. In the User name box, type **Samantha**.

5. In the Password box, type **P@ssw0rd**, and then click **OK**.

6. Click **Start**, click **Run**, in the **Open** box, type **london** and then click **OK**.

7. In the london window, right-click **HPLaserJ** and then click **Connect**.

8. Open Notepad, type some text and attempt to print to **HP LaserJet 5 on london**.

   Did you successfully print the document?

    Yes

9. Close Notepad and do not save changes.

10. Close all windows and log off Bonn.

11. On the Virtual PC window for 2261_Bonn, on the **Action** menu, click **Close**, select **Turn off and delete changes**, and then click **OK**.

12. Pause the 2261_London virtual machine.

Lesson: Troubleshooting User Logon Issues

- How to Reset Passwords
- How to Create a Password Reset Disk
- How to Use Fast User Switching
- Multimedia: Logon and Authentication
- How to Troubleshoot User Logon Issues

Introduction

An essential aspect of Windows XP desktop management is troubleshooting user logon issues. This lesson discusses some of the most common and straightforward issues, such as resetting a forgotten password and enabling multiple users to share a computer without logging off. However, there are more complex logon issues that a DST must know. This lesson discusses some of these logon issues, such as troubleshooting corrupt user profiles, missing domain controllers, and the inability to log on by using cached credentials.

Lesson objectives

After completing this lesson, you will be able to:

- Reset local or domain user passwords.
- Create a password reset disk to change a password.
- Use Fast User Switching.
- Explain logon and authentication.
- Troubleshoot user logon issues.

How to Reset Passwords

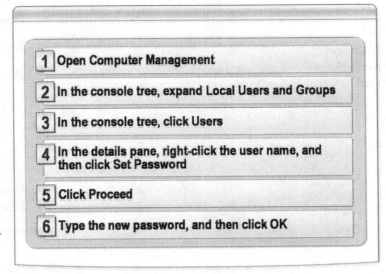

1 | Open Computer Management

2 | In the console tree, expand Local Users and Groups

3 | In the console tree, click Users

4 | In the details pane, right-click the user name, and then click Set Password

5 | Click Proceed

6 | Type the new password, and then click OK

Introduction

As a DST, you will encounter users who have forgotten the password to their local user account. To assist them, you can manually reset a user's password.

Information that is lost after a password reset

Before you reset a user's password, know that following information will be lost:

- E-mail that is encrypted with the user's public key
- Internet passwords that are saved on the computer
- Files that the user has encrypted

There are two types of password resets: local user account passwords and domain passwords.

How to reset a local user account password

To reset a local user account password, the user must log on to the computer with a different account, such as a local Administrator account.

To reset a local user account password:

1. In Control Panel, click **Performance and Maintenance**, click **Administrative Tools**, and then double-click **Computer Management**.

2. In the **Computer Management** box, in the console tree, expand **Local Users and Groups**, and then click **Users**.

3. In the details pane, right-click the user name, and then click **Set Password**.

4. Read the warning message, and then click **Proceed**.

5. In the **New password** and **Confirm password** boxes, type the new password, and then click **OK**.

Note   To perform this procedure, you must be a member of the Administrators group on the local computer, or you must have the appropriate permissions. As a security best practice, consider using the **run as** command to perform this procedure.

How to reset a domain user account password

Users do not normally have access to the Active Directory Users and Groups utility to reset their passwords. If the user does have access to the Active Directory domain controller, use the following procedure on the domain controller.

To reset a domain user account password:

1. In Control Panel, click **Performance and Maintenance**.

2. In **Performance and Maintenance**, click **Administrative Tools**, and then double-click **Active Directory Users and Computers**.

3. In the **Active Directory Users and Computers**, in the console tree, double-click **Users**.

4. In the details pane, right-click the user name, and then click **Reset Password**.

5. In the **New password** and **Confirm password** boxes, type the new password, select the **User must change password at next logon** check box, and then click **OK**.

Note   In most organizations, the DST has the authority to reset passwords on domain user accounts. To reset passwords on domain user accounts from a workstation, you must install Microsoft Windows Server™ 2003 Administrative Tools Pack (Adminpak.msi) on the Windows XP client.

How to Create a Password Reset Disk

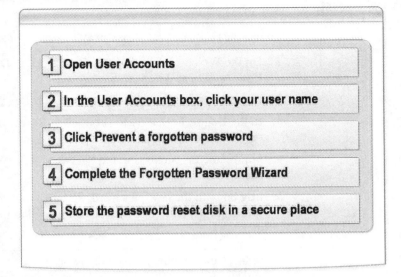

1 Open User Accounts

2 In the User Accounts box, click your user name

3 Click Prevent a forgotten password

4 Complete the Forgotten Password Wizard

5 Store the password reset disk in a secure place

Introduction

To protect a user account in the event that a user forgets the password, every local user should create a password reset disk. Then, if the user forgets his or her password, the password can be reset using the password reset disk, and the user is able to access the local user account again. A *password reset disk* is a floppy disk that contains encrypted password information that allows users to change their password without knowing the old password. As standard practice, every user should create a password reset disk and keep it in a secure location.

Note   A password reset disk can be used only for local user accounts—it cannot be used for domain user accounts.

How to create a password reset disk

The Forgotten Password Wizard enables you to create a password reset disk if you have a computer administrator account or a limited account.

To create a password reset disk:

1. In Control Panel, click **User Accounts**.

2. In the **User Accounts** dialog box, click *your user name*.

3. On the left side of the window, under **Related Tasks**, click **Prevent a forgotten password**.

4. Follow the steps in the Forgotten Password Wizard until the procedure is complete.

5. Store the password reset disk in a secure place.

How to use the password reset disk in a domain environment

If you have a local user account in a domain environment and you made a password reset disk by using the Forgotten Password Wizard, you can use the disk to access the computer.

To use the password reset disk in a domain environment:

1. On the Welcome screen, press CTRL+ALT+DEL, and then in the **Password** box, type your password.

2. If you have forgotten your password, the **Logon Failed** dialog box appears.

3. In the **Logon Failed** dialog box, click **Reset**, and then put your password reset disk in drive A.

4. Follow the instructions in the Password Reset Wizard to create a new password.

5. Log on with the new password, and then return the password reset disk to its safe storage place. The user does not need to make a new password reset disk.

Note   You can change your password after creating a password reset disk and still use the same password reset disk in the future.

Tip   Before you delete a computer from a domain, verify you are able to access that computer using at least one local Administrator account. If you do not know the passwords for any administrator accounts, you will be unable to rejoin that computer to the domain or perform any tasks requiring administrative privileges.

How to use the password reset disk in a workgroup environment

If you have a local user account in a workgroup environment and you made a password reset disk using the Forgotten Password Wizard, you can use the disk to access the computer.

To use the password reset disk in a workgroup environment:

1. On the Welcome screen, click your user name, and then type your password.

   If you have forgotten your password, the **Did you forget your password** message appears.

2. Click **Use your password reset disk**.

   The Password Reset Wizard starts.

3. Follow the instructions in the Password Reset Wizard to create a new password.

4. Log on with the new password, and then return the password reset disk to its safe storage place. The user does not need to make a new password reset disk.

How to Use Fast User Switching

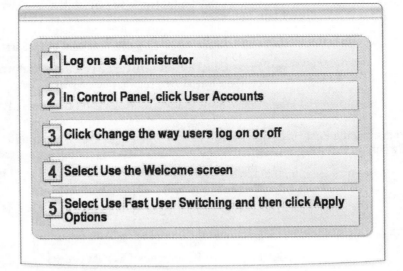

1. Log on as Administrator

2. In Control Panel, click User Accounts

3. Click Change the way users log on or off

4. Select Use the Welcome screen

5. Select Use Fast User Switching and then click Apply Options

Introduction

Fast User Switching enables multiple users to share a computer and to use it simultaneously, switching back and forth without closing programs or logging off the computer.

For example, user A is logged on and is browsing the Internet, and user B wants to log on to his user account to check his e-mail. User A can leave her programs running while user B logs on and checks his e-mail. User A can then return to her session, where her programs are still running.

Note To use Fast User Switching, you must have an administrator account on a computer that is a member of a workgroup or standalone computer. Also, Fast User Switching is not available on computers that are members of an Active Directory domain.

How to enable the Fast User Switching feature

Before you can use Fast User Switching, you must enable it.

To enable Fast User Switching:

1. Log on to the computer as Administrator.

2. In Control Panel, click **User Accounts**.

3. In the User Accounts dialog box, click **Change the way users log on or off**.

4. Ensure that the **Use the Welcome screen** check box is selected, select the **Use Fast User Switching** check box, and then click **Apply Options**.

Note To enable Fast User Switching, you must first select the **Use the Welcome screen** check box.

How to switch users without logging off

After you enable Fast User Switching, the computer returns to the Welcome screen. The current user's session remains active and another user can then log on and use the computer. You can switch users by using one of the following options:

- Click **Start**, click **Log off**, and then click **Switch User**.

- Press CTRL+ALT+DELETE, on the **Windows Task Manger** dialog box, on the **Shut Down** menu, click **Switch User**.

- Press the Windows logo key, and then press L.

How to disable the Fast User Switching feature

Programs run slower when Fast User Switching is enabled if the computer has less than 64 megabytes (MB) of random access memory (RAM). If you have less than 64 MB of RAM on your computer, you may want to consider disabling the feature.

To disable the Fast User Switching feature:

1. Log on to the computer as Administrator.

2. In Control Panel, click **User Accounts**.

3. In the User Accounts dialog box, click **Change the way users log on or off**.

4. Ensure that the **Use the Welcome screen** check box is selected, clear the **Use Fast User Switching** check box, and then click **Apply Options**.

Note   If you leave a lot of programs open when you switch users, you may notice that your computer runs slower than usual. To resolve this issue, quit some programs before you switch users.

Additional reading

For more information about using Fast User Switching, see article 279765 in the Microsoft Knowledge Base (KB).

Multimedia: Logon and Authentication

This activity presents information about:
- Local and domain logon processes
- Secondary logon process
- Smart card logon process

Important points to look for:
- Difference between local and domain authentication
- How to perform a secondary logon
- Contents of an access token

Multimedia   To view the *Logon and Authentication* presentation, open the Web page on the Student Materials compact disc, click **Multimedia**, and then click the title of the presentation. Do not open this presentation unless directed by your instructor.

Key points   The key concepts you should know about authentication are:

- Authentication identifies something or someone.

- Local logon is authenticated by the SAM database on the physical computer.

- Domain logon is authenticated by a domain controller.

- Secondary logon is authenticated by a domain controller.

- Smart cards log on to domain accounts only.

Questions   Review the information and processes in *Logon and Authentication*, and then answer the following questions.

1. What is the difference between authentication of a local logon and authentication of a domain logon?

   local logon authentication is local

2. How do you perform a secondary logon?

    Run as

3. What type of information is contained in an access token?

    SID

    Some kind, security ID changes unique.

How to Troubleshoot User Logon Issues

Issue	Solution
User profile	Ensure the user account has sufficient permissions
Domain controller	Ensure the computer is connected to the network
Cached credentials	Create a new map to a network resource
Password	Log on using a different user account and then reset the password
Domain	Ensure the correct domain is listed

Introduction

As a DST, there are some basic troubleshooting techniques that you can use to troubleshoot user logon issues. Your first priority is to determine whether the problem is on the user's computer or on the user's network. If the problem is on the network, it is may not be within the scope of your responsibilities as a DST, and you should consider escalating the call for further assistance. If you determine that the problem resides on the user's computer, you can troubleshoot the issue. This section describes common user logon issues that originate on users' computers.

Determine if the user profile caused the logon issue

User profile-related issues usually appear during the logon process. You can attempt to resolve some of these issues by starting the computer in safe mode. *Safe mode* is a method of starting Windows when a problem prevents the operating system from starting normally. Safe mode allows you to troubleshoot the operating system to determine what is not functioning properly. For example, standard safe mode troubleshooting procedures can detect and correct user profile issues that are associated with applications that launch at startup.

Note   Troubleshooting issues by using safe mode is discussed in detail in Module 5 of this course, "Resolving Hardware Issues."

If starting in safe mode does not resolve the issue, or if you are unable to locate the cause of the issue by using standard safe mode troubleshooting procedures, you should consider troubleshooting the user profile.

The first step in troubleshooting the user profile is to determine whether the user profile is the issue. This can be accomplished in several ways.

To determine if the local profile caused the issue:

- Is another user able to log on to the same computer by using a different user account? Does the other user experience the same issue? If not, the problem is definitely a user profile issue.

- If no other user accounts can access the computer, try to create a new user account. Then log off the computer, and log on again as the new user account. This forces the creation of a new local profile from the Default User profile. Does the issue go away? If so, this is a user profile issue.

- If either of the preceding steps fails to solve the issue, troubleshoot the All Users profile.

To determine if the roaming profile caused the issue:

- If the user attempts to log on to another computer, does the issue go away? If so, the issue is most likely with the All Users profile on the afflicted computer.

- If the user is unable to log on to another computer, see if another user can log on to the afflicted computer. Does the issue still occur? If so, the issue is most likely with the All Users profile.

How to troubleshoot user profile issues

If you determine that the user profile is the problem, try some or all of the following:

- Examine the amount of space that is available on the volume. If it is extremely low, instruct the user to create some free space.

- If you suspect the problem is within a certain profile subfolder, back up the contents of that folder and then delete its contents.

- Ensure that the user's account has sufficient permissions to access the profile folder.

- Restore the profile to previous settings using System Restore, following the steps outlined in article 306084 in the Microsoft Knowledge Base.

- Use the User Profile Hive Cleanup Service (Uphclean.exe) to help with slow logoff and unreconciled profile issues. For information regarding Uphclean.exe, see article 837115 in the Microsoft Knowledge Base.

If the preceding efforts fail, the user profile is probably corrupt and you must create a new profile. To create a new profile, you must log on to the computer as a user with administrative rights. Once logged on, delete the old profile and then log on to the computer with the user's account. A new profile will be created.

Important   When you create a new profile for a user, all of the user's local configuration settings are reset. This includes desktop settings, favorites, access to the My Documents folder, and so on. Therefore, you should tell the user that some information may be irretrievable.

Additional user profile issues

Other common user profile issues include:

- Changed desktop environment. The probable cause is that the user has logged on with a new user account or has switched from logging on as a local user to logging on as a domain user. Copy the user's old profile into the new profile using the User Profiles copy tool.

- Missing files. The user may have created references in the roaming profile to files that are stored on the local drive of a different computer. Instruct the user either to place these files in the roaming profile or copy them to each computer on which she plans to access these files.

Additional reading

For more information on user profiles, see articles 305506, 319974, 326688, and 314886 in the Microsoft Knowledge Base.

How to troubleshoot domain controller–related issues

When a user joins a domain, a domain controller validates the user's logon. However, sometimes when a user attempts to log on, an error message appears stating that a domain controller could not be located to perform logon. This usually occurs when a user is logging on to a computer on the domain for the first time, and the domain controller is not yet available or the computer is not connected to the domain. When this occurs, ensure that the computer is connected to the network with the correct equipment. If this does not resolve the issue, you should escalate the call for further assistance.

When a computer is unable to contact a domain controller to validate a user's logon, the user can log on to their computer by using cached credentials. *Cached credentials* are a copy of the security credentials that were last used to access the domain.

Note   Usually, if the user has logged on without domain connectivity, the computer logs on with cached credentials.

How to troubleshoot cached credentials-related issues

There are two user logon issues that occur when working with cached credentials:

- A user cannot log on using cached credentials. This occurs when a user installs Windows XP but does not install a service pack. To resolve this issue, the user must install Service Pack 1 (SP1) or greater.

- A user can log on using cached credentials but cannot connect to resources on a mapped drive. This occurs when a user can log on with cached credentials and connect to a network from a remote computer, but cannot connect to resources on a mapped drive because the user did not receive a current access token from the domain. To resolve this issue, the user should create a new map to a network resource so that an access token is reissued to the remote computer.

How to troubleshoot password-related issues

When a user attempts to log on and receives the error message, "Unknown user name or bad password," it indicates that the user is not logging on correctly. This usually occurs because:

- The user is mistyping the user name and/or password.
- The user has the CAPS LOCK key engaged.

If neither of these seems to be the cause of the logon problem and the user is not connected to a domain, the user can use a different user account to log on to the computer and then reset their password in **Users and Computers**. Also, some domain user accounts are configured to prohibit logon if a user incorrectly enters the password after a predetermined number of times. When this occurs, an account reset may be required, which requires you to escalate the call.

How to troubleshoot domain name-related issues

When a user logs on to a domain, the user account must be authenticated by the domain controller. Some corporate infrastructures contain numerous domains and the user must choose the correct domain from a drop-down list at logon. If the user does not know which domain their user account is on, they cannot log on to the computer.

The **Windows Log On** dialog box does not show a list of available domains by default. To ensure that the user is logged on to the appropriate domain, request that the user contact the company's IT department for the domain name. After the user has received the domain name, the user can then click **Options** in the **Windows Log On** dialog box and then select the correct domain name in the **Log on to** list box.

Practice: Troubleshooting User Logon Issues

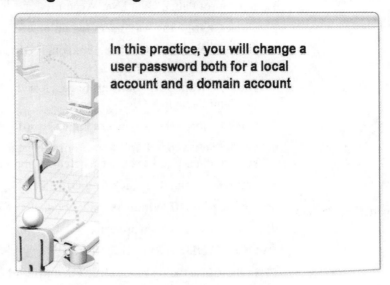

In this practice, you will change a user password both for a local account and a domain account

Objective

In this practice, you will change a user password for a domain account and also for a local account. To complete the second portion of this practice, you must be logged on with an account that is a member of the local Administrators group.

Scenario

Frank Lee has forgotten his password and has asked you to reset it. Frank also says that his team liked the ability to quickly log on and off without having to close their programs and asks you to re-enable that feature.

▶ **Reset Frank Lee's password**

1. Start the 2261_Bonn virtual machine.

2. Log on to Bonn as Administrator with a password of **P@ssw0rd**.

3. Click **Start**, right-click **My Computer**, and then click **Manage**.

4. In **Computer Management**, in the console tree, expand **Local Users and Groups**.

5. In the console tree, click **Users**, and in the details pane, right-click **Frank Lee**, and then click **Set Password**.

6. On the **Set Password for Frank Lee** dialog box, click **Proceed**.

7. In the **New password** and **Confirm password** boxes, type **newP@ssw0rd** and then click **OK**.

8. On the **Local Users and Groups** dialog box click **OK**.

9. Close **Computer Management**.

▶ **Enable Fast User Switching**

1. In Control Panel, click **User Accounts**.

2. Click **Change the way users log on or off**.

3. In the **User Accounts** dialog box, click **OK** to make changes to Offline Files settings.

4. On the **Offline Files Settings** page, clear the **Enable Offline Files** check box, and then click **OK**.

5. Click **Change the way users log on or off**.

6. On the **Select logon and logoff options** page, click **Use the Welcome screen**, click **Use Fast User Switching** and then click **Apply Options**.

7. Click **Start** and then click **Log Off**.

8. On the **Log Off Windows** dialog box, click **Switch User**.

9. The Welcome screen appears.

10. On the **Action** menu, click **Close**.

11. In the **Close** dialog box, select **Turn off and delete changes**, and then click **OK**.

Lesson: Troubleshooting User Configuration Issues

- **How to Configure Folder Views**
- **How to Migrate Files and Settings**
- **How to Configure Accessibility Settings**
- **How to Configure the User Interface Language**
- **How to Troubleshoot User Configuration Issues**

Introduction

One of the most common questions DSTs receive from users is how to configure or customize files and folders. This lesson defines folder views and explains how to access folder views to perform a variety of configuration tasks. This lesson also discusses less common but essential user tasks, such as how to configure accessibility settings for users with special needs and how to configure Windows XP for multilingual support.

Lesson objectives

After completing this lesson, you will be able to:

- Configure folder views.
- Migrate files and settings.
- Configure accessibility settings.
- Configure the User Interface Language.
- Troubleshoot user configuration issues.

How to Configure Folder Views

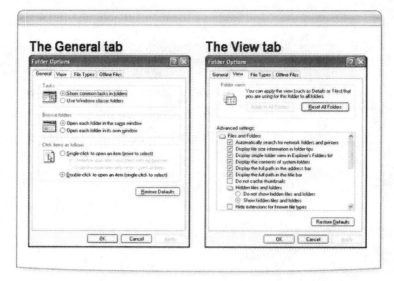

Introduction

Windows Explorer is the tool used to access the file system in Windows XP. Users can customize the way that folders and files are displayed in Windows Explorer to assist them in personalizing their data. As a DST, you will often find it helpful to configure your folder view to match your user's folder view. This enables you to see what the user sees.

How to configure folder views

A *folder view* is a group of settings that is used to customize the way a specific folder looks when shown in Windows Explorer. These settings are controlled in the **Folder Options** dialog box.

To access folder views:

1. In Control Panel, click **Appearance and Themes**.

2. In Appearance and Themes, click **Folder Options**.

In the **Folder Options** dialog box, a user can choose among a number of folder options on the following tabs:

General:

- Choose whether a new window is opened each time a folder is opened.

- Determine single-click or double-click behavior.

- Determine whether common tasks associated with the folder types are displayed in the left pane of the folder window or in Classic view, without tasks.

View:

- Apply settings for the currently selected folder or for all folders.
- Use the **Advanced Settings** list box.
  - Apply various informational settings.
  - Display the contents of system folders or issue a warning when they are accessed.
  - Show hidden files and folders.
  - Hide or display file extensions.
  - Hide system files.
  - Launch each folder opened as a separate operating system process.
  - Show encrypted and compressed files in different colors.
  - Restore system defaults for all settings.

How to configure a default folder view

Some users prefer to configure their folder view one time and then apply it to all folder views within Windows Explorer.

To configure a default view and apply it to all folders:

1. Click the folder whose view you want to change.
2. In Windows Explorer, click the **View** menu, and then select the desired view, such as **Tiles** or **Details**.
3. On the **Tools** menu, select **Folder Options**.
4. On the **View** tab, in the **Advanced Settings** list, select the additional options that you want.
5. Click **Apply to All Folders**, and then click **OK**.

How to Migrate Files and Settings

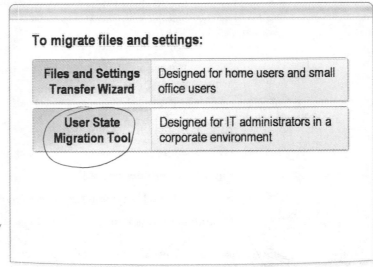

Introduction	Windows XP includes two tools for migrating files and settings that are aimed at different types of users and situations: Files and Settings Transfer Wizard and User State Migration Tool (USMT). This section describes these tools.

Files and settings migration tools

- *Files and Settings Transfer Wizard*. This tool is designed for home users and small-office users. The wizard is also useful in a corporate network environment for employees who receive a new computer and need to migrate their files and settings without the support of an IT department or DST.

    To start the Files and Settings Transfer Wizard:

    - Click **Start**, click **All Programs**, click **Accessories**, click **System Tools**, and then click **Files and Settings Transfer Wizard**.

- *USMT*. This tool is designed for IT administrators for performing large deployments of Windows XP Professional in a corporate environment. USMT provides the same functionality as the wizard, but on a large scale targeted at migrating multiple users. USMT gives administrators command-line precision in customizing specific settings such as unique modifications to the registry.

    For information on accessing USMT, see http://www.microsoft.com/technet/prodtechnol/winxppro/deploy/usermigr.mspx.

Files and Settings Transfer Wizard

Using the Files and Settings Transfer Wizard to copy files and settings reduces:

- Downtime for re-personalizing the desktop.
- Downtime due to missing work files.
- The number of calls to technical support with issues regarding re-personalizing the desktop.
- The ramp-up time using the new operating system.

Files and Settings Transfer Wizard settings

The Files and Settings Transfer Wizard settings are categorized into the following groups:

- *Appearance*. This includes items such as wallpaper, colors, sounds, and the location of the taskbar.

- *Action*. This includes items such as the key repeat rate, whether double-clicking a folder opens it in a new window or in the same window, and whether you need to double-click or single-click an item to open it.

- *Internet*. These settings allow you to connect to the Internet and control how your browser operates. This includes items such as your home page URL, favorites or bookmarks, cookies, security settings, dial-up connections, and proxy settings.

- *Mail*. This includes the information you need to connect to your mail server, your signature file, views, mail rules, local mail, and contacts. The mail clients supported are Microsoft Outlook® and Outlook Express.

USMT

USMT is a command-line tool that collects a user's documents and settings (state) before an operating system migration to Windows XP is performed and then restores them after the installation. The **ScanState** command of the USMT is run before installation to collect a user's state information. After the Windows XP installation is complete, the **LoadState** command of the tool is run to place the user's state on the computer.

USMT tasks

USMT can perform the following tasks without the modification of any associated .inf files:

- Migrate most of the user's settings including:
  - Dial-up Networking (DUN)/Remote Access Service (RAS)
  - Display settings (wallpaper, fonts, color, and so on)
  - Internet Explorer settings
  - Accessibility settings
  - Mapped drives
  - Network printers
  - Folder options
- Migrate Outlook connectivity settings
- Migrate some common types of user files to the My Documents folder

USMT files

USMT consists of the following files:

- Two executable files:
  - *ScanState.exe*. This file collects user data and settings based on the information contained in Migapp.inf, Migsys.inf, Miguser.inf, and Sysfiles.inf.
  - *LoadState.exe*. This file deposits ScanState.exe user state data on a computer running a fresh (not upgraded) installation of Windows XP Professional.

■ Four migration rule information files:

- Migapp.inf
- Migsys.inf
- Miguser.inf
- Sysfiles.inf

How to use USMT

In the simplest case, the default migration rule .inf file (Sysfiles.inf) is used as is for the migration. The administrator must create a script to run on the client workstation. The script should:

■ Run ScanState.exe on the client workstation, copying the user state data to an intermediate store. You can send a shortcut to the script to the users and instruct them to run this program when they leave for the evening, or you can deploy the script automatically or on a schedule.

■ Reformat the disk and install Windows XP Professional and applications as needed. This can be automated by using disk-imaging software.

■ Run LoadState.exe as the local administrator on the client workstation to restore the user settings. (This can be done as a scheduled task running in the local administrator context.)

Note USMT includes the same functionality as the Files and Settings Transfer Wizard, but it also permits administrators to fully customize specific settings such as unique modifications to the registry.

Practice: Migrating User Information in a Domain

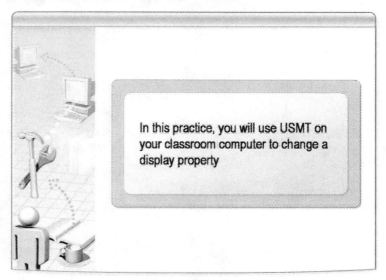

In this practice, you will use USMT on your classroom computer to change a display property

Objective

In this practice, you will use USMT on your classroom computer to change a display property. This practice illustrates the functionality of the tool in a broader, corporate environment.

Practice

► **Use USMT to change a display property**

1. Resume the 2261_London virtual machine.

2. Start the 2261_Acapulco virtual machine.

3. Using Acapulco, log on to the domain as **AcapulcoAdmin** with a password of **P@ssw0rd**.

4. Click **Start**, click **Run**, type **cmd** and then click **OK**.

5. At the command prompt, type **cd c:\program files\microsoft learning\2261\practices\mod03\usmt** and then press ENTER.

6. Type **scanstate /i migsys.inf c:** and then press ENTER.

7. Access the **Display Properties** dialog box, and change the desktop background.

8. Close all windows and log off.

9. Log on to the domain as **AcapulcoAdmin** with a password of **P@ssw0rd**

10. Click **Start**, click **Run**, type **cmd**, and then click **OK**.

11. At the command prompt, type **cd c:\program files\microsoft learning\2261\practices\mod03\usmt** and then press ENTER.

12. Type **loadstate /i migsys.inf c:** and then press ENTER.

13. Close all windows and log off.

14. Log on to the domain as **AcapulcoAdmin** with a password of **P@ssw0rd**.

15. Verify that the display is back to the original background.

16. Pause the 2261_Acapulco virtual machine.

Practice: Migrating User Information in a Workgroup

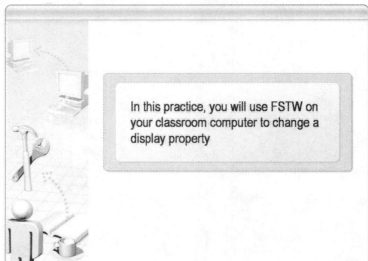

In this practice, you will use FSTW on your classroom computer to change a display property

---

Objective

In this practice, you will use Files and Settings Transfer Wizard (FSTW) on your classroom computer to change a display property. This practice illustrates the functionality of the tool in a workgroup environment.

Practice

▶ **Change a display property and save settings**

1. Start the 2261_Bonn virtual computer.

2. Using Bonn, log on locally as **Frank Lee** with a password of **P@ssw0rd**

3. Click **Start**, point to **All Programs**, point to **Accessories**, point to **System Tools**, and then click **Files and Settings Transfer Wizard**.

4. In the **Files and Settings Transfer Wizard**, click **Next**.

5. On the **Which computer is this?** page, click **Old computer**, and then click **Next**.

6. On the Select a transfer method page, click **Other**, click **Browse**, click **Desktop**, click **OK**, and then click **Next**.

7. On the What do you want to transfer? page, click **Settings Only**, select the **Let me select a custom list of files and settings when I click Next** checkbox, and then click **Next**.

8. Remove the first item under **Settings** by clicking on the item and then clicking **Remove**. Repeat this for every item except **Display properties**, and then click **Next**.

9. If prompted to overwrite, click **Yes**, and then click **Finish**.

10. Right-click the desktop, and then click **Properties**.

11. In the **Display Properties** dialog box, click the **Desktop** tab.

12. Change the desktop background to something other than **Coffee Bean**, and then click **OK**.

► **Restore settings**

1. Click **Start**, point to **All Programs**, point to **Accessories**, point to **System Tools**, and then click **Files and Settings Transfer Wizard**.

2. On the **Files and Settings Transfer Wizard** page, click **Next**.

3. On the Which computer is this? page, click **New computer**, and then click **Next**.

4. On the Do you have a Windows XP CD? page, click **I don't need the Wizard Disk. I have already collected my files and settings from my old computer**, and then click **Next**.

5. On the Where are the files and settings? page, click **Other**, and then click **Browse**, click **USMT2.UNC**, click **OK**, click **Next**, and then click **Finish**.

6. In the **File Settings Transfer Wizard** dialog box, click **Yes** to log off.

7. Log on as **Frank Lee** to verify that the background has changed back to the original.

8. Log off and pause Bonn.

How to Configure Accessibility Settings

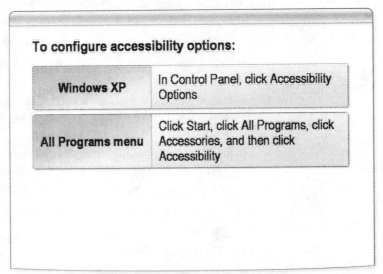

To configure accessibility options:

Windows XP	In Control Panel, click Accessibility Options
All Programs menu	Click Start, click All Programs, click Accessories, and then click Accessibility

Introduction

As a DST, you might receive a call from a user with special needs who wants to know how to set accessibility options. The accessibility options are also useful to users without special needs. For example, many users want to know how to change a cursor's blink rate or how to use FilterKeys to ignore brief or repeated keystrokes.

How to configure accessibility options

To configure accessibility options in Control Panel:

- In Control Panel, click **Accessibility Options**.

Accessibility options

You can set accessibility options for the following components:

- *Keyboard*. Includes options for enabling users to press single keystrokes to accomplish multiple-keystroke combinations or ignore brief or repeated keystrokes.

- *Sound*. Includes captions for speech and sounds or visual warning when Windows plays a sound.

- *Display*. Includes options for high-contrast colors and fonts for users with visual impairments.

- *Mouse*. Includes options such as a mouse pointer that can be controlled from the keyboard.

- *General*. Includes options such as features that automatically shut off once the system has been idle for a period of time or notifications when accessibilities features are turned on and off.

- *Administrative Options*. Determine whether to apply the current accessibility settings to only the current user or to all users that log on to this computer.

How to Configure the User Interface Language

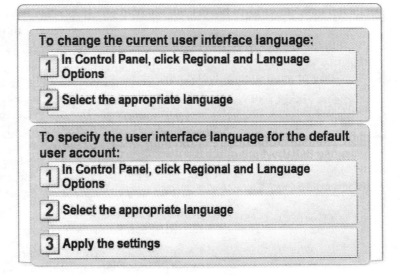

To change the current user interface language:

1. In Control Panel, click Regional and Language Options

2. Select the appropriate language

To specify the user interface language for the default user account:

1. In Control Panel, click Regional and Language Options

2. Select the appropriate language

3. Apply the settings

Introduction

Windows XP provides two levels of multilingual support: Localization and Regional and Language Options. *Localization* refers to the language that is displayed by the operating system in the user interface. *Regional and Language Options* provide the ability to view, to edit, and to print Unicode-enabled documents for users within *any* localized version of Windows. The Unicode standard enables almost all the written languages of the world to be represented using a single character set.

Localization options

To address worldwide language requirements, Windows XP Professional is offered in three distinct variations:

- English version—Standard U.S. version

- Localized versions—24 different varieties in Windows XP

- Windows XP Multilanguage User Interface (MUI)

Users can change the language options only for Unicode-based applications. Users cannot change the localization of the operating system unless they are using a computer running Windows XP with MUI.

How to configure regional and language options

Windows XP provides users with the ability to change their *input language*. This is the language they use to enter text and to view and edit Unicode-compliant documents. The operating systems also provide the ability to change the standards and formats in the operating system. Changing standards and formats allows users to specify local currency units, number formatting, and so on. Collectively, format and style settings are referred to as *regional settings*.

To configure regional and language options:

- In Control Panel, click **Date, Time, Language, and Regional Options**, and then click **Regional and Language Options**.

In the **Regional and Language Options** dialog box, you can access the following options:

- *Standard and Formats*. Customizes the unit of currency, numerical notation, and other styles. There can be any number of regional group settings.

- *Input Language Settings*. This allows the user to specify additional languages to use when viewing, editing, and printing Unicode-compliant documents. By selecting various language groups and a matching keyboard device from within this dialog box, users can gain access to the different character sets necessary to make edits to Unicode documents written in other languages. Activating this feature by adding additional languages places the **Language** toolbar on the Windows desktop, which provides the user with the ability to quickly change the language in which she is currently working. If the user has administrative privileges, she can also add support for scripted languages and East Asian languages.

  For more information on using the language bar in Windows XP, see article 306993 in the Microsoft Knowledge Base.

- *Support for non-Unicode character mapping*. If the user has administrative privileges, the **Advanced** tab can be used to manually map code-page conversion tables to documents represented in non-Unicode-based editing applications.

How to configure the user interface language

Windows XP MUI allows users to change user interface languages for the operating system only if support for additional user interface languages has been installed and an administrator has not locked the desktop by using Group Policy settings.

How to change the current user interface language

To change the current user interface language:

1. In Control Panel, click **Date, Time, Language, and Regional Options**, and then click **Regional and Language Options**.

2. Click the **Languages** tab, and then under **Language used in menus and dialogs**, select the appropriate language.

Note   This option is only available in the Windows Multilingual User Interface Pack.

How to set the language for the default user account

To set the user interface language for the default user account:

1. In **Control Panel**, click **Date**, **Time**, **Language, and Regional Options**, and then click **Regional and Language Options**.

2. In the **Regional and Language Options** dialog box, on the **Languages** tab, and then under **Language used in menus and dialogs**, select the appropriate language.

3. On the **Advanced** tab, select the **Apply all settings to the current user account and to the default user profile** check box.

Note   This option is only available in the Windows Multilingual User Interface Pack.

How to Troubleshoot User Configuration Issues

Introduction

Troubleshooting user configuration issues usually involves answering "How do I...?" questions. Users could be experiencing problems logging on to their desktop or with other profile-related issues.

How to answer configuration questions

When you are presented with configuration questions, begin by getting a clear picture of the problem and then assist the user with making the appropriate system configuration changes. Answers to many common desktop, Start menu, and taskbar issues can be found in Help and Support and in the Knowledge Base by using keywords such as "start menu," "taskbar," and "desktop."

Accessibility features. These issues are either questions regarding configuring accessibility features or disabling features that were accidentally enabled, such as StickyKeys. An excellent resource for troubleshooting accessibility is the Microsoft Accessibility Support Center at http://support.microsoft.com /default.aspx?scid=fh;EN-US;enable&Product=winxp.

Practice: Troubleshooting User Configuration Issues

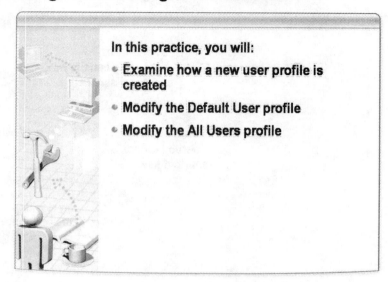

In this practice, you will:

- Examine how a new user profile is created
- Modify the Default User profile
- Modify the All Users profile

Objective

In this practice, you will:

- Examine how a new user profile is created.
- Modify the Default User profile.
- Modify the All Users profile.

Scenario

A user calls and says someone deleted all their documents in the My Documents folders as well as every link in the Favorites folder. The user also indicates they had some difficulty logging on.

▶ **Examine how a new user profile is created**

1. Resume the 2261_London virtual machine.

2. Start the 2261_Acapulco virtual machine.

3. Using Acapulco, log on to NWTRADERS as **Samantha**, and then log off.

4. Using Acapulco, log on locally as **Administrator** with a password of **P@ssw0rd**.

5. Click **Start**, and then click **Run**.

6. In the **Open** box, type **c:\documents and settings** and then click **OK**.

   The Documents and Settings folder contains the profiles that exist on the computer. There is a profile called Samantha. Where did this profile come from?

   Created when Samantha logon.

7. Close the Documents and Settings window.

▶ **Modify the Default User profile**

1. Using Acapulco, click **Start**, click **Run**, type **c:**, and then click **OK**.

2. In the **Local Disk (C:)** window, click **Show the contents of this folder**.

3. On the **File** menu, point to **New**, and then click **Text Document**, type **M3PracticeC_default**, and press ENTER.

4. Close all windows.

5. Click **Start**, and then click **Run**.

6. In the **Open** box, type **c:\documents and settings \default user\desktop**, and then click **OK**.

Note   Since, by default, the Default User folder is hidden, default user will not auto-complete as you are typing in the **Open** box.

---

7. In the **Desktop** window, on the **File** menu, point to **New**, and then click **Shortcut**.

8. In the **Create Shortcut** dialog box, in the **Type the location of the item** box, type **C:\M3PracticeC_default .txt**, and then click **Next**.

9. Click **Finish**.

10. Click **Start**, right-click **My Computer**, and then click **Manage**.

11. In the **Computer Management** console, in the console tree, expand **Local Users and Groups**.

12. In the console tree, right-click **Users**, and then click **New User**.

13. In the **User name** box, type **mod3user_c**, and in the **Password** and **Confirm Password** boxes, type **P@ssw0rd**.

14. Clear the **User must change password at next logon** check box, click **Create**, and then click **Close**.

15. Close all windows and log off of Acapulco.

16. Using Acapulco, log on locally as **mod3user_c** with a password of **P@ssw0rd**.

    Notice that the text document appears on the desktop of mod3user_c. Why does the shortcut appear in mod3user_c's profile?

    Added it to the default profile new user will see it

17. Log off Acapulco.

18. Log on locally to **Acapulco** as **Samantha Smith** with a password of **P@ssw0rd**.

    Does the text document not appear on Samantha Smith's desktop?

    No she is not new user does not use default. Yes because she has not logon.

▶ **Modify the All Users profile**

1. Log off the Acapulco.

2. Using Acapulco, log on locally as **Administrator** with a password of **P@ssw0rd**

3. Click **Start**, click **Run**, in the Open box, type **c:**, and then click **OK**.

4. If you are unable to see the contents of the folder, click **Show contents of this folder**.

5. In the Local Disk (C:) window, on the **File** menu, point to **New**, and then click **Text Document**.

6. Name the document **All User's Text Document**.

7. Close all windows.

8. Click **Start**, and then click **Run**.

9. In the **Open** box, type **c:\documents and settings\all users**, click **OK**, and then double-click **Desktop**.

10. In the Desktop window, on the **File** menu, point to **New**, and then click **Shortcut**.

11. In the **Create Shortcut** dialog box, type **c:\all user's text document.txt**, click **Next**, and then click **Finish**.

12. Close all windows, log off of Acapulco, and then log on to Acapulco again as **mod3user_c** with a password of **P@ssw0rd**.

    Why do both icons appear on mod3user_c's desktop?

    Yes all users

13. Using Acapulco, close all windows and log off.

14. Pause the 2261_Acapulco and 2261_London virtual machines.

Lesson: Troubleshooting Security Issues

- **Windows XP Security in a Local Security Environment**
- **How to Protect a Computer on the Internet**
- **How to Audit Events**
- **How to Troubleshoot Security Issues**

Introduction

A major concern of any computer user is how to ensure that their computer and network are secure. Windows XP users often want to protect business data by encrypting files and folders or managing access to the network and the resources located on it. Regardless of whether you will work with home users or corporate users, you will need to address a wide variety of security-related issues.

Lesson objectives

After completing this lesson, you will be able to:

- Describe Windows security in a local security environment.
- Identify methods for protecting a computer on the Internet.
- Use audit logs for troubleshooting.
- Troubleshoot security and local policy settings.

Windows XP Security in a Local Security Environment

- **Local Security Policy Controls:**
  - Who accesses the computer
  - Which resources are available
  - Whether actions are recorded in the Event Log

Introduction

Security policy is a combination of the security settings that affect the security on a computer. To view and configure security settings on a local computer, you must have administrative rights to the computer. Local Security Policy is a Windows XP Professional administrative tool that you can use to view and configure security settings.

What is Local Security Policy?

A *local security policy* refers to the security information on a local computer. It can be implemented on any computer to grant or deny rights to user accounts and groups that are local to that computer. A local security policy enables you to control:

- Who accesses the computer.

- Which resources users are authorized to use on their computer.

- Whether a user or group's actions are recorded in Event Log. (*Event Log* is a service that records in the system, security, and application logs.)

Note   When a local security policy is changed, it affects only the computer on which the change was made. To apply changes to an entire workgroup, you must make the change on each local computer.

Security settings that can be configured

Windows XP Professional enables you to configure security settings in the following areas:

- *Account Policies*. Includes password policies, such as minimum password length.

- *Local Policies*. Includes auditing policy, assignment of user rights and privileges, and various security options.

- *Event Log Settings*. Used to control auditing for security events, such as failed logon and logoff attempts.

- *Public Key Policies*. Used to configure encrypted data and other public key policies.

- *Software Restriction Policies.* Used to prevent unwanted applications, such as viruses or other harmful software, from running.

- *IP Security Policies.* Used to configure network Internet Protocol (IP) security.

- *Restricted Groups.* Used to manage the members of built-in groups that have predefined capabilities, such as Administrators, Power Users, and so on.

- *System Services.* Used to manage security settings for areas such as network services, file and print services, and so on.

- *Registry.* Used to manage the security descriptors on registry subkeys and entries.

- *File System.* Used to configure and manage security settings on the local file system.

You can use Local Security Settings to modify account policies, local policies, public key policies, and IP security policies for a local computer.

How to configure Local Security Settings

To configure the **Local Security Settings**:

1. In Control Panel, click **Performance and Maintenance**, click **Administrative Tools**, and then double-click **Local Security Policy**.

2. In the **Local Security Settings** box, perform the following procedures:

    - To edit Password Policy or Account Lockout Policy, click **Account Policies** in the console tree.

    –Or–

    - To edit an Audit Policy, User Right Assignment, or Security Options, click **Local Policies** in the console tree.

3. In the details pane, double-click the policy that you want to modify.

4. Make the appropriate changes, and then click **OK**.

5. To change other policies, repeat steps 3 and 4.

Important   If the Windows XP Local Security Policy tool is used incorrectly, it can cause serious problems with a computer, such as the inability to perform certain tasks or to log on to the computer.

Windows XP Security in a Domain Environment

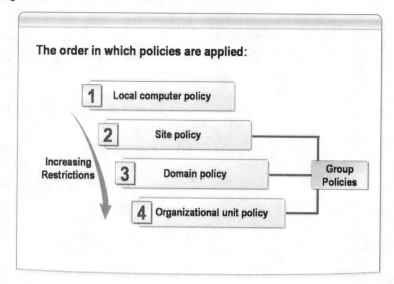

Introduction	Ensuring Windows XP security in a domain environment is significantly different than in a workgroup environment. This section describes how Group Policy is used to provide security in a domain environment.
What is Group Policy?	Windows security in a domain environment is managed by using Group Policy. *Group Policy* is the primary administrative tool for defining and controlling how applications, network resources, and the operating system function for users and computers in an organization. For example, you can use Group Policy to control user access to files and folders, to control user logon rights, and to configure user account lockout restrictions.
	Group Policy applies not only to users and client computers, but also to member servers, domain controllers, and any other computers running Windows 2000 within the scope of management. By default, Group Policy that is applied to a domain affects all computers and users in the domain. The Active Directory Users and Computers snap-in also provides a built-in domain controllers organizational unit (OU). If you keep your domain controller accounts here, you can use the Group Policy object Default Domain Controllers Policy to manage domain controllers separately from other computers.
Benefits of Group Policy and its extensions	■ Manage registry-based policy with Administrative Templates. Group Policy creates a file that contains registry settings that are written to the User or Local Machine portion of the registry database. User profile settings that are specific to a user who logs on to a given workstation or server are written to the registry under **HKEY_CURRENT_USER** (HKCU), and computer-specific settings are written under **HKEY_LOCAL_MACHINE** (HKLM).
	■ Assign scripts. This includes such scripts as computer startup, shutdown, logon, and logoff.
	■ Redirect folders. You can redirect folders, such as My Documents and My Pictures, from the Documents and Settings folder on the local computer to network locations.

- Manage applications. With Group Policy, you can assign, publish, update, or repair applications by using the Software Installation extension.
- Specify security options.

Order of Group Policy application

In an Active Directory environment, Group Policy is applied to users or computers on the basis of their membership in sites, domains, or OUs. As a result, policies can come from more than one source and are applied in the following order:

1. First, local computer policy
2. Second, site policy
3. Third, domain policy
4. Fourth, organizational unit policy

Note If a conflict occurs when applying policies, the last policy overrides all previous policies.

Warning When you modify security settings on a local computer using the Local Security Policy tool, you are directly modifying the settings on the computer. On a local computer, the security settings are applied immediately; however, the settings remain in effect only until the security settings are refreshed. On a workstation or server, the security settings are refreshed every 90 minutes, and on a domain controller, they are refreshed every five minutes. The settings are refreshed every 16 hours, regardless of whether settings were modified.

Tools for Troubleshooting Group Policy

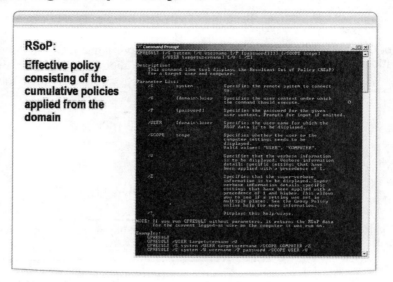

RSoP:

Effective policy consisting of the cumulative policies applied from the domain

---

Introduction

Windows XP includes tools and features that enable administrators to plan, monitor, and troubleshoot Group Policy computers in a domain environment. As a DST, you can use the tools described in this section to troubleshoot your users' issues regarding Group Policy.

Command-line tools for Group Policy

Windows XP includes the following command-line tools for Group Policy:

- Gpresult. Use this troubleshooting tool to see what policy is in effect.

- Gpupdate. Use this tool to force Group Policy to immediately refresh and to permit certain options to be specified on the command line.

What is RSoP?

Resultant Set of Policy (RSoP) is an addition to Group Policy that makes policy implementation and troubleshooting easier. Specifically, RSoP is a query engine that polls existing policies and then reports the results of the query. In addition to checking the policies set by Group Policy, RSoP also checks Software Installation for any applications that are associated with a particular user or computer and reports the results of these queries as well. RSoP details all the policy settings that are configured by an administrator. When policies are applied on multiple levels, the results can be in conflict. If a conflicting policy is set, it can be difficult to track down and change. RSoP makes troubleshooting easier because you can use it to determine the final set of policies that is applied and then track down policy precedence. RSoP includes two modes:

- Planning mode. Enables administrators to plan how Group Policy changes will affect a user or group.

- Logging mode. Enables administrators to verify the policies that are currently in effect on a specific computer.

How to use RSoP to determine a user's policy settings

You can use the command-line tool Gpresult.exe to display Group Policy settings and RSoP for a user or a computer.

To use Gpresult to display Group Policy settings and RSoP:

- Click **Start**, click **Run**, and then in the **Run** box, type **gpresult**

    For information about other options, in the **Run** box, type **gpresult /?**

Note   As a DST, you might not be able to change the policy settings on a user's local computer because of domain policy restrictions.

What is the Group Policy tool?

Windows XP Help and Support includes the Group Policy tool, which lists and describes a user's Group Policy settings. For example, this tool provides computer information, such as computer name, domain, site, and the last time the Group Policy was applied; applied Group Policy objects; security group membership when Group Policy was applied; security settings, and so on. When you receive the data from this tool, you can teach the user how to export the information to a file. The user can then e-mail the file to you for examination and troubleshooting.

How to use the Group Policy tool

To access the Group Policy tool:

1. Click **Start**, and then click **Help and Support**.
2. In the **Help and Support Center** dialog box, in the right pane, click **Tools**.
3. In the left pane, click **Advanced System Information**.
4. In the right pane, click **View Group Policy settings applied**.

The Group Policy tool data may take a few moments to display.

The Group Policy Management Console (GPMC)

Another tool that is more extensive in managing Group Policy settings is the Group Policy Management Console (GPMC). The GPMC allows administrators to manage Group Policy for multiple domains and sites within one or more forests, all in a simplified user interface with drag-and-drop support. The functionality of this tool includes backup, restore, import, copy, and reporting of Group Policy objects (GPOs).

However, this tool must be downloaded and installed separately. For more information on GPMC, see http://www.microsoft.com/windowsserver2003/gpmc/gpmcwp.mspx

How to Protect a Computer on the Internet

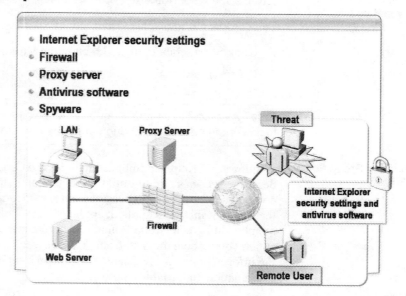

Introduction

To establish a secure Internet connection, users need a combination of Internet Explorer security settings, firewall, proxy server, antivirus software, and spyware. Without these tools, users risk leaving their computers vulnerable to damage caused by hackers and computer viruses.

Internet Explorer security settings

Microsoft Internet Explorer is capable of downloading active content. *Active content* is material on a Web page that changes on the screen with time or in response to user action. Active content is normally implemented through Microsoft ActiveX® controls and Java applets and scripts.

Because active content can be used to run viruses, Internet Explorer provides security settings that can prevent certain types of scripts, controls, or applets from downloading. Security zones in Internet Explorer let a user divide Internet sites into four categories, or *zones*, according to a site's perceived level of trustworthiness. The zones are:

- Local Intranet. Initially, any site that a user connects to on an internal network is automatically assigned to the Local Intranet zone. Internet Explorer gives this zone a medium-low level of security.

- Internet. Internet Web sites are assigned to the Internet zone, which is given a medium level of security.

- Trusted Sites. If a user implicitly trusts a site, the user can move the site into the Trusted Sites zone. By default, Internet Explorer applies a low level of security to the Trusted Sites zone.

- Restricted Sites. Sites that warrant a high degree of watchfulness are in the Restricted Sites zone. By default, Internet Explorer applies a high level of security to this zone.

Warning *Never* accept a download for a component from a site that is not in the Trusted Sites zone.

Firewalls	A *firewall* acts as a protective boundary between a network or local computer and the Internet. Firewall software can monitor Internet connections and block unwanted connections to the local computer. In Windows XP, the Windows Firewall protects a user's connection to the Internet.
How to enable the Windows Firewall	To enable the Windows Firewall in Windows XP:

1. In Control Panel, click **Security Center**, and then click **Windows Firewall**.
2. In the Windows Firewall window, verify **On (recommended)** is selected and then click **OK**.

How to set a proxy in Internet Explorer	A *proxy server* is a firewall component that manages Internet traffic to and from a local area network (LAN). The proxy server can also provide other features, such as document caching and access control.

Some networks use a proxy server to connect to the Internet. In this environment, a user must specify the server name in Microsoft Internet Explorer settings.

To set a proxy in Internet Explorer:

1. In Control Panel, click **Security Center**, and then click **Internet Options**.
2. On the **Connections** tab, click **LAN Settings**.
3. Select **Use a proxy server for your LAN**.
4. In the **Address** box, enter the name of the proxy, and in the **Port** box, enter the port setting.

Note   The port setting is typically 80.

---

5. Select **Bypass proxy server for local addresses**.
6. Click **OK** twice.

Antivirus software	Antivirus software can protect a local computer from viruses. Antivirus software scans all files on a computer and looks for malicious code. Antivirus software includes an active scanner that scans files as they are loaded into memory. Microsoft does not provide antivirus software; users must use third-party software.
Spyware	Spyware is software that sends personal information to a third party without a user's permission or knowledge. This can include information about Web sites a user visits or more sensitive information, such as a user name and password. Unscrupulous companies often use this data to send users unsolicited targeted advertisements.

How to Audit Events

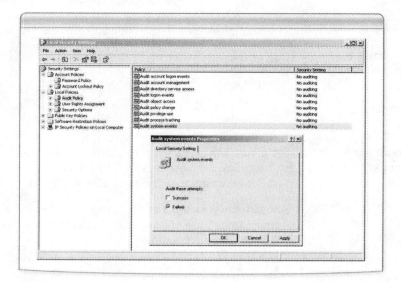

Introduction

Security auditing monitors security-related events to detect intruders and to detect attempts to compromise data on a system. A failed logon attempt is an example of an event that can be audited.

Auditing can also help in troubleshooting events within the operating system. DSTs can use audit logs to determine behavior of the operating system over a period of time.

Types of auditing events

The most common types of events that you can audit are:

- Access to objects, such as files and folders.

- Management of user and group accounts.

- Attempts by users to log on and off the system.

In addition to auditing security-related events, a security log is generated that provides a way for users to view the security events reported in the log. Users can view the security log with Event Viewer.

How to configure local security auditing

To complete this procedure, you must be logged on as an administrator or a member of the Administrators group. If your computer is connected to a network, network policy settings may prevent you from completing an audit.

To configure local security auditing:

1. Log on as Administrator.

2. In Control Panel, click **Performance and Maintenance**.

3. In Performance and Maintenance, click **Administrative Tools**.

4. In the **Administrative Tools** dialog box, double-click **Local Security Policy** to start the Local Security Settings snap-in in Microsoft Management Console (MMC).

5. Double-click **Local Policies**, and then double-click **Audit Policy**.

6. In the right pane, double-click the policy you want to enable or disable.

7. Select **Success** or **Fail,** as appropriate.

Note   If you are connected to a domain, and a domain-level policy is defined, domain-level settings override the local policy settings.

How to view the security log

To view the security log:

1. In **Administrative Tools**, double-click **Computer Management**.

2. In the console tree, click **Event Viewer**.

3. In the details pane, double-click **Security**.

4. To see more information on an event, in the details pane, double-click the event.

Additional reading

For more information on auditing security-related events, see articles 310399, 248260, and 252412 in the Microsoft Knowledge Base.

How to Troubleshoot Security Issues

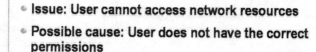

- Issue: User cannot access network resources
- Possible cause: User does not have the correct permissions

Introduction

When users call about security issues, they generally cannot access files, printers, or some other network resource. It is the job of the DST to determine whether the user has the correct permissions to access that resource.

The DST typically does not have access to edit security or local policy settings in a domain environment. However, the DST can use RSoP to determine whether the user has the correct permissions to allow access to resources. If the issue is one that requires a domain policy change, that issue must be escalated.

Troubleshooting tips

Gather the following information when working with security and local policy settings:

Is the user having issues accessing a resource? Is it a local or network resource? What kind of network is the user on: workgroup or domain? Is it an issue of connectivity or a security problem?

Many applications fail and issue error messages that are related to security and policy settings. When a user reports an application error, consider what the application might be doing and investigate the possibility of policy restrictions as the cause. As always, ask the user when the problem first began and whether the application has ever worked properly.

Additional reading

For more information on working with security and local policies, see articles 289289, 269799, and 307882 in the Microsoft Knowledge Base.

Practice: Troubleshooting Security

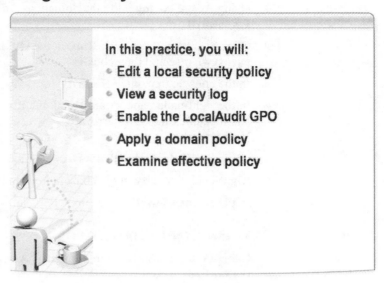

In this practice, you will:
- Edit a local security policy
- View a security log
- Enable the LocalAudit GPO
- Apply a domain policy
- Examine effective policy

Objective

In this practice, you will:

- Change a local policy and verify that the policy was successfully applied.
- Enable a GPO on the domain that overrides the local policy.
- Examine the effective policy, also known as the RSoP.

Scenario

You are troubleshooting a policy issue and notice that even though you set a local policy, it does not take effect.

▶ **Edit a local security policy**

1. Resume both 2261_London and 2261_Acapulco virtual machines.

2. Using Acapulco, log on to the NWTRADERS domain as **Administrator** with a password of **P@ssw0rd**.

3. Click **Start**, and then click **Run**.

4. In the **Open** box, type **secpol.msc** and then click **OK**.

5. In the **Local Security Settings** console, expand **Local Policies** in the console tree, and then click **Audit Policy**.

6. In the details pane, double-click **Audit logon events**.

7. Select the **Success** checkbox, and then click **OK**.

8. Close the **Local Security Settings** console.

9. Log off Acapulco.

▶ **View the security log**

1. Using Acapulco, log on to the domain as **Administrator** with a password of **P@ssw0rd**.

2. Click **Start**, and then click **Run**, in the **Open** dialog box, type **eventvwr.msc** and then click **OK**.

3. In the console tree, click **Security**.

4. In the right-hand pane, double-click the first audit event to see its details, and then click the down arrow to view each of the events. If the **Event Viewer** dialog box appears, click **No**.

5. Click **OK** in the **Event Properties** dialog box.

6. Right-click **Security** in the console tree, and then click **Clear all Events**.

7. In the **Event Viewer** dialog box, click **No**.

▶ **To enable the LocalAudit GPO:**

1. Using London, log on to the domain as **Administrator** with a password of **P@ssw0rd**.

2. Click **Start**, point to **Administrative Tools**, and then click **Active Directory Users and Computers**.

3. Right-click **nwtraders.msft**, and then select **Properties**.

4. Click the **Group Policy** tab.

5. Click **localaudit**, and then click **Options**.

6. Clear the **Disabled** check box, and then click **OK**.

7. In the **nwtraders.msft Properties** dialog box, click **OK**.

▶ **To apply a domain policy**

1. Using Acapulco, click **Start**, and then click **Run**.

2. In the **Open** box, type **gpupdate /force** and then click **OK**.

3. Using Acapulco, log on to the domain as **Administrator** with a password of **P@ssw0rd**.

4. Click **Start**, and then click **Run**, in the **Open** box, type **secpol.msc** and then click **OK**.

5. In the **Local Security Settings** console, expand **Local Policies** in the console tree, click **Audit Policy**, and then double-click one of the policies in the details pane.

   Can you change the Audit logon events?

   No

6. Close all windows.

► **Examine effective policy**

1. Using Acapulco, click **Start**, and then click **Run**, in the **Open** box, type **cmd** and then click **OK**.

2. At the command prompt type **gpresult /v > c:\gpo.txt** and press ENTER.

3. At the command prompt type **notepad c:\gpo.txt** and press ENTER.

4. In Notepad, scroll down the window to find Applied Group Policy Objects.

5. Is localaudit listed as one of the Applied Group Policy Objects?

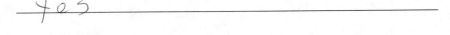

6. On the 2261_London – Microsoft Virtual PC 2004 window, on the **Action** menu, click **Close**.

7. On the **Close** dialog box, click **Turn off and delete changes**, and then click **OK**.

8. Close all windows and log off Acapulco.

9. Pause the 2261_Acapulco virtual machines.

Lesson: Troubleshooting System Performance

- Multimedia: Creating a Performance Baseline
- Tools for Maintaining System Performance
- Tools for Troubleshooting System Performance
- How to Troubleshoot System Performance

Introduction

Poor system performance is one of the most common end-user complaints. Computers become slower over time for a variety of reasons: files become disorganized, unnecessary software consumes resources, too many programs run at startup, a virus invades a computer, and so on. As a DST, you must determine the cause of poor performance and then use the appropriate tool to solve the performance issue. This lesson describes various tools that you can use to improve system performance.

Lesson objectives

After completing this lesson, you will be able to:

- Explain the purpose of monitoring system performance.
- Describe the tools that help maintain system performance.
- Describe the tools that help troubleshoot system performance.
- Troubleshoot system performance.

Multimedia: Creating a Performance Baseline

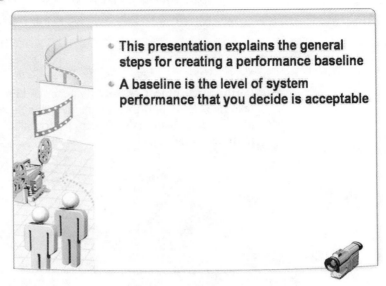

Introduction

Users can experience sudden, unexplained slowdowns in system performance. Routine actions that normally take a few microseconds suddenly cause the computer to stop responding and the hard disk to make excessive noise. These are symptoms of poor system performance.

Multimedia

To view the *Creating a Performance Baseline* presentation, open the Web page on the Student Materials compact disc, click **Multimedia**, and then click the title of the presentation. Do not open this presentation unless directed to do so by your instructor.

Key points

System performance is typically measured in two ways: CPU usage and page file usage.

- *CPU usage* is a measurement of the amount of time the CPU is being used to execute a program. If a program has excessive CPU utilization, it will slow down the computer.

- *Page file usage* is a measure of memory usage, or how much RAM is currently being used. If all RAM is currently in use, Windows will create additional virtual memory by using a page file to increase the amount of memory available. The process of adding information to a page file is called *paging*. When a computer is paging excessively, system performance suffers.

Key points from the presentation are:

- Baseline. Take samples of counter values every 30 to 45 minutes for one week, during peak, low, and normal operations.

- General steps for creating a baseline:

  a. Identify resources.

  b. Capture data.

  c. Store data.

- Four major system resources for performance baselines:
  - Memory
  - Processor
  - Physical disk
  - Network
- Performance object. Is the data generated by a system component or resource? Each performance object provides *counters,* which represent data about specific aspects of system performance. Performance objects can have multiple instances.

Tools for Maintaining System Performance

- **Disk Defragmenter:**
  - Consolidates fragmented files and folders
  - Increases efficiency
- **Check Disk (Chkdsk):**
  - Displays status report for a disk
  - Lists and corrects errors on disk
- **Disk Cleanup:**
  - Finds unnecessary files that may be deleted
  - Creates space on the hard drive

Introduction

Windows comes with a set of tools that help maintain system performance. These tools can organize information on the hard disk, remove unused files, and report damaged files.

Disk Defragmenter

Disk Defragmenter consolidates fragmented files and folders on a computer's hard disk so that each file and folder occupies a single, contiguous space on the volume. As a result, a computer can gain access to files and folders and save new ones more efficiently. By consolidating files and folders, Disk Defragmenter also consolidates the volume's free space, making it less likely that new files will be fragmented.

To use Disk Defragmenter:

- Click **Start**, point to **All Programs**, point to **Accessories**, point to **System Tools**, and then click **Disk Defragmenter**.

Check Disk (Chkdsk)

Check Disk is a program that verifies the logical integrity of a file system. If Chkdsk encounters logical inconsistencies in file system data, it performs actions that repair the file system data, assuming that the data is not in read-only mode. As Chkdsk runs, the program creates a status report of the disk, including the errors it encounters and corrects.

To use the Check Disk tool to fix errors:

- Click **Start**, click **Run**, type **chkdsk /f** and then click **OK**.

When it is used without parameters, Chkdsk displays the status of the disk in the current drive.

Disk Cleanup

Disk Cleanup helps create available space on the hard disk. Disk Cleanup searches the hard disk drive, and then shows temporary files, Internet cache files, and unnecessary program files that a user can safely delete. A user can direct Disk Cleanup to delete some or all files.

To open Disk Cleanup:

- Click **Start**, point to **All Programs**, point to **Accessories**, point to **System Tools**, and then click **Disk Cleanup**.

Tools for Troubleshooting System Performance

- **Task Manager:**
  - Information about computer performance
  - Details about programs and processes
- **System Configuration Utility:**
  - Automates troubleshooting steps
  - Modifies system configuration
  - Enables access to the System Restore utility
- **Perfmon:**
  - System Monitor: View data about memory, disk, processor, and network
  - Performance: Logs data and alerts, and provides system information

Introduction

When a user thinks that his computer is performing poorly, he will often contact technical support for assistance. Performance issues are time-dependent; they do not have the characteristics common to other types of issues in that they rarely involve error messages, specific actions taken, or "How do I...?" questions on the part of the user.

Many of these issues require making an initial attempt to clean up and streamline the operating system in a general sense and asking the user to monitor the performance of the computer for a specified period of time, necessitating a callback. Very difficult issues may require the implementation of advanced performance monitoring tools to log performance data. In this case, you may need to escalate an issue.

However, the DST has many useful tools to assist in diagnosing and resolving the most common performance problems.

Task Manager

Windows Task Manager provides information about computer performance and displays details about programs and processes that are running on a computer. By using Task Manager, a user can view network status when connected to the network, end programs or processes, start programs, and view a dynamic display of the computer's performance. Task Manager contains the following tabs:

- **Applications**. Shows the status of the programs running on the computer. On this tab, users can end, switch to, or start a program.

- **Processes**. Shows information about the processes running on the computer. For example, this tab displays CPU and memory usage information, page faults, handle counts, and a number of other parameters.

- **Performance**. Displays a dynamic overview of the computer's performance, including:
  - Graphs for CPU and memory usage.
  - Totals for the number of handles, threads, and processes running on the computer.
  - Totals, in kilobytes, for physical, kernel, and commit memory.
- **Networking**. Displays a graphical representation of network performance. This tab provides a qualitative indicator that shows the status of the network(s) running on the computer. The **Networking** tab is displayed only if a network card is present.
- **Users**. Displays users who can access the computer and session status and names in Windows XP. The **Users** tab is displayed only if the computer has Fast User Switching enabled and is a standalone computer or a member of a workgroup. The **Users** tab is unavailable on computers that are members of a network domain.
  - Client Name. Specifies the name of the client computer using the session, if applicable.
  - Session. Provides a name for users to use to perform such tasks as sending another user a message or connecting to another user's session.

To start Task Manager:

- Press CTRL+ALT+DEL or right-click on an open part of the taskbar, and then in the **Windows Securities** box, click **Task Manager**.

To end a program that hangs or crashes:

- In Task Manager, on the **Applications** tab, click the program you want to end, and then click **End Task**.

Important   When you use Task Manager to end a program, any data changes entered or made in that program are lost.

To end a process that hangs or crashes:

- In Task Manager, on the **Process** tab, click the process you want to end, and then click **End Process**.

To end a process and all processes directly or indirectly related to it:

- In Task Manager, on the **Process** tab, right-click the process you want to end, and then click **End Process Tree**.

Important   Be careful when using Task Manager to end a process. If you end a system service, some part of the system may not function properly.

System Configuration Utility

The System Configuration Utility automates the routine troubleshooting steps used by the DST when diagnosing Windows configuration issues. In addition, the System Configuration Utility provides access to the System Restore feature of Windows XP.

Users can use System Restore to undo harmful changes to their computer. To open System Restore:

1. Click **Start**, click **Run**, type **msconfig** and then click **OK**.

2. On the **General** tab of the System Configuration Utility, click **Launch System Restore**.

Windows Performance tool (Perfmon)

The Windows Performance tool (Perfmon) has two parts: System Monitor and Performance Logs and Alerts.

With System Monitor, users can collect and view real-time data about memory, disk, processor, network, and other activity in graph, histogram, or report form.

With Performance Logs and Alerts, users can configure logs to record performance data and set system alerts to notify them when a specified counter's value is above or below a defined threshold.

To open the Windows Performance tool:

- In Control Panel, click **Administrative Tools**, and then double-click **Performance**.

How to Troubleshoot System Performance

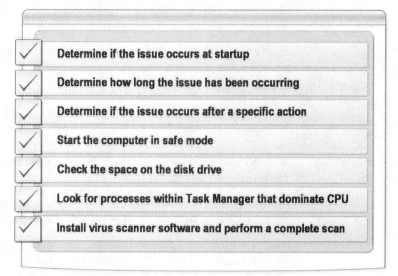

✓	**Determine if the issue occurs at startup**
✓	**Determine how long the issue has been occurring**
✓	**Determine if the issue occurs after a specific action**
✓	**Start the computer in safe mode**
✓	**Check the space on the disk drive**
✓	**Look for processes within Task Manager that dominate CPU**
✓	**Install virus scanner software and perform a complete scan**

Introduction

Performance issues can be generated by many different, unconnected factors and can be difficult to find and eliminate. Additionally, performance issues may be caused by other problems that are beyond the control of the DST or user. It can be challenging to explain these issues to users and to direct them to the appropriate location for additional help.

How to address performance problems

Use your judgment in selecting the best place to start, based upon the user's description of the problem. The following steps are available for troubleshooting performance issues:

- Does the issue occur at startup? If so, troubleshoot in safe mode or perform a virus scan.

- Does the issue occur over a period of time? If so, it could be a leaking memory application or service. Use msconfig to analyze the computer, direct the user to reboot, and wait the prescribed amount of time with the computer in this state. Issue a ticket number, have the user test the issue, document what you did, and instruct the user to call back with the results.

- Does the issue occur when a specific action is taken, such as opening an application? Identify the application and troubleshoot its installation and configuration.

- Start the computer in safe mode. If the issue goes away, perform standard boot issue troubleshooting procedures.

- Check the space on the disk drive. If there is less than 100 MB of free space, direct the user to clean up the disk drive using one or more of the following steps:

  - Delete temporary Internet files in Internet Explorer.

  - Empty the C:\Temp directory.

  - Search for and delete .chk files.

  Warning   Do not assist the user in making decisions about other types of files because this could lead to a potential data-loss issue.

  - Run the Check Disk and Disk Defragmenter programs.

- Some performance issues are related to networking; for example, problems with mapped drives may cause Windows Explorer to stop responding.

- Look for processes within Task Manager that dominate the available CPU usage. Check the memory performance.

- If all else fails, direct the user to install or update virus scanner software and then perform a complete scan of the computer.

Additional reading   For more information on troubleshooting system performance, see articles 308219 and 308417 in the Microsoft Knowledge Base, and also see the Windows XP Professional Resource Kit.

Practice: Troubleshooting System Performance

In this practice, you will:

- Run a CPU stress test
- Examine and monitor high CPU and memory usage effects
- Run an application that simulates memory leaks and examine its effects

Objective

In this practice, you will:

- Run a CPU stress utility.
- Examine and monitor high CPU and memory usage effects by using the **Performance** tab in Task Manager.
- Run an application that simulates a memory leak and examine its effects.

Practice

▶ **Run a CPU stress test and monitor CPU usage**

1. Resume Acapulco, log on locally as **Administrator** with a password of **P@ssw0rd**.
2. Right-click the **taskbar**, click **Task Manager**, and then click the **Performance** tab.
3. Click **Start**, and then click **Run**, in the **Open** box, type **c:\program files\ microsoft learning\2261\practices\mod03** and then click **OK**.
4. Double-click **cpustres**.
5. Position the Task Manager and the CPU Stress windows so that you can view both simultaneously.
6. In the CPU Stress window, select the **Thread 2**, **Thread 3**, and **Thread 4 Active** check boxes. Note the change in Task Manager.

7. In the CPU Stress window, select **Busy** from each thread's **Activity** drop-down list. Note the changes in Task Manager.

   What happens if you increase the Thread Priority for each thread to Highest?

   _____

   _____

8. Close **CPU Stress**.

▶ **Run a memory-leaking application and monitor memory usage**

1. In the Mod03 folder, double-click **leakyapp**.

2. Position the Task Manager and the My Leaky App windows so that you can view both simultaneously.

3. In My Leaky App, click **Start Leaking**.

   In Task Manager, notice the increase in page file usage.

4. In My Leaky App, click **Stop Leaking**, and then click **Reset** to release the memory used.

5. Close My Leaky App.

6. Close all windows and log off.

▶ **To close virtual machines without saving changes**

1. Using Acapulco, on the **Action** menu, click **Close**.

2. On the **Close** dialog box, select **Turn off and delete changes**.

Lab: Resolving Desktop Management Issues

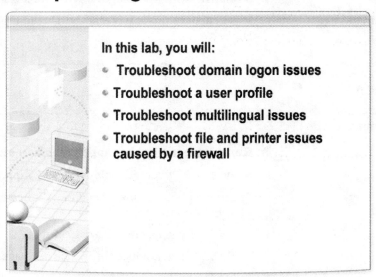

In this lab, you will:

- **Troubleshoot domain logon issues**
- **Troubleshoot a user profile**
- **Troubleshoot multilingual issues**
- **Troubleshoot file and printer issues caused by a firewall**

Objectives

After completing this lab, you will be able to:

- Troubleshoot domain logon issues.
- Troubleshoot a user profile.
- Troubleshoot multilingual issues.
- Troubleshoot file and printer issues caused by a firewall.

Prerequisites

Before working on this lab, you must have an understanding of how to use Microsoft Virtual PC.

Before You Begin

Before you begin this lab, you must close each image and delete changes.

For each exercise in this lab, use a password of P@ssw0rd.

In Virtual PC, <right> ALT+DEL is the equivalent of CTRL+ALT+DEL.

Scenario

You are a DST for Northwind Traders, a company whose workers use Microsoft Windows XP Professional. Two users call with various desktop configuration and customization questions.

Estimated time to complete this lab: 45 minutes

Exercise 1
Troubleshooting Domain Logon Issues

In this exercise, you will troubleshoot two domain logon issues.

Scenario

A user calls stating that he cannot log on to the domain. He recently received a new desktop computer, and this is the first time he has tried to log on to the domain.

Tasks	Guidance for completing the task
1. Start the 2261_London and 2261_Bonn virtual machines, and log on to London as NWTRADERS\ Administrator.	■ Use the Virtual PC console. ■ Allow London to start completely before starting Bonn.
2. On London, navigate to C:\Program Files\ Microsoft Learning\2261\ Labfiles\Lab03\ and run 2261_Lab03_Ex1.exe.	■ This step introduces the problem.
3. On the Bonn virtual machine, log on to the NWTRADERS\ domain as AcapulcoUser.	■ Press <right> ALT+DEL.
4. Were you able to log on to the NWTRADERS domain? If not, why?	No not on
5. Resolve the issue, and then log on to the NWTRADERS\ domain as AcapulcoUser.	■ Refer to the How to Determine if a User Is a Member of a Domain or Workgroup topic page in the module. join Domain
6. Were you able to log on to the NWTRADERS domain? If not, why?	No disabled
7. Resolve the second logon issue.	■ Refer to the How to Troubleshoot User Logon Issues topic page in the module.
8. Close Bonn and delete changes.	Active directory enabled.

Exercise 2
Troubleshooting a User Profile Issue

In this exercise, you will troubleshoot a user profile issue.

Scenario

A user calls stating that his files have disappeared from his My Documents folder. Specifically, the user created a folder titled My Very Important Documents that is no longer in the My Documents folder.

Tasks	Guidance for completing the task
1. Start the Bonn virtual machine, and log on to the Bonn computer as Frank Lee.	
2. Open My Documents, and create a folder titled My Very Important Documents.	
3. Log off the Bonn computer, and then log on again as Administrator.	
4. Navigate to C:\Program Files\ Microsoft Learning\ 2261\Labfiles\Lab03\ and run 2261_Lab03_Ex2.exe.	■ This step introduces the problem.
5. Log off the Bonn computer, and log on again as Frank Lee.	
6. Were you able to log on successfully?	_yes_
7. Open My Documents, and verify that the folder titled My Very Important Documents is located in the folder.	
8. Does the My Very Important Documents folder appear in the My Documents folder?	_No_
9. Resolve this issue.	■ Refer to the How to Troubleshoot User Logon Issues topic page in the module. ■ Successful resolution of this issue enables Frank Lee to log on and access his files in the My Documents folder.
10. Close all windows, and log off Bonn.	

Exercise 3
Troubleshooting Multilingual Issues

In this exercise, you will troubleshoot multilingual issues.

Scenario

A user calls stating that her keyboard is malfunctioning because she can no longer type certain characters. She believes someone may have spilled water or some other liquid on the keyboard. You inquire further and learn that when she presses certain keys, unexpected characters are displayed. Some of the malfunctioning keys include: [(left bracket),] (right bracket), ' (single apostrophe), and ? (question mark). You also examine the keyboard and find no evidence of spilled liquid.

Tasks	Guidance for completing the task
1. Using Bonn, log on as Student with a password of **P@ssw0rd**.	
2. Navigate to C:\Program Files \Microsoft Learning\2261 \Labfiles\lab03, and double-click 2261_Lab03_Ex3.exe.	▪ This step introduces the problem.
3. Log off and back on to Bonn as Student.	
4. Reproduce the problem.	▪ Open Microsoft Notepad and type the malfunctioning characters.
5. Resolve the keyboard issue.	▪ Refer to the topic How to Troubleshoot the User Interface Language. ▪ Successful resolution of this issue enables Student to type without seeing unexpected characters.
6. Close Bonn, and delete changes.	*Reginol language changed*

Keyboard layot

Exercise 4
Troubleshooting File and Printer Issues Caused by Firewalls

In this exercise, you will troubleshoot file and printer issues related to firewall configuration.

Scenario

A user calls and says the network is down. The caller and his manager share a folder and a printer, but now they are suddenly unable to share files. When the manager, Frank, attempts to access the folder or printer, he receives an error message stating, "The network resource cannot be found."

Tasks	Guidance for completing the task
1. Start the 2261_Bonn and 2261_Acapulco virtual machines.	
2. Using Acapulco, log on locally as Frank Lee.	
3. Map a network drive to \\BONN\public.	
4. Were you able to map the drive? If not, why?	*No not found*
5. Connect to the shared printer on Bonn.	▪ Browse Bonn, right-click the printer, and then click **Connect**.
6. Were you able to connect to the printer? If not, why?	*No*
7. Resolve the connectivity issue.	▪ Refer to the topic How to Protect a Computer on the Internet in this module. ▪ Successful resolution of this issue enables Frank to access both the Public folder and Printer.
8. Close 2261_Bonn and 2261_Acapulco virtual machines without saving changes.	*Firewall enable exeptions*

Module 4: Resolving Network Connectivity Issues

Contents

Overview

- **Managing Computer Addressing Issues**
- **Troubleshooting Name Resolution Issues**
- **Troubleshooting Remote Network Connectivity Issues**

Introduction

As a desktop support technician (DST), you may be called on to support users who are having problems connecting to networks by using their computers running Microsoft® Windows® XP Professional and Microsoft Windows XP Home Edition. They may be having problems with the physical connection, networking protocols, or the way in which their computer is addressed.

In this module, you will learn how to help users troubleshoot connectivity issues, how to help users manage computer addressing, and how to use a variety of tools to troubleshoot name resolution issues. You will also learn about the different types of remote connections and how to assist users to properly configure these connections.

Objectives

After completing this module, you will be able to:

- Manage computer addressing issues.
- Troubleshoot name resolution issues.
- Troubleshoot remote network connectivity issues.

Lesson: Managing Computer Addressing Issues

- What Is a TCP/IP Address?
- How TCP/IP Addresses Are Assigned
- How to Identify a TCP/IP Address
- How to Configure a TCP/IP Address
- How to Renew a TCP/IP Address Lease
- How to Use Ping to Troubleshoot Network Connectivity Issues

Introduction

Before you troubleshoot network connectivity issues, you must understand the purpose and function of Transmission Control Protocol/Internet Protocol (TCP/IP) and how TCP/IP addresses are assigned, identified, and renewed. Windows XP includes a variety of command-line tools that you can use to identify a TCP/IP address and to monitor how the protocol is functioning. These command-line tools automate a variety of management tasks and include a number of parameters that enable you to customize your task. This lesson discusses these tools and how you can use them to manage computer addressing.

Objectives

After completing this module, you will be able to:

- Describe the function of TCP/IP addresses and how they work.
- Explain how TCP/IP addresses are assigned.
- Identify the TCP/IP address that is assigned to a computer.
- Configure a TCP/IP address.
- Renew a TCP/IP address lease.
- Use Ping to troubleshoot network connectivity issues.

What Is a TCP/IP Address?

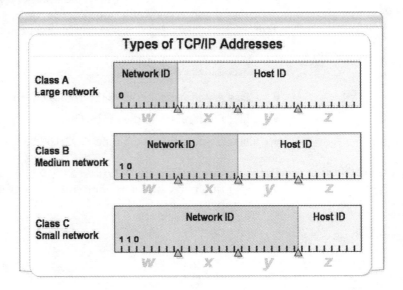

Introduction

TCP/IP is an industry-standard protocol suite that enables communication over the Internet. To communicate and send information over the Internet, your computer must have the TCP/IP protocols installed. TCP/IP can also be used as a communications protocol in a private network.

How TCP/IP works

TCP assembles a message or file into smaller packets that are transmitted over the Internet where they are received by a TCP layer that reassembles the packets into the original message. IP addresses each packet so that it gets to the right destination. Each computer on the network checks the IP address to determine where to forward the message. Although some packets are routed differently than other packets from the same message, the packets are reassembled at the destination.

Note For more information on how TCP/IP works, see the multimedia presentation *How an IP Packet Moves Through the Suite of TCP/IP Protocols* under Multimedia on the Web page on the Student Materials compact disc.

What is an IP address?

A *TCP/IP address*, in the current IP standard (IPv4), is defined as a logical 32-bit numeric address. The main purpose of an IP address is to uniquely identify networked devices so that accurate routing can be achieved. For example, a Web server transmits Web pages to requesting client by disassembling the text and graphics of a Web page into tiny pieces, called packets. Each packet contains the IP address of the source *host* (in our example, a Web server), as well as the IP address of the destination *host,* (again in our example, the client computer.) The client re-assembles all the packets into a single coherent Web page.

IP addresses are usually expressed in four-octet, dotted-decimal form in which each octet ranges in value from 0 to 255, with some restrictions.

The three classes of IP addresses for use in intranets

For an IP network to function, each device must have a unique IP address. In the 1990s, the explosive growth of the Internet made it clear that soon the demand for addresses would soon exceed the largest number of possible addresses. To manage this issue, the Internet Engineering Task Force (IETF) designated three blocks of IP addresses to be reserved exclusively on intranets.

The three blocks of private IP addresses specified by the IETF are:

- Class A addresses in the range 10.0.0.0 through 10.255.255.255.
- Class B addresses in the range 172.16.0.0 through 172.31.255.255.
- Class C addresses in the range 192.168.0.0 through 192.168.255.255.

Additional reading

For more information on TCP/IP, see the white paper, *Introduction to TCP/IP*, at http://msdn.microsoft.com/library/default.asp?url=/library/en-us/dniph/html/tcpipintro.asp.

How TCP/IP Addresses Are Assigned

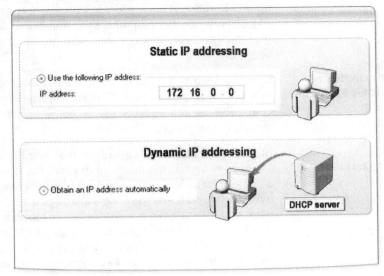

Introduction

IP addresses are assigned to host computers either manually or automatically. An IP address that is assigned manually is called a *static IP address* because it remains the same unless it is changed manually. An IP address that is assigned automatically is called a *dynamic IP address* because it is assigned automatically by using the Dynamic Host Configuration Protocol (DHCP).

What is DHCP?

DHCP enables a network administrator to supervise and distribute IP addresses automatically from a central point. When a computer connects to the network, DHCP automatically sends a new IP address to the computer. Without DHCP, a network administrator must manually assign an IP address to each computer on the network, and if a computer is moved, a new address must be manually assigned.

How DHCP works

DHCP functions in a client-server relationship in which the DHCP client computer broadcasts a request to the DHCP server. The DHCP server includes a pool of available IP addresses that it can distribute to clients. The DHCP client leases an IP address from the pool for a specific period of time, usually several days. When the lease is about to expire, the client contacts the server to arrange for renewal.

In a typical Windows domain environment, DHCP runs as a service on a server. But often in small-office or home networks, DHCP is provided by a dedicated appliance, such as a combination firewall and/or router.

Remotely connected computers also typically obtain their IP addresses through DHCP. The IP address assigned to a dial-up user connecting to the Internet is normally provided by DHCP servers at the Internet service provider (ISP). DHCP is also often used for clients using a virtual private network (VPN) connection.

APIPA used when DHCP is unavailable

When a computer is configured to use DHCP but the DHCP server is not available, the operating system automatically assigns an IP address in a specific private IP range. This process is called *Automatic Private IP Addressing* (APIPA). When all computers on a subnet use APIPA to assign IP addresses, the computers can communicate with one another without additional configuration.

When to manually or automatically assign an IP address

DHCP is usually the preferred method of assigning IP addresses. With a properly configured server, DHCP centralizes updating, greatly simplifies IP configuration, and protects against possible errors that can occur when manually assigning an IP address.

In certain situations, however, you may want to control the IP address that is assigned to certain computers. For example, if you want to set up a Web server, a mail server, a VPN gateway, or any other computer that must be accessible over the Internet, you may want to assign a static IP address to the computer. If you are using a router in a network connecting a group of computers located within a relatively limited area, such as a local area network (LAN), you may want to configure the router so that the packets entering the network on a specific port are forwarded to a specific computer.

DHCP dynamically assigns addresses within the local network. Some applications require that a computer be assigned an IP address that will not change. One way to ensure that a computer always has the same address is to statically assign an IP address to the computer's network adapter.

Additional reading

For more information on TCP/IP addressing and subnetting, see article 164015 in the Microsoft Knowledge Base.

How to Identify a TCP/IP Address

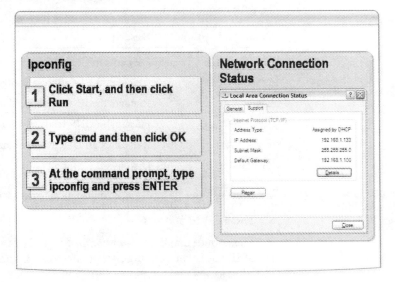

Introduction

Windows XP includes TCP/IP and numerous utilities that you can use to identify a TCP/IP address and monitor how the protocol is functioning. TCP/IP usually does not require manual configuration; however, when a user encounters network connectivity problems, such as problems connecting to computers on the same network or to external Web sites, the issue may be related to TCP/IP. Therefore, you must know how to access TCP/IP configuration information to troubleshoot issues. The most commonly used utilities are described in this section.

What is the Ipconfig command-line utility?

The Ipconfig command-line utility displays the current TCP/IP configuration parameters on your computer. Use Ipconfig to:

- Display current TCP/IP network configuration values.

- Update or release DHCP allocated leases.

- Display, register, or flush (delete) Domain Name System (DNS) names. *DNS* is an Internet service that translates domain names into IP addresses.

Note   The Ipconfig command-line utility is most useful for managing computers that obtain an IP address automatically by using DHCP or APIPA.

The following table lists and describes the Ipconfig command options that you can use to display TCP/IP configuration information and release or renew TCP/IP connections.

Command option	Description
/all	Displays full configuration information
/release	Releases the IP address for the specified adapter
/renew	Renews the IP address for the specified adapter
/flushdns	Purges the DNS resolver cache
/registerdns	Refreshes all DHCP leases and re-registers DNS names
/displaydns	Displays the contents of the DNS resolver cache

How to use Ipconfig to identify a TCP/IP address

You can use the Ipconfig command-line utility to identify:

- The TCP/IP address.
- The subnet mask. (A *subnet mask* is a 32-bit value that enables the recipient of IP packets to distinguish the network ID and host ID portions of the IP address.)
- Default gateway information. A *default gateway* is the gateway in a network that a computer uses to access another network.

You can use Ipconfig to identify the TCP/IP address, subnet mask, and default gateway information for each network interface card (NIC) and to determine if the IP address is statically or dynamically assigned. A *NIC* is an expansion board that is inserted into a computer to connect the computer to a network.

To use the Ipconfig command-line utility to identify TCP/IP settings:

1. Click **Start**, and then click **Run**.
2. In the **Run** dialog box, type **cmd** and then click **OK**.
3. At the command prompt, type **ipconfig** and then press ENTER.

   The IP address, subnet mask, and default gateway information is displayed for each NIC.
4. For additional IP settings information, at the command prompt, type **ipconfig /all** and then press ENTER.

How to use Network Connections to identify a TCP/IP address

You can also use Network Connections in Control Panel to identify a TCP/IP address, subnet mask, and default gateway information for each NIC and to determine if the IP address is statically or dynamically assigned.

To use Network Connections to identify TCP/IP settings:

1. Click **Start**, and then click **Control Panel**.
2. In Control Panel, click **Network and Internet Connections**.
3. In the **Network and Internet Connections** window, click **Network Connections**.
4. In the **Network Connections** window, under **LAN or High-Speed Internet**, double-click **Local Area Connection**.
5. In the **Local Area Connection Status** dialog box, on the **Support** tab, view the address type, IP address, subnet mask, and default gateway information.

How to use an IP address to troubleshoot a network connectivity issue

After you have located the IP address, you can use it to solve connection problems. For example:

- If the format of the IP address is 169.254.*x.y*, the computer is probably using APIPA, which means the computer's DHCP client was unable to reach a DHCP server to assign an IP address. When this occurs, check the connection to the network.

- If the IP address is located in Class A, B, or C (the IP addresses reserved for use on private networks), make sure that another computer (an Internet Connection Sharing host) or a router or residential gateway is routing Internet requests to a properly configured public IP address.

- If the IP address appears as 0.0.0.0, either the computer is disconnected from the network or the static IP address is a duplicate of an address that already exists on the network or the IP address is released.

- Make sure that the user is using the correct subnet mask for computers on the local network. Compare the IP settings on the computer that is having problems with the IP settings on other computers on the network. The subnet mask settings must be identical on all network computers. The first, second, or third sets of numbers in the IP address for each computer should also be identical, depending on the subnet mask.

  For example, if a subnet mask is 255.255.255.0, it means that the first three sets of numbers of the IP address must be identical. In this example, 192.168.0.83 and 192.168.0.223 can communicate, but 192.168.5.101 cannot communicate because it is not on the same network.

  Likewise, if a subnet mask is 255.255.0.0, the first two numbers in each IP address must match. For example, 172.16.2.34, 172.16.4.56, and 172.16.83.201 are all valid addresses on a subnet with this mask.

  In every case, the gateway computer must also be a member of the same subnet. If a router, switch, or residential gateway for Internet access is used, the local address on that device must be part of the same subnet as the computers on the network.

How to Configure a TCP/IP Address

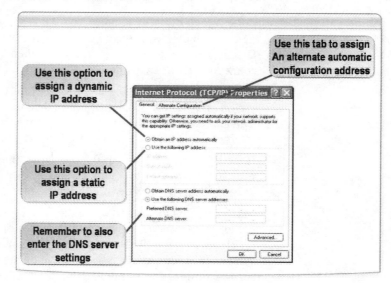

Introduction

As a DST, you may need to configure a computer to use a specific (static) IP address. Although this method takes more time and is more complex than obtaining an automatic (dynamic) IP address, it gives you greater control over the addressing process.

How to assign a static IP address

You can change the way that a computer receives an IP address from using DHCP to using a static IP address.

To assign a static IP address:

1. In Control Panel, click **Network and Internet Connections**.

2. In the Network and Internet Connections window, click **Network Connections**.

3. In the Network Connections window, right-click **Local Area Connection**, and then click **Properties**.

4. In the **Local Area Connection Properties** dialog box, on the **General** tab, under the **This connection uses the following items** box, double-click **Internet Protocol (TCP/IP)**.

5. In the **Internet Protocol (TCP/IP) Properties** dialog box, click **Use the Following IP Address**, and then type in the IP address, subnet mask, and default gateway.

6. Under **Use the following DNS server addresses**, type the preferred DNS server address and the alternate DNS server address.

7. Click **OK** to save your changes.

How to assign an alternate static IP address

Windows XP enables you to specify an alternate IP address for use when a DHCP server is not available. This feature is very useful for portable computers that regularly connect to different networks. For example, a laptop user can configure the connection to automatically acquire an IP address from an available DHCP server while at work, and while at home to automatically assign a preconfigured set of TCP/IP settings.

To assign a user-configured alternate IP address:

1. In Control Panel, in Category View, click **Network and Internet Connections**.

2. In the Network and Internet Connections window, click **Network Connections**.

3. In the Network Connections window, right-click **Local Area Connection**, and then click **Properties**.

4. In the **Local Area Connection Properties** dialog box, on the **General** tab, under **This connection uses the following items** box, double-click **Internet Protocol (TCP/IP)**.

5. On the **General** tab, click **Obtain an IP address automatically**.

6. On the **Alternate Configuration** tab, click **User configured**, and supply values for the TCP/IP connection.

7. To close the **Internet Protocol (TCP/IP) Properties** dialog box, click **OK**.

8. To close the network adapter dialog box, click **OK**.

How to Renew a TCP/IP Address Lease

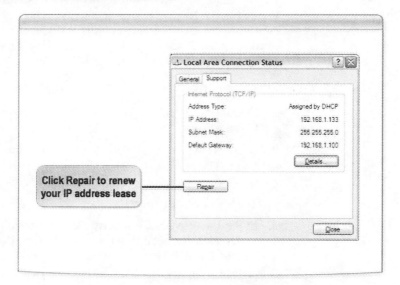

Introduction

When an IP address lease expires on a DHCP client, it automatically requests a new lease from the server. This process is called *renewing an IP address lease.*

When to renew a TCP/IP address lease

There are instances in which you will want to renew the lease of an IP address before the current lease expires. For example:

- The default gateway that is part of the IP lease has been changed. In this situation, you must renew the lease on the DHCP client to obtain the new default gateway address.

- A computer cannot find a DHCP server and APIPA has assigned default IP settings. When proper communication with the DHCP server is restored, you must renew the IP lease to obtain the correct settings for the network.

How to renew a TCP/IP address lease

In Windows XP, you can easily renew your IP address lease by using the Repair function.s

To renew an IP address lease by using Control Panel:

1. In Control Panel, click **Network and Internet Connections**.

2. In the Network and Internet Connections window, click **Network Connections**.

3. In the Network Connections window, double-click **Local Area Connection**.

4. In the **Local Area Connection Status** box, on the **Support** tab, click **Repair**.

You can also renew an IP address lease by using the Ipconfig command.

To renew an IP address lease by using the Ipconfig command:

1. Click **Start**, and then click **Run**.

2. Type **cmd** and then click **OK**.

3. At the command prompt, type **ipconfig /renew** and then press ENTER.

How to release an IP address lease

It is a best practice to always release an IP address prior to renewing it. By following this practice, you will ensure that you receive the correct IP address from the DHCP server.

To release an IP lease:

1. Click **Start**, and then click **Run**.

2. Type **cmd** and then click **OK**.

3. At the command prompt, type **ipconfig /release** and then press ENTER.

Additional reading

For more information about the Repair tool, see article 289256 in the Microsoft Knowledge Base. For more information about the Ipconfig command-line utility, see article 223413 in the Microsoft Knowledge Base.

How to Use Ping to Troubleshoot Network Connectivity Issues

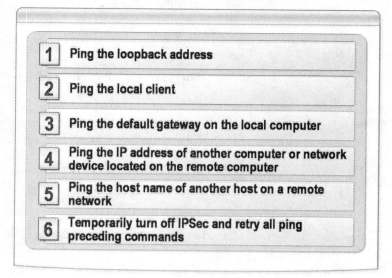

1	Ping the loopback address
2	Ping the local client
3	Ping the default gateway on the local computer
4	Ping the IP address of another computer or network device located on the remote computer
5	Ping the host name of another host on a remote network
6	Temporarily turn off IPSec and retry all ping preceding commands

Introduction

The Ping utility is the primary TCP/IP command-line utility that is used to troubleshoot network connectivity issues.

What is the Ping command-line utility?

Ping verifies connections to one or more remote hosts by using the Internet Control Message Protocol (ICMP) echo request and echo reply packets to determine whether a particular IP system on a network is functional. *ICMP* is a required maintenance protocol in the TCP/IP suite that reports errors and allows simple connectivity. If the Ping test fails, it may return one of the following error messages:

- Destination host unreachable. This error message indicates that there is a problem at the IP routing level between your computer and the remote host.

- Unknown host host name. This error message indicates that none of the client's name resolution mechanisms recognize the name that you typed. In this case, you must check that you typed the host name correctly.

- Request timed out. This error message indicates that at least one of the name resolution mechanisms recognized the name, but the target either did not receive the request or did not respond to it. In this case, you must check connectivity to the target host.

Ping can also perform a loopback test to the computer that it is running on. At a command prompt, type **ping 127.0.0.1** or **ping loopback**. If this loopback test fails, there is a problem with the IP configuration. For example, your computer may not have been set up to use IP, or it may not have restarted after TCP/IP was installed and configured.

Ping can accept an IP address or a host name. In this way, Ping can also be used to test name resolution. If the **ping** command that uses an IP address connects, but the **ping** command that uses a host name fails to connect, there is a problem with name resolution.

Note For security reasons, many Internet resources are configured to not respond to Ping. If you attempt to ping one of these hosts, you will receive a "Request timed out" error message because the address has been configured to disregard Ping requests.

How to use Ping to test connectivity to a remote host

The following steps describe how to use the Ping utility to perform progressively more distant tests on your network connectivity.

1. Ping the loopback address—type **ping 127.0.0.1**

   Successfully pinging the loopback address verifies that TCP/IP is both installed on and correctly configured on the local client. If the loopback test fails, the IP stack is not responding. Lack of response can occur if the TCP drivers are corrupted, if the network adapter is not working, or if another service is interfering with IP. Look for problems reported by Setup in the setup.log files.

2. Ping the local client—type **ping *IP address of local client***

   Successfully pinging the IP address of the local client verifies that the client was correctly added to the network. If you cannot successfully ping the local IP address after successfully pinging the loopback address, check the following:

   - The local client's IP address to ensure that the IP address is valid.

   - The routing table to ensure that it contains the correct IP address. A *routing table* contains the information necessary to forward an IP data packet to its destination.

   - The network adapter driver to ensure that it is functioning properly. A *network adapter driver* is a device that a computer uses to connect to a network.

3. Ping the default gateway on the local computer—type **ping *IP address of the default gateway***

   Successfully pinging the default gateway of the local client verifies both that the default gateway is functioning and that you can communicate with a local host on the local subnet. If you cannot successfully ping the default gateway after successfully pinging the local client, check the default gateway.

4. Ping the IP address of another computer or network device located on a remote network—type **ping *IP address of remote host***

   Successfully pinging the IP address of the remote host verifies that the local client can communicate with the remote host through a router.

   If you cannot successfully ping the remote host IP address after successfully pinging the default gateway, this can indicate that the remote host is not responding, or that there is a problem in the network hardware between the source host and the destination host. To rule out the possibility of a problem in the network hardware, ping a different remote host on the same subnet where the first remote host is located.

5. Ping the host name of another host on a remote network—type
    ping *host name of remote host*

    Successfully pinging the name of a remote host verifies that Ping can
    resolve the remote host name to an IP address. If you cannot successfully
    ping the remote host name after successfully pinging the IP address of the
    remote host, the problem is host name resolution, not network connectivity.
    When pinging the host name of the target host, Ping attempts to resolve the
    host name to an IP address first through a DNS server, and next through a
    Windows Internet Naming Service (WINS) server, if one is configured.
    WINS is a software service that dynamically maps IP addresses to computer
    names. After Ping resolves the host name to an IP address, it attempts to
    broadcast or send the IP address to all the hosts on the network. Check
    TCP/IP properties to see whether the client has DNS server and WINS
    server addresses configured, either typed manually or assigned
    automatically. If DNS server and WINS server addresses are configured in
    TCP/IP properties, and if they appear when you type **ipconfig /all**, then try
    pinging the server addresses to ascertain whether they are accessible.

    On a network that uses DNS for name resolution, if the name entered is not
    a fully qualified domain name (FQDN), the DNS name resolver appends the
    computer's domain name or names to generate the FQDN. Name resolution
    might fail if you do not use an FQDN for a remote name. These requests fail
    because the DNS name resolver appends the local domain suffix to a name
    that resides elsewhere in the domain hierarchy.

6. Temporarily turn off IPSec—retry all of the preceding **ping** commands.

    If none of the preceding **ping** commands are successful, check whether IP
    Security (IPSec) is enabled. If IPSec is enabled locally, temporarily stop the
    IPSec Services service in the Services snap-in, and then try pinging again. If
    network connectivity between hosts works after you stop IPSec, ask the
    security administrator to troubleshoot the IPSec policy.

Demonstration: Managing Computer Addressing

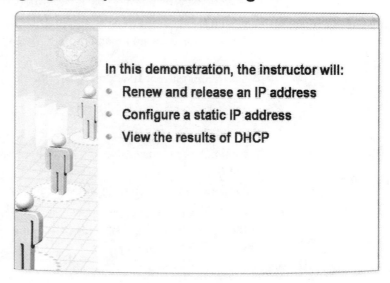

In this demonstration, the instructor will:
- Renew and release an IP address
- Configure a static IP address
- View the results of DHCP

Objectives

In this demonstration, your instructor will use the Ipconfig command-line utility to:

- Renew and release an IP address
- Configure a static IP address
- View the results of DHCP

Scenario

A user calls and states that he cannot access the network. You investigate and determine that the user does not have a TCP/IP address assigned by the DHCP server. Instead, the user has an address that begins with 169.254. To resolve this issue, you decide to configure a static IP address, verify connectivity, and then configure the user's computer to obtain an IP address dynamically.

▶ **Use Ipconfig to renew and release IP addresses**

1. Start the 2261_London virtual machine.

2. Wait for London to display the Windows log on screen, and then start 2261_Acapulco, and 2261_Bonn virtual machines.

3. Using Bonn, log on to the computer as Administrator with the password of **P@ssw0rd**.

4. Using Acapulco, log on to the domain as Administrator with the password **P@ssw0rd**.

5. On Acapulco, click **Start**, click **Run**, type **cmd** and then click **OK**.

6. At the command prompt, type **ipconfig /all** and then press ENTER.

   What is your current IP address?

7. On London, log on as Administrator, open a command prompt, type **net stop "dhcp server"** and then press ENTER.

   The DHCP Server service stops.

8. On Acapulco, at the command prompt, type **ipconfig /release** and then press ENTER.

   What is your current IP address?

   _____

9. Repeat step 8 on Bonn.

10. On Acapulco, at the command prompt, type **ipconfig /renew** and then press ENTER.

    After a minute or so an error message appears.

11. Read the error message that appears in the command-line window, and then at the command prompt, type **ipconfig /all** and then press ENTER.

    What is your IP address now?

    _____

    _____

12. On Acapulco, at the command prompt, type **ping 192.168.1.1** which is London's IP address, and then press ENTER.

    Are you able to ping London? Why?

    _____

    _____

▶ **Configure a static IP address**

1. Using Acapulco, in Control Panel, in Category View, click **Network and Internet Connections**.

2. In the Network and Internet Connections window, click **Network Connections**.

3. In the Network Connections window, right-click **Local Area Connection**, and then click **Properties**.

4. In the Local Area Connection Properties window, double-click **Internet Protocol (TCP/IP)**.

5. In the **Internet Protocol (TCP/IP) Properties** dialog box, click **Use the following IP address,** and then enter the following information:

   IP Address: See table below.

Computer Name	IP Address
Acapulco	192.168.1.213
Bonn	192.168.1.206

   Subnet mask: 255.255.255.0

   Default gateway: blank

   Preferred DNS Server: 192.168.1.1

6. To close the **Internet Protocol (TCP/IP)** dialog box, click **OK**.

7. To close the **Local Area Connection Properties** dialog box, click **OK**.

8. Using Acapulco, at the command prompt, type **ping 192.168.1.1** which is London's IP address, and then press ENTER.

   Were you able to ping London? Why?

   _____

   _____

9. Leave the **Network Connections** dialog box open.

▶ **View the results of DHCP**

1. On London, at the command prompt, type **net start "dhcp server"** and press ENTER.

2. Using Acapulco, in the Network Connections window, right-click **Local Area Connection**, and then click **Properties**.

3. In the **Local Area Connection Properties** dialog box, double-click **Internet Protocol (TCP/IP)**.

4. In the **Internet Protocol (TCP/IP) Properties** dialog box, select **Obtain an IP address automatically**, and then click **OK** twice.

5. At the command prompt, type **ipconfig /release** and then press ENTER.

6. At the command prompt, type **ipconfig /renew** and then press ENTER.

7. At the command prompt, type **ipconfig /all** and then press ENTER.

   What is your IP address?

   _____

   _____

8. Repeat steps 2-6 using Bonn.

9. On all three virtual machines, close all windows, log off, and then on the **Action** menu click **Pause**.

Lesson: Troubleshooting Name Resolution Issues

- What Is Name Resolution?
- How Client Names Are Resolved
- How to Use Net Config and Nbtstat for Name Resolution
- How to Use Nslookup for Name Resolution

Introduction

Although computers and other devices are given friendly names such as London to make them easier to remember, every computer name must be translated to an IP address for a computer to communicate across a network. The process of translating a computer name to an IP address is called *name resolution*. Proper name resolution is essential for fast network communication. If IP addresses are not correctly resolved, the network will be slow or network host computers will be inaccessible. This section discusses name resolution and explains how to use Windows XP network utilities and tools to isolate common connectivity issues.

Lesson objectives

After completing this lesson, you will be able to:

- Explain the concept of name resolution and describe how it works.
- Explain how client names are resolved using the hosts and Lmhosts files.
- Use Net Config and Nbtstat to troubleshoot network basic input/output system (NetBIOS) name resolution issues.
- Use Nslookup to troubleshoot DNS name resolution issues.

What Is Name Resolution?

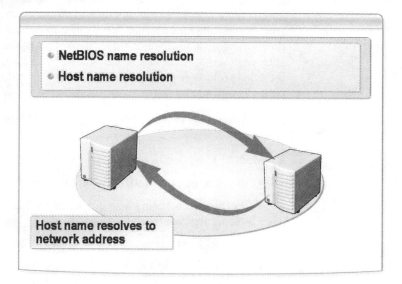

Introduction

TCP/IP identifies source and destination computers by their IP addresses. However, because computer users are much better at remembering and using names than numbers, common or user-friendly names are assigned to the computer's IP address. These names are either NetBIOS names or host names.

NetBIOS

NetBIOS is an application programming interface (API) that can be used by programs on a LAN. NetBIOS provides applications with a uniform set of commands for requesting the lower-level services that are required to manage names, conduct sessions, and send datagrams between nodes on a network.

Name resolution

Name resolution is the process of translating, or resolving, the name of a host on a network into its associated network address. Name resolution plays an important part of network communication because the logical names of hosts on the network must be resolved into their network addresses before actual communication can take place between them.

NetBIOS name

A *NetBIOS name* is a 16-character name that is used to identify a NetBIOS resource on the network. A NetBIOS name can represent a single computer or a group of computers. The first 15 characters may be used for the name. The final character is used to identify the resource or service that is being referred to on the computer.

For example, one NetBIOS resource is File and Printer Sharing for the Microsoft Networks component on a computer running Microsoft Windows Server™ 2003. When this component uses NetBIOS name resolution, the component registers a unique NetBIOS name based on the name of the computer and the character identifier that represents the component.

Host name

A host name is a user-friendly name that is assigned to a computer's IP address to identify it as a TCP/IP host. The host name can be up to 255 characters in length and can contain alphabetic and numeric characters, hyphens, and periods. Host names can take various forms. The two most common forms are alias and domain name. An *alias* is a single name that is associated with an IP address, such as *payroll*. A *domain name* is structured for use on the Internet and includes periods as separators. An example of a domain name is *payroll.contoso.com*.

TCP/IP networks running Windows operating systems support two basic name resolution methods:

- Method 1: NetBIOS name resolution. This method is:

  - Used to resolve NetBIOS computer names into IP addresses.

  - Performed by using broadcasts, or by querying a Windows Internet Name Service (WINS) server.

- Method 2: Host name resolution. This method is:

  - Used to resolve FQDNs in DNS into IP addresses.

  - Performed either by using a local hosts file on the computer or by querying a name server.

Note NetBIOS is used by previous versions of Windows for host name resolution. In Windows XP, DNS has superseded NetBIOS, but these operating systems still include support for NetBIOS to ensure compatibility with computers running Windows NT, Windows 95, Windows 98, Windows Millennium Edition, and Windows 2000.

How name resolution works

In the name resolution process, if you access the command prompt of a computer running Windows XP and type **ping** followed by a host name or FQDN of another host on the network, the host name or FQDN of the target host must be resolved into its IP address before the TCP/IP utility Ping can occur.

Note For information about NetBIOS over TCP/IP and troubleshooting tips see Microsoft Knowledge Base Article - 818092 "Description of NetBIOS Browsing Console (Browcon.exe)."

How Client Names Are Resolved

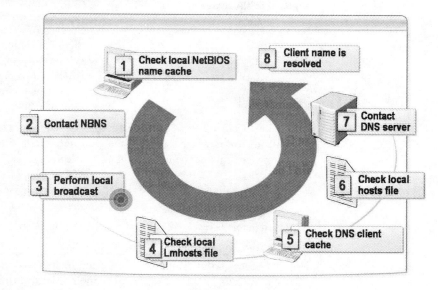

Introduction	Many applications access computers through a network connection. When you download your e-mail, view a Web site, and so on, the application that you use must resolve a host name or FQDN to an IP address.
Example of NetBIOS name resolution	The following table shows the order in which methods of name resolution are attempted when the NetBT node type of the client is H-node, **Enable Lmhosts Lookup** is selected on the **WINS** tab of **Advanced TCP/IP Properties,** and the **Enable DNS** registry setting is set to 1.

Method in the order applied	Comments
1. Check local NetBIOS name cache	The cache contains recently resolved NetBIOS names.
2. Contact NBNS	This method works only if NBNS is configured. WINS is usually the NBNS on a Microsoft network. The requestor tries three times to contact the name server, and then tries three times to contact a secondary WINS server if there is one.
3. Perform local broadcast	The requestor broadcasts a NetBIOS name query request packet. The requestor tries three times before giving an error.
4. Check local Lmhosts file	The requestor checks if an Lmhosts file exists.
5. Check DNS client cache	The requestor checks its DNS client cache for the name.

(*continued*)

Method in the order applied	Comments
6. Check local hosts file	On Windows Server 2003, the requestor checks the Hosts file if **Enable DNS For Windows Resolution** is selected on the **WINS Address** tab of the TCP/IP property sheet. This option is not available for Windows 2000.
7. Contact DNS server (if all methods fail, an error message states that the computer could not be found on the network)	The requestor contacts the DNS server if **Enable DNS For Windows Resolution** is selected on the **WINS Address** tab of the TCP/IP property sheet and the **DNS** tab has a DNS server specified on it. The requestor also tries 5, 10, 20, and 40 seconds later.
8. Client name is resolved	The requestor resolves the client name.

Note These resolution methods are tried in succession until the host name is resolved into its IP address or until name resolution finally fails. Some methods may not be available, such as when there is no DNS server or NetBIOS Name Server (NBNS) on the network. If all methods fail, an error message states that the computer could not be found on the network.

Use hosts files to resolve domain names

The first name resolution method that is used is the hosts file. A hosts file is used to resolve a host name or FQDN into its associated IP address. Hosts files are a local alternative to using distributed DNS servers to perform name resolution.

Hosts files are text files that consist of a series of FQDN-to-IP address mappings, one per line. Each line in the hosts file contains the IP address of a host followed by the FQDN of the host, followed by an optional comment prefixed with a pound sign (#). Hosts files should contain mappings for hosts on both local and remote networks. Mappings can consist of an IP address and one or more host names (aliases). If you are using hosts files to resolve host names on a network, each computer on the network should have a hosts file. You can find the file in *systemroot*\system32\ drivers\etc\Hosts in Windows NT, Windows XP, and Windows Server 2003.

Although DNS has largely eliminated the need for maintaining hosts files, these files are still useful in two scenarios:

- On small TCP/IP networks not connected to the Internet, it may be easier to maintain a hosts file than to run a DNS server.

- As a backup in case the DNS server goes down. Typically, in this case, you would keep the hosts file small, adding only entries for your servers and for gateways to remote networks, plus a line for localhost, which maps to 127.0.0.1, the loopback address for testing IP communications.

Use Lmhosts files to resolve NetBIOS names

While the hosts file is used to resolve domain names, the *Lmhosts file* is used to resolve NetBIOS computer names. The Lmhosts file usually contains mappings for hosts on remote networks only. Mappings are usually not required for hosts on local networks because these can be resolved using broadcasts. If you are using Lmhosts files to resolve NetBIOS names on a network, each computer on the network should have an Lmhosts file. You can find the Lmhosts file in *systemroot*\system32\drivers\etc in Windows NT, Windows XP, and Windows Server 2003.

Each line in the Lmhosts file contains the IP address of a NetBIOS computer on the network, followed by the NetBIOS name of the computer. The computer name can be followed by optional prefixes that identify domains and domain controllers and allow entries to be loaded into the NetBIOS name cache at startup. Comments are prefixed with the pound sign (#). Place the NetBIOS names that need to be resolved most frequently near the top of the Lmhosts file because the file is parsed linearly from the beginning.

How to Use Net Config and Nbtstat for Name Resolution

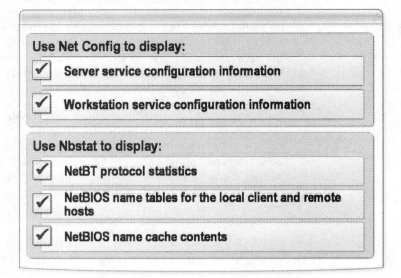

Use Net Config to display:
- ✓ Server service configuration information
- ✓ Workstation service configuration information

Use Nbstat to display:
- ✓ NetBT protocol statistics
- ✓ NetBIOS name tables for the local client and remote hosts
- ✓ NetBIOS name cache contents

Introduction

You can use Net Config and Nbtstat to check NetBIOS-to-IP name resolution.

The Net Config command-line utility

The Net Config command-line utility is primarily used for viewing network settings for the computer. The main Net Config command that is used for testing NetBIOS name resolution is the **net config workstation** command. The **net config workstation** command reports the NetBIOS name and the domain name of the computer. For more information about the Net Config, at a command prompt, type **net help**.

The Nbtstat command-line utility

You can use the Nbtstat command-line utility to isolate NetBIOS name resolution problems, such as whether a specific NetBIOS name is registered. The **nbtstat** command checks the state of current NetBIOS over TCP/IP connections, updates the Lmhosts cache, and determines your registered name. This command is also useful for troubleshooting and preloading the NetBIOS name cache.

When a network is functioning correctly, NetBIOS over TCP/IP (NetBT) resolves NetBIOS names to IP addresses. NetBT uses several options for NetBIOS name resolution, including local cache lookup, WINS server query, broadcast, LMHOSTS lookup, HOSTS lookup, and DNS server query.

You can use **nbtstat** to display a variety of information, including:

- NetBT protocol statistics.
- NetBIOS name tables both for the local client and for remote hosts. The NetBIOS name table is the list of NetBIOS names that corresponds to NetBIOS applications running on the client.
- The contents of the NetBIOS name cache. The NetBIOS name cache is the table that contains NetBIOS name–to–IP address mappings.

How to run nbtstat

Nbtstat is run from the command line and includes a number of options for troubleshooting TCP/IP connections.

To run **nbtstat**:

1. Click **Start**, click **Run**, type **cmd** and then click **OK**.

2. At the command prompt, type **nbtstat** and then press ENTER.

   The following table shows the **nbtstat** command options that you can use to diagnose protocol statistics and TCP/IP connections.

Command	Description
nbtstat -n	Lists the NetBIOS names registered by the client
nbtstat -c	Displays the NetBIOS name cache
nbtstat -R	Manually reloads the NetBIOS name cache by using entries in the Lmhosts file with a #PRE parameter

3. At the command prompt, type **nbtstat /?** for more information about the **nbtstat** command.

How to Use Nslookup for Name Resolution

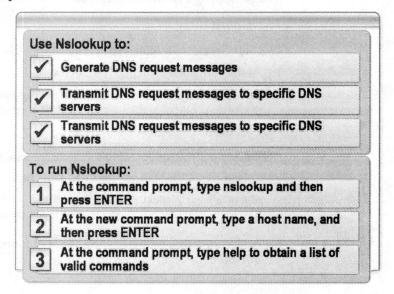

Use Nslookup to:

✓ Generate DNS request messages

✓ Transmit DNS request messages to specific DNS servers

✓ Transmit DNS request messages to specific DNS servers

To run Nslookup:

1. At the command prompt, type nslookup and then press ENTER

2. At the new command prompt, type a host name, and then press ENTER

3. At the command prompt, type help to obtain a list of valid commands

---

Introduction

You can use Nslookup to check DNS name–to–IP name resolution. For example, a user states that she occasionally receives an error when attempting to browse an internal company Web site. You suspect one of the internal DNS servers may have an incorrect DNS record for the Web site. One of the ways you can verify the DNS record is by using Nslookup to query the DNS server in question.

What is the Nslookup command-line utility?

Nslookup enables you to generate DNS request messages and also to transmit them to specific DNS servers on the network. Use Nslookup to determine what IP address a particular DNS server has associated with a host name. The advantage of Nslookup is that you can test the functionality and the quality of the information on a specific DNS server by specifying it on the command line.

How to run Nslookup

You can run the Nslookup utility in interactive mode.

To run Nslookup in interactive mode:

1. At a command prompt, type **nslookup** and then press ENTER.

   The command displays its own prompt.

2. At the command prompt, type a host name, and then press ENTER.

   The computer name is translated to an IP address.

3. At the command prompt, type **help** to obtain a list of valid commands.

   For example, type **nslookup WKS1 DNSServer3** to query DNSServer3 for the IP address of the host, WKS1.

Practice: Resolving FQDNs to IP Addresses

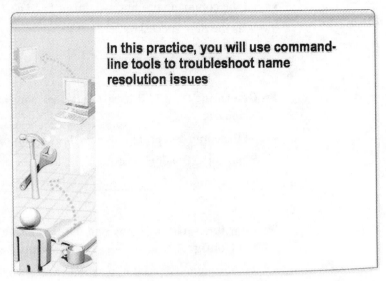

In this practice, you will use command-line tools to troubleshoot name resolution issues

Objective

In this practice, you will use command-line tools to troubleshoot name resolution issues.

Scenario

A user calls and says that she cannot access her file server (named London). During your troubleshooting session, you decide to verify that the name London is correctly resolving to its IP address, 192.168.1.1.

Practice

To complete this practice, you need to log on to the domain with an account that has local administrative rights on the computer.

▶ **Verify name server settings by using Ipconfig**

1. Resume 2261_London and 2261_Acapulco virtual machines.

2. Using Acapulco, log on to the NWTraders domain as **Administrator** with the password **P@ssw0rd**.

3. Click **Start**, click **Run**, in the **Open** box, type **cmd** and then click **OK**.

4. At the command prompt, type **ipconfig /all** and then press ENTER.

   What is the IP address of this computer's DHCP server?

   _____

   What is the IP address of this computer's DNS server?

   _____

   What is the IP address of this computer's Primary WINS server?

   _____

▶ **Verify connectivity with DNS and WINS servers by using Ping**

- At the command prompt, type **ping 192.168.1.1** and then press ENTER. Was the ping successful?

_____

▶ **Determine the IP address of another computer on the network by using Nslookup**

- At the command prompt, type **nslookup london** and then press ENTER. What is the IP address of London?

_____

▶ **View the NetBIOS name and domain name of the computer by using Net Config**

- At the command prompt, type **net config workstation** and then press ENTER.

   What is the computer name of your computer?

_____

   What is the full computer name of your computer?

_____

▶ **Display the full list of NetBIOS names registered to the computer using Nbtstat**

1. At the command prompt, type **nbtstat -n** and then press ENTER. What is the result?

_____

_____

2. Using Acapulco, close all windows, log off, and pause the virtual machine.
3. Repeat step 2 for London.

Lesson: Troubleshooting Remote Network Connectivity Issues

- Types of Remote Connections
- What Is Connection Manager?
- How to Configure a VPN Connection
- How to Configure an ICS Connection
- How to Configure a Dial-Up Connection
- How to Use Remote Desktop
- How to Use Remote Assistance
- How to Troubleshoot Remote Connection Issues

[handwritten annotations: "tunnel", "Internet Connection Sharing", "take over system", "asking Someone else"]

Introduction

A remote access connection allows users to securely access organization intranets when the users are working at remote locations. However, because there are many components involved in a remote connection, when connection fails, it can be difficult to determine what went wrong. This lesson describes the components that are used to establish a remote connection and how to configure these components. Finally, this lesson describes how to troubleshoot common remote connection issues.

Lesson objectives

After completing this lesson, you will be able to:

- Identify the types of remote connections.
- Describe the function of Connection Manager and how it is used to establish remote connections.
- Configure a VPN connection.
- Configure an Internet Connection Sharing (ICS) connection.
- Configure a dial-up connection.
- Use Remote Desktop.
- Use Remote Assistance.
- Troubleshoot remote connection issues.

Types of Remote Connections

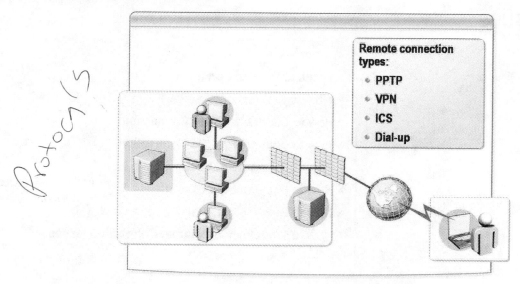

Introduction

A remote connection provides the means for users to connect to a network from a remote location, such as when a user is working from home and needs access to resources that are only available on the office LAN. There are several types of remote connections, including Point-to-Point Tunneling Protocol (PPTP) and VPN connections.

PPTP

PPTP is a data-link layer protocol based on the Internet standard Point-to-Point Protocol (PPP). PPTP was developed by Microsoft to enable network traffic to be encapsulated and sent over an unsecured public IP network such as the Internet. PPTP does this through the creation of VPNs, which securely tunnel network traffic through the Internet. Remote users can use PPTP to securely access resources on their corporate network over the Internet instead of using direct modem connections or costly leased lines.

VPN

A VPN connection uses both private and public networks to create a network connection. There are two main types of VPNs:

- Network-network VPNs: For example, a branch office network or an enterprise that is connected to corporate headquarters by a VPN. Network-network VPNs offer a low-cost alternative to deploying expensive, dedicated leased lines such as T1 lines at all branch offices. In spite of the cost advantage, however, network-network VPNs have been slow to gain a foothold in the enterprise environment due to the proven reliability of leased lines and the relative unreliability of the Internet in comparison.

- Host-network VPNs: For example, a mobile knowledge worker uses his or her laptop or personal digital assistant (PDA) and modem to dial in to a local ISP and connect securely to a company intranet or portal by means of an encrypted VPN connection. Use of VPNs for this purpose has proliferated in the enterprise environment because it is more cost-effective than traditional remote access solutions involving modem pools, dedicated phone lines, and toll-free numbers.

For a typical host-network VPN scenario, the remote user first establishes a dial-up connection with a local ISP to connect to the Internet. When the user connects, the client contacts the VPN server to connect to the corporate intranet. The VPN server authenticates the VPN client, negotiates which tunneling and encryption protocols to use, and establishes the secure VPN connection.

The result is the formation of a secure encrypted tunnel that connects the VPN client to the VPN server. The effect is as if both client and server are on the same LAN. For the connection to work, however, the VPN client must be assigned an IP address that makes it appear to the VPN server that it is on the same LAN as the server. VPN clients thus generally have two IP addresses: one for the VPN connection and one for the intermediate or transit network, such as the Internet.

ICS

Internet Connection Sharing (ICS) enables a computer that is connected to the Internet to share the Internet service with several computers on a home or small-office network. The computer with the active Internet connection acts as the ICS host computer and shares its Internet connection. Other computers that are configured for ICS on your network route their Internet traffic through the ICS host computer. ICS is most effective with high-speed (cable or DSL) connections, although it works acceptably with dial-up Internet connections. The ICS host computer must have a second network adapter to share a broadband connection; and, of course, the shared connection is only available if the ICS host computer is turned on.

Dial-up

The term *dial-up* usually refers to the use of an analog modem and ordinary phone line to establish a remote connection. Dial-up lines are generally much less expensive to use, but they have less available bandwidth compared to dedicated or leased lines, which are digital lines with dedicated circuits.

Companies often use dial-up lines for occasional, low-bandwidth usage, such as remote access networking, or as a backup for the more costly dedicated lines.

In addition to dial-up lines using analog modems over local loop connections, there are some digital services that can be dialed instead of dedicated, such as Integrated Services Digital Network (ISDN) and X.25.

What Is Connection Manager?

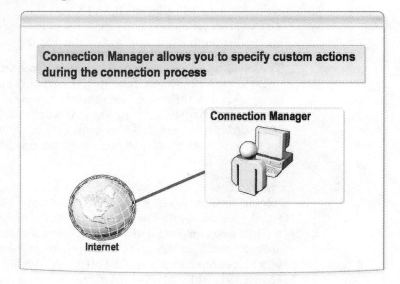

Introduction

Connection Manager is software that is installed on remote access client computers and allows users to easily connect to a remote network. It limits the number of configuration options that a user can change, ensuring that the user can always connect successfully.

Connection Manager functionality

Connection Manager enables users to:

- Select from a list of phone numbers to use, based on physical location.

- Use customized graphics, icons, messages, and help.

- Automatically create a dial-up connection before the VPN connection is made.

- Run custom actions during various parts of the connection process, such as preconnect and postconnect actions. These actions are executed before or after the dial-up or VPN connection is completed.

Connection Manager profiles

A customized Connection Manager client dialer package, also known as a profile, is a self-extracting executable file that is created by a network administrator with the Connection Manager Administration Kit (CMAK). The Connection Manager profile is distributed to VPN users via CD-ROM, e-mail, Web site, or file share. When the user runs the Connection Manager profile, it automatically configures the appropriate dial-up and VPN connections.

How to Configure a VPN Connection

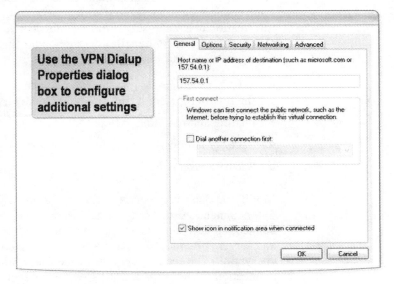

Use the VPN Dialup Properties dialog box to configure additional settings

Introduction	To configure a VPN connection in Windows XP, you can use the New Connection Wizard. The PPTP protocol that you need for VPN connections is automatically installed in Windows. To complete the wizard, you only need the host name or IP address of the remote computer to which you are connecting.
How to create a new VPN connection	A new VPN connection enables you to create different connections to accommodate multiple hosts, provide additional security options, and so on.

To create a new VPN connection:

1. In Control Panel, click **Network and Internet Connections**, and then click **Network Connections**.
2. Click **Create a new connection**, and then click **Next**.
3. Click **Connect to the network at my workplace**, and then click **Next**.
4. Click **Virtual Private Network connection**, and then click **Next**.
5. Type a descriptive name for your company, and then click **Next**.
6. Click **Do not dial the initial connection**, and then click **Next**.
7. Type the host name or IP address of the computer to which you are connecting, and then click **Next**.
8. On the **Completing the New Connection Wizard** page, click **Finish**.

How to configure VPN settings

After you create a VPN connection, you can view and edit settings for this connection by right-clicking the connection's icon and selecting **Properties**. Each connection is configured with general settings that are the minimum information needed to successfully connect. These options are found on the **General** tab of the **Properties** dialog box for that connection. You can configure additional settings, such as:

- Whether the operating system should connect to the public network, such as the Internet, before it tries to establish the virtual connection.

- Dialing and redialing options.

- Security options.

- Security protocols.

Modifying these connection settings does not modify or affect the settings of other connections that may already exist. For example, you may have a VPN connection that requires data encryption for all traffic between the VPN client and server. You may also have a second connection that does not require any encryption. The security settings of the first connection never cause the second connection to challenge the VPN server for encryption.

You can modify connection settings while you are connected. However, the connection may need to be reinitiated to save the changes. The connection will be terminated, the changes will be saved, and the connection will be reestablished immediately.

Additional reading

For more information on how to configure a VPN connection in Windows XP, see article 305550 in the Microsoft Knowledge Base.

How to Configure an ICS Connection

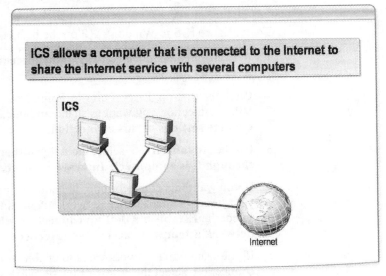

ICS allows a computer that is connected to the Internet to share the Internet service with several computers

ICS

Internet

Introduction

When you enable ICS, the LAN connection to the home or small-office network is given a new static IP address and configuration. Consequently, TCP/IP connections that are established between any home or small-office computer and the ICS host computer at the time ICS is enabled are lost and must be reestablished. For example, if Microsoft Internet Explorer is connecting to a Web site when you enable ICS, you must refresh the browser to reestablish the connection.

You must configure client computers on your home or small-office network so that TCP/IP on the local area connection obtains an IP address automatically. Home or small-office network users must also configure Internet options for ICS.

ICS requirements

To enable and configure ICS on a network, the ICS host computer needs these network connections:

- A local area connection, automatically created by installing a network adapter that connects to the computers on your home or small-office network

- A second connection, by means of a 56-kilobyte modem, ISDN, DSL, or cable modem, linking the home or small-office network and the Internet

You must ensure that ICS is enabled on the connection to the Internet. By doing this, the shared connection can link your home or small-office network to the Internet, and users outside your network are not at risk of receiving inappropriate addresses from your network.

How to configure ICS on the host computer

To take advantage of the security features of Windows XP, it is recommended that you install ICS on the computer that you use to connect to the Internet, which is called the *host computer*.

To configure ICS in Windows XP on the host computer:

1. In Control Panel, click **Network and Internet Connections**, and then click **Network Connections**.

2. Click the dial-up, LAN, Point-to-Point Protocol over Ethernet (PPPoE), or VPN connection you want to share, and then, under **Network Tasks**, click **Change settings of this connection**.

3. On the **Advanced** tab, select the **Allow other network users to connect through this computer's Internet connection** check box.

4. If you want this connection to dial automatically when another computer on your home or small-office network attempts to access external resources, select the **Establish a dial-up connection whenever a computer on my network attempts to access the Internet** check box.

5. If you want other network users to enable or disable the shared Internet connection, select the **Allow other network users to control or disable the shared Internet connection** check box.

How to configure ICS on the client computer

The other computers on the LAN that use the host computer to connect to the Internet are called *client computers*.

To configure Internet options on your client computers for ICS:

1. Click **Start**, click **All Programs**, and then click **Internet Explorer**.

2. On the **Tools** menu, click **Internet Options**.

3. On the **Connections** tab, click **Never dial a connection**, and then click **LAN Settings**.

4. In **Automatic configuration**, clear the **Automatically detect settings** and **Use automatic configuration script** check boxes.

5. In **Proxy Server,** clear the **Use a proxy server** check box.

Additional reading

For information on installing and troubleshooting ICS in Windows XP Professional and Windows XP Home Edition, refer to article 308006 in the Microsoft Knowledge Base.

How to Configure a Dial-Up Connection

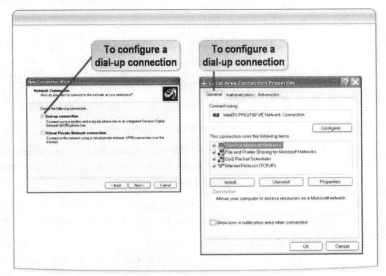

Introduction

To dial in to and log on to a network, you must create and configure a connection. This section describes how to create and configure a dial-up connection.

How to configure a dial-up connection

You can use the **Network Connections** dialog box to automatically configure connections according to the devices that are available. For example, when you use a laptop's docking station in the office, the connection is configured to use the docking station modem. When you are out of the office, and the docking station is not available, the connection is automatically configured to use the laptop's modem.

To configure a dial-up connection:

1. In Control Panel, click **Network and Internet Connections**.

2. Click **Create a connection to the network at your office**.

3. In the **Location Information** dialog box, enter the appropriate information.

4. Click **OK**, and then click **OK** again to close the **Phone and Modem Options** dialog box and start the New Connection Wizard.

5. In the New Connection Wizard, click **Dial-up connection**, and then click **Next**.

6. Type a name for the network to which you are connecting, and then click **Next**.

7. Type the phone number for the network to which you are connecting, including, if necessary, the area code and "1" prefix.

8. Specify whether you want this connection to be available for anyone's use, meaning for any user on this computer, or for your use only, meaning only for the user who is now logged on.

9. Specify whether you want a shortcut to the connection on your desktop.

10. Click **Finish**.

How to use dial-up connections

One of the most common procedures users require assistance with is using a dial-up connection.

To use a dial-up connection:

1. Click **Start**, click **Connect to**, and then click the connection that you want to use.

2. In the **User Name** box, type your user name.

3. In the **Password** box, type your password.

4. Choose one of the following options:

   - To save the user name and password so that you will not have to type them in the future, select the **Save this user name and password for the following users** check box.

   - If you want only the current user to have access to the saved user name and password, select the **Me only** check box.

   - If you want all users to have access to the user name and password, select the **Anyone who uses this computer** check box.

5. Click **Dial**.

How to modify an existing dial-up connection

You may need to modify some of the parameters in your dial-up connection to successfully connect to the Internet.

To modify an existing dial-up connection:

1. Click **Start**, click **Control Panel**, click **Network and Internet Connections**, and then click **Network Connections**.

2. Click the connection, and then click **Change settings of this connection**.

   - On the **General** tab, you can change the server name or IP address.

   - On the **Networking** tab, you can change the type of secure protocol.

   - On the **Advanced** tab, you can enable Windows Firewall protection to prevent access to your computer from the Internet.

     To do this, select the **Protect my computer and network by limiting and preventing access to this computer from the Internet** check box.

Note   When you enable Windows Firewall protection to prevent access to your computer from the Internet, you may also create problems with the connection to your server. After you enable Windows Firewall protection, verify that the connection to your server is still working.

Important   A firewall is designed to help protect your computer from attack by malicious users or by malicious software such as viruses that use unsolicited incoming network traffic to attack your computer. If the connection to your server is working and you decide to disable your firewall, you must disconnect your computer from all networks including the Internet.

How to Use Remote Desktop

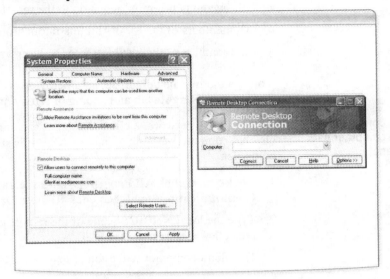

Introduction

Remote Desktop allows a computer to control another computer remotely over the Internet or on a local intranet. For example, you can use Remote Desktop to access files on your work computer from your home computer. A user might need your assistance to configure a Remote Desktop connection, or you might use Remote Desktop to connect to a remote computer for troubleshooting.

Requirements for Remote Desktop

The computer that establishes the connection is called the *client computer*, and the computer to which the client computer connects is called the *remote computer*. By using a Remote Desktop connection, you can perform tasks on the remote computer directly. The requirements for Remote Desktop are:

- The remote computer must be running Windows XP Professional.
- The remote computer must have Remote Desktop connections enabled.
- The client computer must be running Windows 95 or a more recent version of Windows, and it must have the Remote Desktop Connection client software installed.
- Only one connection (local or remote) is possible.

How to configure the remote computer

To connect to a remote computer running Windows XP Professional by using the Remote Desktop utility, the remote computer must have Remote Desktop enabled.

To enable Remote Desktop:

1. In Control Panel, click **System**.
2. On the **Remote** tab, select the **Allow users to connect remotely to this computer** check box.

How to modify permissions

By default, the users that can connect to the remote computer include:

- The account currently logged on to the remote computer.
- All members of the local Administrators group.
- All members of the local Remote Desktop Users group.

You can modify the default account permissions by clicking **Select Remote Users** on the **Remote** tab and adding or removing accounts.

How to connect to a remote computer over an intranet

Within a local network, a client computer can connect to any Remote Desktop–enabled computer running Windows XP Professional. To connect to a remote computer:

1. Click **Start**, click **All Programs**, click **Accessories**, click **Communications**, and then click **Remote Desktop Connection**.
2. Type the local NetBIOS name of the remote computer or its IP address, and then click **OK**.

   The client computer will attempt to connect to the remote computer.

How to connect to a remote computer over the Internet

Connecting to a remote computer over the Internet requires more considerations than connecting over an intranet:

- If the remote computer uses a modem to connect to the Internet, the modem must be installed and functioning properly.
- If the remote computer is located behind a firewall, such as Windows Firewall, the Remote Desktop port must be opened. The port number for Remote Desktop connection is TCP port number 3389.
- If the remote computer is on another intranet and not directly connected to the Internet, you must create a VPN to the other intranet to connect to the computer.
- If the remote computer is assigned a dynamic IP address for connectivity, you must first determine the IP address to make a connection to the remote computer. Use the remote computer's Ipconfig command-line utility to determine its current IP address.

Note For more information about Remote Desktop, refer to Knowledge Base (KB) articles 300698 and 281262.

How to Use Remote Assistance

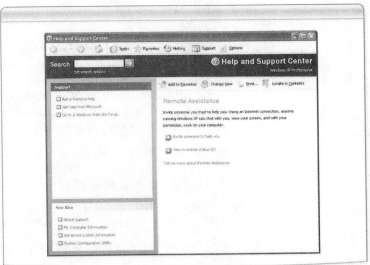

Introduction

Remote Assistance is another remote access tool that is available to the DST. Remote Assistance is similar to Remote Desktop in that both use TCP port number 3389. Remote Assistance differs from Remote Desktop in several ways:

- Both users must be present at their computers and must agree to the establishment of a Remote Assistance connection.
- Remote Assistance can be used to connect to a computer running Windows XP Home Edition.

How to initialize a Remote Assistance session

The two parties that are involved in a Remote Assistance session are referred to as the *novice* and the *expert*. The process for initializing a Remote Assistance session is as follows:

1. The novice sends a Remote Assistance request, using either Windows Messenger, e-mail, or by saving an invitation. This can also be initiated by clicking **Start**, clicking **All Programs**, and then clicking **Remote Assistance**.

2. The expert accepts the invitation, which opens a terminal window that displays the desktop of the novice's computer.

    The expert can view the desktop in a read-only window and can exchange messages with the novice by using voice or chat. The expert can request to take control of the novice's computer by clicking the **Take Control** button in the **Expert** console. This sends a message to the novice's computer. The novice must allow the expert to take control of the computer before the expert can work with objects on the novice's computer.

Note On computers that are in the same domain, the expert can offer Remote Assistance to the novice, thereby bypassing the need for the novice to send the invitation to the expert.

Remote Assistance issues when using NAT

Using Remote Assistance is fairly simple in a local home network, intranet, or on the Internet if both computers have direct connections to the Internet utilizing public IP addresses.

However, in many cases, one or both of the computers involved in the interaction may be using a Network Address Translation (NAT) connection. NAT essentially maps multiple computers to one or more IP addresses to maximize the number of Internet connections that are available using a minimum of IP addresses. How NAT performs its task determines the success or failure of Remote Assistance, since problems might occur if one or both computers are behind a NAT connection.

- ICS listens for Remote Assistance data on port 5001 and forwards it to port 3389. If either computer is using a public IP address or ICS to connect to the Internet, Remote Assistance functions correctly.

- Universal Plug and Play (UPnP)–compatible routers and/or gateways allow computers behind them to establish Remote Assistance connections.

- Non-UPnP-compatible routers and/or gateways do not allow computers behind them to establish Remote Assistance connections. However, a computer that is *not* located behind a non-UPnP-compatible router may establish a connection to one that is, if the novice initiates a connection by using Windows Messenger on a random port and the expert uses this port to initiate a connection back.

- Non-UPnP-compatible routers and/or gateways without Windows Messenger require some advanced configuration of the Remote Assistance ticket file, which is an eXtensible Markup Language (XML) file created for the connection.

Additional reading

For more information on configuring and troubleshooting Remote Assistance, refer to Knowledge Base articles 300692 and 306298.

How to Troubleshoot Remote Connection Issues

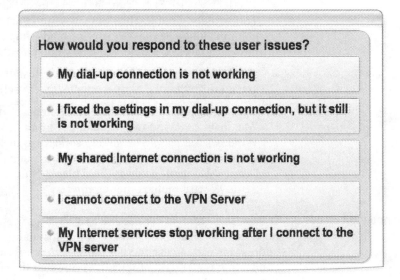

How would you respond to these user issues?

- My dial-up connection is not working

- I fixed the settings in my dial-up connection, but it still is not working

- My shared Internet connection is not working

- I cannot connect to the VPN Server

- My Internet services stop working after I connect to the VPN server

Introduction

This section describes the common problems that you may encounter when troubleshooting remote connection issues and provides some possible solutions.

Dial-up connection issues

Problems with a dial-up connection may be caused by the modem hardware, the phone line, or software settings.

To verify that a modem is functioning properly:

1. Click **Start**, click **Control Panel**, and then in Classic View, double-click **Phone and Modem Options**.

2. In the **Phone and Modem Options** dialog box, on the **Modems** tab, select the modem, and then click **Properties**.

3. In the **Properties** box, on the **Diagnostics** tab, click **Query Modem**.

   If the modem is working correctly, a series of diagnostics responses are returned. If the modem is faulty, try reinstalling the modem or consult the modem manufacturer for more information.

4. For additional information about the attempted connection, on the **Diagnostics** tab, click **View log**.

   The modem session log information can help to pinpoint a variety of problems that you might encounter while attempting to make a dial-up connection.

Also verify that the phone cord and the phone jack that the computer is connected to work properly by testing each with a phone.

Finally, if a user has attempted to resolve an issue by reconfiguring dial-up settings multiple times, the connection may have become corrupted. If you have verified that the settings are correct but the connection still is not working, delete the connection and create a new one using the New Connection Wizard.

Shared ICS issues

Any of the following circumstances can prevent ICS from working properly:

- The ICS service is not running. In Control Panel, open the Administrative Tools folder, double-click **Services**, and then check to see that the Status column alongside the ICS service reads Started. If necessary, on the shortcut menu, right-click the Service entry and click **Start** or **Restart**.

- The wrong network adapter is shared. Restart the Network Setup Wizard and confirm that the correct adapters were selected.

- The settings on other network computers are incorrect. Computers running Windows 98, Windows Millennium Edition, Windows 2000, or Windows XP should be able to connect to the Internet through an ICS host when configured to obtain an IP address and DNS servers automatically. Leave the default gateway field blank. If necessary, rerun the Network Setup Wizard on the other computers.

VPN connection issues

If there is a problem connecting to a VPN server, first verify that the correct host name or IP address is used. If the host name is correct, try using the IP address instead in case there is a problem with name resolution. Also, if the connection is through a firewall, ensure that the correct ports are open at the firewall to allow the VPN connection through the firewall. Another reason for VPN connection failure can be using NAT. If the network uses NAT to protect internal IP addressing, certain VPN protocols cannot pass through.

Another common problem that may occur with a VPN connection is that Internet services stop working after a VPN connection is established. This occurs when the VPN connection is configured to use the default gateway on the remote network for Internet access. When connecting to a single computer or a small workgroup, it is usually not necessary to use the remote gateway.

To disable the default gateway on the remote network:

1. Right-click the VPN connection and choose **Properties**.

2. On the **Networking** tab, click **Internet Protocol (TCP/IP)**, and then click **Properties**.

3. In the **Internet Protocol (TCP/IP) Properties** dialog box, click **Advanced**.

4. In the **Advanced TCP/IP Settings** dialog box, on the **General** tab, clear the **Use default gateway on remote network** check box.

When connecting to a corporate network, it may be necessary to leave the **Use default gateway on remote network** check box selected for security reasons. In this situation, configure Internet Explorer to use a Web proxy for the VPN connection.

To configure Internet Explorer to use a Web proxy:

1. In Internet Explorer, on the **Tools** menu, click **Internet Options**.

2. In the **Internet Options** dialog box, on the **Connections** tab, in the **Dial-up and Virtual Private Network Settings** box, select the connection type, and then click **Settings**.

3. Enter the Proxy server settings provided by your network administrator.

Demonstration: Managing Remote Connection Issues

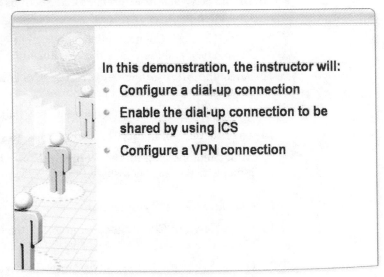

In this demonstration, the instructor will:
- Configure a dial-up connection
- Enable the dial-up connection to be shared by using ICS
- Configure a VPN connection

Objectives

In this practice, your instructor will:

- Configure a dial-up connection.
- Enable the dial-up connection to be shared by using Internet Connection Sharing.
- Configure a VPN connection.

Scenario

A user calls while traveling and says that she needs to connect to the network to access the company intranet. She needs to create both a dial-up connection and a VPN connection.

▶ **Configure a dial-up connection and enable ICS**

1. Resume London and Acapulco.

2. On Acapulco, log on to the domain as **Administrator** with a password of **P@ssw0rd**.

3. In Control Panel, click **Network and Internet Connections**.

4. In the **Network and Internet Connections** dialog box, click **Create a connection to the network at your workplace**.

5. On the **Network Connection** page, click **Dial-up connection** and then click **Next**.

6. On the **Connection Name** page, in the **Company Name** box, type **Northwind Traders** and then click **Next**.

7. On the **Phone Number to Dial** page, in the **Phone number** box, type **206 555-0100** and then click **Next**.

8. On the **Connection Availability** page, verify **Anyone's use** is selected, and then click **Next**.

9. On the **Completing the New Connection Wizard** page, click **Finish**.

10. On the **Network and Internet Connections** page, click **Network Connections**.

11. In the Network Connections window, right-click **Northwind Traders**, click **Properties**, and then click the **Advanced** tab.

12. Select the **Allow other network users to connect through this computer's Internet connection** checkbox.

13. Read the information in the message box and click **OK**.

14. To close the **Northwind Traders Properties** dialog box, click **OK**.

    Notice that the icon for the Northwind Traders connection has changed to indicate that it has been shared.

▶ **Configure a VPN connection**

1. In the Network Connections window, on the task pad, click **Create a New Connection**.

2. On the **Welcome to the New Connection Wizard** page, click **Next**.

3. On the **Network Connection Type** page, click **Connect to the network at my workplace** and then click **Next**.

4. On the **Network Connection** page, click **Virtual Private Network connection**, and then click **Next**.

5. On the **Connection Name** page, in the **Company Name** box, type **Northwind VPN** and then click **Next**.

6. On the **Public Network** page, click **Do not dial the initial connection**, and then click **Next**.

7. On the **VPN Server Selection** page, in the **Host name or IP address** box, type **nwtraders.msft** and then click **Next**.

8. On the **Connection Availability** page, click **Anyone's use**, and then click **Next**.

9. On the **Completing the New Connection Wizard** page, click **Finish**.

10. On the **Connect Northwind VPN** dialog box, click **Cancel**.

    Notice the Northwind VPN connection is displayed under Virtual Private Network.

11. For all three virtual machines, on the Virtual PC window, on the **Action** menu, click **Close**.

12. On the **Close** dialog box, select **Turn off and delete changes** and then click **OK**.

Lab: Resolving Network Connectivity Issues

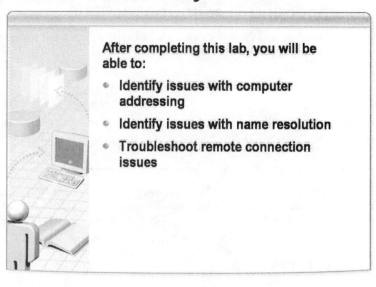

After completing this lab, you will be able to:

- Identify issues with computer addressing
- Identify issues with name resolution
- Troubleshoot remote connection issues

Objectives

After completing this lab, you will be able to:

- Identify issues with computer addressing.
- Identify issues with name resolution.
- Troubleshoot remote connection issues.

Prerequisites

Before working on this lab, you must have an understanding of how to use Microsoft Virtual PC.

Before You Begin

- For each exercise in this lab, use a password of **P@ssw0rd**.
- Inside a virtual machine, <right>ALT+DEL is the equivalent of CTRL+ALT+DEL.

Scenario

You are a DST for Northwind Traders, a company whose workers use Windows XP Professional. Two users call with various desktop configuration and customization questions.

Estimated time to complete this lab: 30 minutes

Exercise 1
Troubleshooting TCP/IP Connections

In this exercise, you will troubleshoot a situation in which a corporate user cannot connect her laptop to her home network.

Scenario

A user calls and says that she is working from home and that she cannot connect her laptop to her home network. To simulate this scenario, you use Acapulco to connect to a share on Bonn.

Tasks	Guidance for completing the task
1. Start the London, Acapulco, and Bonn virtual machines, and using London, log on to the NWTRADERS domain as Administrator with a password of **P@ssw0rd**.	▪ Use the Virtual PC console. ▪ Wait for London to display the log on screen before starting Acapulco.
2. On London, stop the DHCP Server service.	▪ Command-line command is **net stop "dhcp server"**
3. Using the Virtual PC Console, pause 2261_London.	▪ Press \<right> ALT+P
4. Using Acapulco, log on locally as Administrator, navigate to C:\Program Files \Microsoft Learning\2261 \Labfiles\Lab04\ and run 2261_Lab04_Ex1_Acapulco .exe	▪ Press \<right> ALT+DEL.
5. Using Bonn, log on locally as Administrator, navigate to C:\Program Files\ Microsoft Learning\ 2261\Labfiles\Lab04\ and run 2261_Lab04_Ex1_Bonn.exe	
6. What is Bonn's IP address? What is Acapulco's IP address? Are they on the same network?	169.254.172.53 169.254.136.1 No

(continued)

Tasks	Guidance for completing the task
7. Resolve the issue so that the user will be able to connect her laptop to the office without reconfiguring it again.	▪ Refer to the topic How to Configure a TCP/IP Address in this module. ▪ The issue is considered resolved when both computers are on the same home network (10.1.1.0) and the user can simply connect to the corporate network without having to reconfigure the network connection again. To test the corporate network environment, resume London, restart the DHCP Server service on London, then renew the IP address on Acapulco. If you receive a 192.168.1.x address from the DHCP server, you have successfully resolved the issue.
8. Resume London and restart the DHCP Server service.	
9. Pause Bonn.	

Exercise 2
Troubleshooting a Name Resolution Issue

In this exercise, you will troubleshoot a name resolution issue.

Scenario

A user calls and says while using Acapulco, he ping London. Other connections are erratic. He is able to log on and connect to shared printers and folders, but when he pings London, the request times out. You have been asked to enable the user to successfully ping London.

Tasks	Guidance for completing the task
1. Verify London is running, then using Acapulco log on to the domain as **Administrator**.	
2. On Acapulco, navigate to C:\Program Files \Microsoft Learning\2261 \Labfiles\Lab04\ and run 2261_Lab04_Ex2.exe.	▪ This step introduces the problem.
3. Using Acapulco, log off and log to the NWTRADERS domain as Administrator, and then ping London.	
4. Were you able to successfully ping London?	
5. Resolve the name resolution issue.	▪ Refer to the topic page title How Client Names Are Resolved. ▪ This issue is considered resolved when you successfully ping London.

Microsoft®

Module 5: Resolving Hardware Issues

Contents

Overview

- Managing Drivers
- Troubleshooting Drivers by Using Safe Mode
- Troubleshooting Storage Devices
- Troubleshooting Display Devices
- Troubleshooting I/O Devices
- Troubleshooting ACPI

Introduction

Every device, such as a disk drive, a monitor, or a modem, requires a device driver to ensure that the hardware functions properly with the computer. Most drivers come with the operating system, such as Microsoft® Windows® XP Professional or Windows XP Home Edition, and they are installed and configured automatically without user intervention. However, some devices require the user to install a new driver for the computer to communicate with the device. Because any driver installed in a computer can cause startup and stability problems, it is important that you, as a desktop support technician (DST), are familiar with common issues so that you can diagnose and troubleshoot your users' hardware issues related to drivers. This module describes how to troubleshoot drivers within several device categories: storage devices, display devices, and input/output (I/O) devices. Finally, this module explains the purpose of Advanced Configuration and Power Interface (ACPI) and describes how to troubleshoot issues related to ACPI.

Objectives

After completing this module, you will be able to:

- Manage drivers.
- Troubleshoot drivers by using safe mode.
- Troubleshoot storage devices.
- Troubleshoot display devices.
- Troubleshoot I/O devices.
- Troubleshoot ACPI issues.

Lesson: Managing Drivers

* What Is a Device Driver?
* What Is Device Manager?
* How to Update a Driver
* How to Roll Back a Driver
* What Are Digitally Signed Drivers?
* How to Adjust Digitally Signed Driver Policies
* How to Troubleshoot Drivers

Introduction

Before you troubleshoot storage devices, display devices, and I/O devices, you must know how to locate and install drivers, how to roll back a driver, how to determine if a driver is digitally signed, and how to configure a computer to allow only digitally signed drivers. You can perform all these functions by using Device Manager. This lesson explains how to use Device Manager to perform these tasks and how to perform general troubleshooting procedures.

Lesson objectives

After completing this lesson, you will be able to:

* Explain the function and purpose of device drivers.
* Explain the function and purpose of Device Manager.
* Update a driver.
* Roll back a driver.
* Explain the function and purpose of digitally signed drivers.
* Configure a computer to allow or not allow digitally signed drivers.
* Troubleshoot driver issues.

What Is a Device Driver?

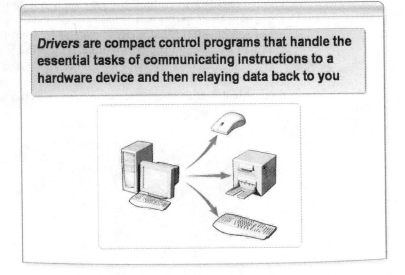

Drivers are compact control programs that handle the essential tasks of communicating instructions to a hardware device and then relaying data back to you

Introduction

Before the Windows operating system can work with any hardware device, it requires a compatible, properly configured device driver.

Definition

A *device driver* is a compact program that enables peripheral devices to communicate with the operating system. Specifically, a device driver enables a device to communicate with the program that uses the device by accepting generic commands from the program and then translating the commands into specialized commands for the device.

Driver library

Although most drivers for standard devices come with the operating system, devices that are added later usually require a corresponding driver. Windows XP includes a large library of drivers for keyboards, pointing devices, printers, scanners, digital cameras. By default, when a user installs a new device, Windows XP searches the library for the appropriate device driver.

The driver library is a single compressed filed called Driver.cab that is located in the *systemroot%*\Driver Cache\I386 folder. All the drivers in this file are certified to be fully compatible with Windows XP and are digitally signed by Microsoft.

Windows XP Service Pack 1 (SP1) and Service Pack 2 (SP2) include Sp1.cab, and Sp2.cab files respectively. The service pack that is installed determines the cab file that is installed. For example, if SP4 is installed, Sp4.cab is installed in the *systemroot%*\Driver Cache\I386 folder along with the original Driver.cab file.

Locating the appropriate driver

When you install any new Plug and Play–compatible device, Windows XP searches for drivers in %systemroot%*platform*\driver cache folder (where *platform* is the type of platform on which Windows XP is installed, typically I386) as well as in original Windows XP installation source. *Plug and Play* is a set of specifications that were developed by Intel that allows a computer to automatically detect and configure a device and install the appropriate device drivers. If Windows XP finds a suitable driver, the installation proceeds automatically. If Windows XP does not find a suitable driver, you must provide a suitable driver from another source, such as the hardware device manufacturer or the Web.

What Is Device Manager?

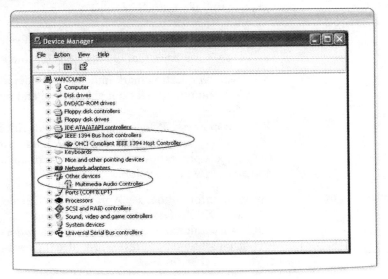

Introduction

Device Manager is a Windows XP administrative tool that you can use to manage the devices on a computer. Administrators or users with administrative rights typically use Device Manager to examine the status of hardware and to update device drivers. Administrators who have a thorough understanding of computer hardware might also use the diagnostic features of Device Manager to resolve device conflicts and change resource settings. In general, use Device Manager to:

- View the status of device drivers.
- Update device drivers.
- Configure device driver settings.
- Remove device drivers.
- Troubleshoot device driver–related issues.

How to access Device Manager

You can access Device Manager to view information about hardware that is installed on users' computers, but you must have administrative rights to modify or update hardware.

To access Device Manager:

1. In Control Panel, click **Performance and Maintenance**, and then click **System**.
2. In the **Systems Properties** dialog box, on the **Hardware** tab, click **Device Manager**.

How Device Manager displays the status of a device

The Device Manager window displays a tree that lists all the devices configured for the computer. The status of a particular device is indicated in Device Manager by the following icons:

- A yellow exclamation point indicates a problem with the device.
- A red X indicates that the device is disabled.
- A yellow question mark indicates the device was installed on the computer but Windows XP was not able to find and install a driver for it.

When Windows XP encounters a problem with a device or its driver, it changes the icon in Device Manager and displays an error code on the **General** tab of the device's properties window. Each error code is associated with a number and a brief text description.

Additional reading

For more information, see Appendix F, "Device Manager Error Codes," in the Windows XP Professional Resource Kit at http://www.microsoft.com/technet/treeview/default.asp?url=/TechNet /prodtechnol/winxppro/reskit/prjk_dec_lgsc.asp.

How to Update a Driver

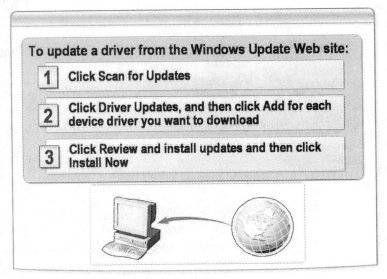

To update a driver from the Windows Update Web site:

1 Click Scan for Updates

2 Click Driver Updates, and then click Add for each device driver you want to download

3 Click Review and install updates and then click Install Now

Introduction

Microsoft and other device manufacturers frequently issue updates for device drivers. In some cases, the updates enable new features. In other cases, the update corrects a bug that could affect users. Device driver updates can usually be obtained from the manufacturer of the hardware device or from the Windows Update Web site.

Important　Make sure that you read the instructions that are provided by the manufacturer before installing any new device drivers.

How to obtain device driver updates from the manufacturer

A common method of updating a device driver is for the device manufacturer to provide a CD-ROM or downloadable executable file that automatically installs the device driver.

To install these device drivers, close all open programs and run either the CD-ROM or the executable file that installs the device driver.

Tip　Typically, a universal serial bus (USB) device driver must be installed before you plug in a USB device. A *USB* is a device that supports Plug and Play installation, which enables you to connect and disconnect devices without shutting down or restarting your computer.

How to obtain device driver updates from Windows Update

Some manufacturers submit updated drivers to Microsoft and then Microsoft posts the updated drivers on the Windows Update Web site.

To connect to the Windows Update Web site:

1. In Windows XP, click **Start**, click **All Programs**, and then click **Windows Update**.

   The Windows Update Web site opens.

2. On the Windows Update Web site, click the **Scan for updates** link.

   Windows Update scans the computer and displays the appropriate updates.

3. Leave the Windows Update Web site open.

To download device driver updates from the Windows Update Web site:

1. On the Windows Update Web site, click **Driver Updates**, and then click **Add** for each device driver you want to download.

2. To install the updates, click **Review and install updates**, and then click **Install Now**.

How to install drivers that do not include setup programs

Occasionally, manufacturers release drivers that do not include their own setup program. This type of setup uses a *setup information* file (with the extension .inf). This is a text file that contains detailed information about the device to be installed, including the names of device files, where to install the device, any required registry settings, and version information.

In general, this type of driver is available as a downloadable .zip file. A *.zip file* is a compressed archive file that contains all the files needed to install the device driver. Windows XP Professional and Windows XP Home Edition include a program that can uncompress a .zip file. After a file is uncompressed, you can install the driver by using the Update Driver Wizard in Device Manager.

To install the uncompressed driver:

1. Open **Device Manager**.
2. Right-click the device whose driver you want to update, and then click **Update Driver**.
3. Click **Install from a list or a specific location**, and then click **Next**.
4. Click **Don't search. I will choose the driver to install.** and then click **Next**.
5. Click **Have Disk**, and then click **Browse**.
6. In the **Locate File** dialog box, navigate to the folder where the new driver is located, and then click **Open**. Click **OK**.
7. Select the driver that matches your hardware, and then click **Next**.
8. Click **Next** again, and then click **Finish**.

Additional reading

For more information on updating device drivers, see Microsoft Knowledge Base (KB) article 283658.

How to Roll Back a Driver

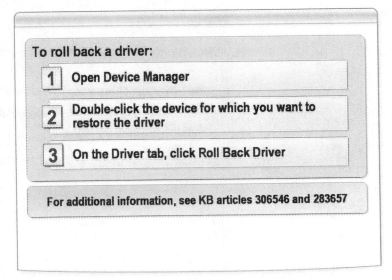

To roll back a driver:

1 Open Device Manager

2 Double-click the device for which you want to restore the driver

3 On the Driver tab, click Roll Back Driver

For additional information, see KB articles 306546 and 283657

Introduction

Sometimes a new device driver causes a computer to become unstable and unusable. When this occurs, you can use the Roll Back Driver feature to replace the device driver with a previously installed version of the driver so that you can continue to use the computer.

How to roll back a device driver

To roll back a device driver:

1. Open **Device Manager**.

2. In the Device Manager window, double-click the device for which you want to restore the driver.

3. On the **Driver** tab, click **Roll Back Driver**.

Note You cannot roll back a printer driver because you cannot restore printer drivers with the Device Driver Roll Back feature.

Additional reading

For more information on the Roll Back Driver feature, see KB articles 306546 and 283657.

What Are Digitally Signed Drivers?

How to verify digitally signed drivers:

- View the driver properties in Device Manager
- Run the File Signature Verification utility
- Run the Driverquery utility

Introduction

Microsoft digitally signs each device driver to assure users that the driver was tested for compatibility with Windows and that the driver has not been altered since testing. Windows XP determines whether to install a device driver based on whether the driver is digitally signed. If a driver is not digitally signed, Windows XP warns the users when they attempt to install the driver. System administrators and individual computer owners can also choose to set operating system policies that prevent the installation of drivers that do not have digital signatures.

How to verify a digitally signed driver

There are several ways to verify whether a device driver is digitally signed. You can:

- View the driver properties in Device Manager.

  Open **Device Manager**, double-click the device and then click the **Driver** tab.

- Run the File Signature Verification utility. This utility scans all digitally signed files on the local computer and provides a report of the files that are signed and those that are not signed. By default, this utility notifies you of any files that are not signed, and it logs the results in *systemroot*\SIGVERIF.TXT.

  To run File Signature Verification, click **Start**, click **Run**, and then in the **Run** box, type **sigverif.exe** and then click **OK**.

- Run the Driverquery utility. This utility creates a list of the drivers installed on the local computer. The following example shows how to use Driverquery to create a file that lists all the drivers. This file can be viewed in Microsoft Office Excel.

  For example: driverquery /v /fo csv > drvlist.csv

Additional reading

For more information on digitally signed drivers, see KB articles 308514, 259283, and 224404. For more information on the Driverquery utility, see the Microsoft Windows XP Resource Kit.

How to Adjust Digitally Signed Driver Policies

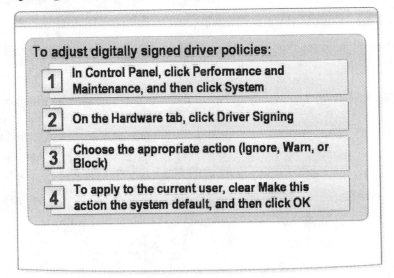

To adjust digitally signed driver policies:

1 In Control Panel, click Performance and Maintenance, and then click System

2 On the Hardware tab, click Driver Signing

3 Choose the appropriate action (Ignore, Warn, or Block)

4 To apply to the current user, clear Make this action the system default, and then click OK

Introduction

The Windows XP default setting is to issue a warning when a user attempts to install an unsigned device driver. However, experienced Windows users who can identify and select compatible drivers sometimes choose to configure the computer to ignore this warning. In contrast, there are circumstances in which it is appropriate to prevent users from installing an unsigned driver, such as when a novice user could undermine system stability by attempting to install an incompatible device.

How to adjust driver-signing policies

To adjust driver-signing policies:

1. In Control Panel, click **Performance and Maintenance**, and then click **System**.

2. In the **System Properties** dialog box, on the **Hardware** tab, click **Driver Signing**.

3. In the **Driver Signing Options** dialog box, choose the action you want Windows to take when a user attempts to install an unsigned driver. These options include:

   - **Ignore**. Allows users to install an unsigned driver without receiving a warning message.

   - **Warn**. (default) Allows users to override the warning message and install an unsigned driver.

   - **Block**. Does not allow users to install an unsigned driver.

4. To apply the selected option only to the current user, clear the **Make This Action the System Default** check box. Select this check box to apply the action to all users. (This option is available only if you are logged on as an administrator.) Click **OK** to apply the changes.

How to Troubleshoot Drivers

Troubleshooting driver issues

- If the user downloaded a beta version of the device driver, perform a driver rollback
- If the driver is corrupt, disable it in Device Manager
- If the computer runs normally with the device disabled, roll back the driver and install an updated driver that is digitally signed

Introduction

When a DST receives a call relating to device drivers, the user may say something like, "I just installed an update for my network card, but now my computer keeps rebooting on its own."

Obtain information from the user

To troubleshoot this issue, ask the user where she obtained the driver update and if she knows the version, manufacturer, and model of the driver. When you have this information, go to the manufacturer's Web site and determine if the correct driver version was installed. The user may have installed a beta-release driver or the incorrect driver for her specific hardware. The manufacturer's Web site might also contain information about known issues between its products and other hardware.

Important   Depending on the severity of the computer's instability, you might need to start the computer in safe mode to troubleshoot, disable, or roll back the driver. (*Safe mode* is a method of starting Windows XP that uses only basic files and the minimal set of drivers that the operating system must have to function. Safe mode is discussed in more detail later in this module.) Starting in safe mode can be a valuable troubleshooting tool. For example, if a problem exists with the computer's video driver, you might be unable to see the screen to change the driver. In this case, you can start the computer in safe mode, which uses a generic video driver so that you can troubleshoot the problem.

Perform troubleshooting procedures

Based on the scenario presented, you might try the following troubleshooting actions:

- If the user downloaded a beta version of the device driver, perform a driver rollback.

- If the driver might be corrupt, disable the device in Device Manager. If the computer starts successfully after disabling the device, this may indicate that the driver is the cause of the computer's instability.

- If the computer runs normally with the device disabled, you should roll back the driver and then install an updated driver that is digitally signed.

- If you cannot roll back the driver, uninstall the driver by removing it from Device Manager in safe mode, restart the computer, and then scan for new hardware to reinstall the driver. To scan for new hardware, in Device Manager, on the **Action** menu, click **Scan for hardware changes**.

- If Device Manager reports an error that is not resolved by performing the previous steps, reference Appendix F, "Device Manager Error Codes," in the Windows XP Professional Resource Kit at http://www.microsoft.com /technet/treeview/default.asp?url=/TechNet/prodtechnol/winxppro/reskit /prjk_dec_lgsc.asp.

- If you cannot access Device Manager, such as when a computer will not boot normally, use Recovery Console. *Recovery Console* is a command-line interface that provides a limited set of administrative commands that are useful for repairing a computer.

Practice: Troubleshooting Drivers

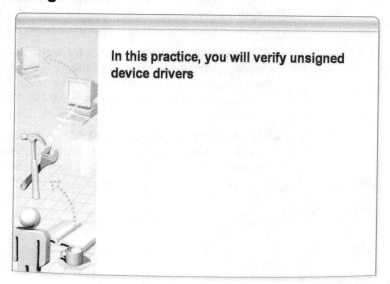

In this practice, you will verify unsigned
device drivers

Objective

In this practice, you will use the File Signature Verification utility to verify unsigned device drivers.

Scenario

A user calls and says that when he starts his computer, a dialog box is displayed that says a driver is not signed. You need to determine if other drivers are unsigned and replace those drivers.

Practice

▶ **Determine unsigned device drivers**

1. Start the 2261_Bonn virtual machine.

2. Log on to Bonn as **Administrator** with a password of **P@ssw0rd**.

3. Click **Start**, click **Run**, in the **Open** box, type **sigverif**, and then click **OK**.

4. On the **File Signature Verification** dialog box, click **Advanced**.

5. On the **Advanced File Signature Verification Settings** dialog box, click **Look for other files that are not digitally signed**.

6. In the **Look in this folder** box, type **C:\Windows\system32\drivers**.

7. On the **Logging** tab, confirm that the **Save the file signature verification results to a log file** check box is selected, and then click **OK**.

8. On the **File Signature Verification** dialog box, click **Start**.

9. In the **SigVerif** dialog box, click **OK**.

10. On the **File Signature Verification** dialog box, click **Advanced**.

11. In the **Advanced File Signature Verification Settings** page, on the **Logging** tab, click **View Log**.

    View the list of drivers, their versions and the signed status.

    Note   The log file is named Sigverif.txt, and it is saved in the Windows folder. Third-party drivers that are unsigned are displayed as *Not signed*. Use the drivers in this list as your troubleshooting starting point. Pay particular attention to files with an .inf extension. These are drivers.

    ---

12. Close all windows, log off, and then pause the 2261_Bonn virtual machine.

Lesson: Troubleshooting Drivers by Using Safe Mode

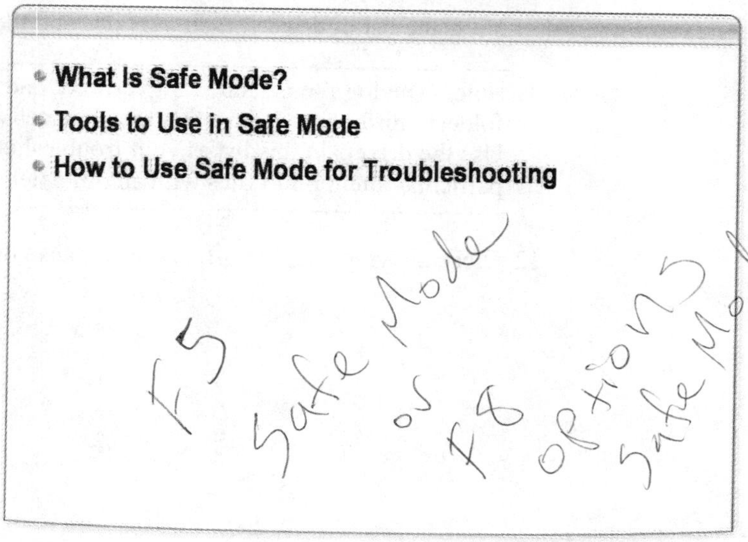

- What Is Safe Mode?
- Tools to Use in Safe Mode
- How to Use Safe Mode for Troubleshooting

[handwritten: F5 Safe Mode or F8 options Safe Mode]

Introduction

Windows XP has significantly improved device compatibility; nevertheless, hardware compatibility issues continue to be among the top questions facing DSTs. This is largely due to the increasing variety of hardware and because more users are building their own computers by piecing together hardware in unique combinations.

If a newly added device or changed driver is causing problems for your user, you can use safe mode to remove the device and reverse the change. This lesson describes safe mode and explains how to use it to troubleshoot drivers.

Lesson objectives

After completing this lesson, you will be able to:

- Explain the purpose of safe mode and the startup options available in Windows XP Professional.
- Describe the tools to use in safe mode.
- Use safe mode for troubleshooting.

What Is Safe Mode?

Startup option	Description
Safe mode	Loads the minimum set of drivers and system services
Safe mode with networking	Includes the drivers and services needed for network connectivity
Safe mode with command prompt	Starts the computer in safe mode but displays the command prompt rather than the GUI
Last known good configuration	Restores the registry and driver configuration in use last
Debugging mode	Starts the computer in kernel debugging mode

Introduction

When a computer appears to have a problem with a device that prevents either the device or the computer from starting up, the first step in solving the problem is to start the computer in safe mode. *Safe mode* is a method of starting Windows XP that uses only basic files and the minimal set of drivers that the operating system must have to function. By using safe mode, which disables startup programs, nonessential services, and support for devices such as audio devices, most USB devices, and IEEE 1394 devices, it is easier to identify and diagnose the cause of startup problems, stop messages, or system instability.

Startup options

Windows XP provides the startup options described in the following table.

Startup option	Description
Safe mode	Loads the minimum set of device drivers and system services required to start Windows XP Professional. User-specific startup programs do not run.
Safe mode with networking	Includes the drivers and services needed for network connectivity. This option enables you to log on to the network, logon scripts, security, and Group Policy settings. Nonessential services and startup programs not related to networking do not run.
Safe mode with command prompt	Starts the computer in safe mode, but displays the command prompt rather than the Windows graphical user interface (GUI).
Enable boot logging	Creates a log file (Ntbtlog.txt) in the %Systemroot% folder, which contains the file names and status of all drivers loaded into memory. *%Systemroot%* is an environment variable that can vary from one system running Windows XP Professional to another.

(*continued*)

Startup option	Description
Enable VGA mode	Starts the computer in standard video graphics adapter (VGA) mode. This option helps you recover from distorted video displays caused by using incorrect settings for the display adapter or monitor.
Last known good configuration	Restores the registry and driver configuration in use the last time the computer started successfully.
Debugging mode	Starts Windows XP Professional in kernel debugging mode, which allows you to use a kernel debugger for troubleshooting and system analysis.
Start Windows normally	Starts Windows XP Professional in normal mode.
Reboot	Restarts the computer.

Logging on to the computer in safe mode does not update Last Known Good Configuration information. This means that if you log on to your computer in safe mode and then decide you want to use the Last Known Good Configuration startup option, the option is still available.

To start your computer using the last known good configuration:

1. While starting or restarting the computer, press F8 immediately after the BIOS screen.

2. After the **Please select the operating system to start** page is displayed, press F8.

3. Use the arrow keys to select Last **Known Good Configuration**, and then press ENTER.

Tools to Use in Safe Mode

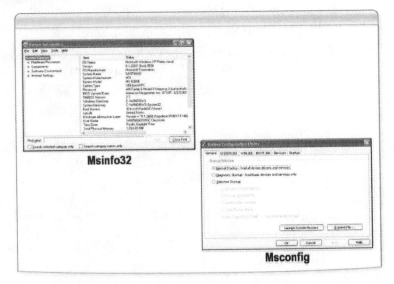

Msinfo32

Msconfig

Introduction

Windows XP Professional includes two tools you can use to diagnose and troubleshoot driver issues while in safe mode: the System Configuration utility (Msconfig) and the System Information utility (Msinfo32).

What is the System Configuration utility?

Use the System Configuration utility to disable components that are launched during startup and have the potential of causing conflict within the operating system. When all the components listed in Msconfig are disabled, the computer will start in normal mode.

To access the System Configuration utility:

1. Click **Start**, click **Run**, and then in the **Open** box, type **cmd**.

2. At the command prompt, type **msconfig**.

What is the System Information utility?

Use the System Information utility to troubleshoot problems that are related to drivers, hardware, and services. This tool queries the operating system to retrieve all sorts of detailed information, such as:

- System summary
- Hardware resources
- Hardware components
- Software environment

To access the System Information tool:

- At the command prompt, type **msinfo32**.

  –Or–

- Click **Start**, click **All Programs**, click **Accessories**, click **System Tools**, and then click **System Information**.

How to Use Safe Mode for Troubleshooting

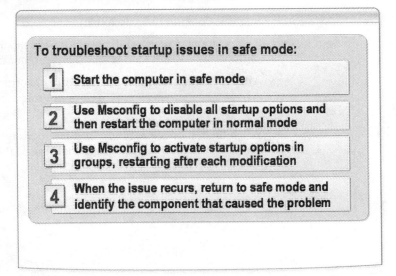

To troubleshoot startup issues in safe mode:

1. Start the computer in safe mode

2. Use Msconfig to disable all startup options and then restart the computer in normal mode

3. Use Msconfig to activate startup options in groups, restarting after each modification

4. When the issue recurs, return to safe mode and identify the component that caused the problem

---

Introduction

Safe mode enables you to troubleshoot the operating system to determine what is not functioning properly. For example, because new drivers that are added for a hardware device can cause conflicts with existing programs, you can use safe mode to identify the problem by using the process of elimination.

When to use safe mode

Starting a computer in safe mode is a good idea under the following circumstances:

- When there is a startup or shutdown issue. Safe mode eliminates all but the most basic components needed to start the operating system. Note that these same components can affect the shutdown process as well.

- When the computer experiences errors, poor performance, or any other negative behavior during normal operations. The minimal configuration of safe mode may remove processes that are causing the problem in normal mode.

Use the following method to start a computer running Windows XP in safe mode:

- Press F8 immediately following the basic input/output system (BIOS) post and before the Windows logo screen appears.

How to troubleshoot startup issues in safe mode

By using the following approach to troubleshooting startup, you can isolate the cause of an issue relatively quickly:

1. Start the computer in safe mode.

2. If the computer successfully starts in safe mode, use Msconfig to disable all startup options, and then restart the computer in normal mode.

3. After the computer successfully starts in normal mode, use Msconfig to activate the various startup options in groups, restarting after each modification.

4. When the issue recurs, return to safe mode and identify the specific component within the last group that caused the problem.

Practice: Starting the Computer in Safe Mode

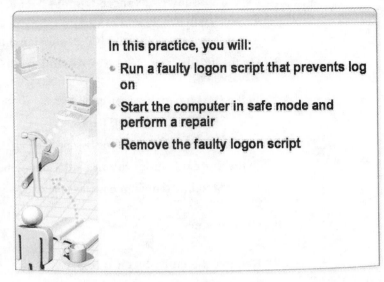

In this practice, you will:

- Run a faulty logon script that prevents log on
- Start the computer in safe mode and perform a repair
- Remove the faulty logon script

Objectives

In this practice, you will:

- Run a faulty logon script that prevents you from logging on.
- Start the computer in safe mode and perform a repair.
- Remove the faulty logon script.

Practice

▶ **Run a logon script and display the Advanced Options menu**

1. Resume the 2261_Bonn virtual machine.

   You should already be logged on as Administrator.

2. Click **Start**, click **Run**, and then in the **Open** box, type
   c:\program files\microsoft learning\2261\practices\mod05, and click **OK**.

3. Double-click **2261_M05b_break**.

4. In the **WARNING** dialog box, click **OK**.

5. After your computer logs you off, attempt to log on to Bonn as
   Administrator with a password of **P@ssw0rd**.

   You are automatically logged off.

6. Restart Bonn and immediately upon restart, following the BIOS, press **F8**.

7. When prompted to select the operating system to start, press **F8** to display
   advanced startup options for Windows.

▶ **Start Bonn in Safe Mode**

1. On the **Windows Advanced Options Menu**, verify that **Safe Mode** is selected, and then press ENTER.

2. Verify Microsoft Windows **XP Professional** is selected, and press ENTER.

3. On the logon screen, log on as **Administrator** with a password of **P@ssw0rd**.

4. In the **Desktop** dialog box, click **Yes**.

5. Click **Start**, and then click **Run**.

6. In the **Open** box, type **msconfig** and then click **OK**.

7. In the **System Configuration Utility** dialog box, click the **Startup** tab.

8. In the **Startup Item** column, clear the check box next to **Logoff**, and then click **OK**.

9. Click **Restart**.

▶ **Remove the faulty logon script**

1. On the logon screen, log on to the 2261_Bonn virtual machine as **Administrator** with a password of **P@ssw0rd**.

   Notice that the logoff script did not execute as a result of the Msconfig configuration implemented in the previous step.

2. In the **System Configuration Utility** dialog box, click **OK**.

3. In the **System Configuration Utility** dialog box, on the **General** tab, click **Normal Startup—load all device drivers and services**, and then click **OK** to close.

4. In the **System Configuration Utility** dialog box, click **Exit Without Restart**.

5. Click **Start**, and then click **Run**.

6. In the **Open** box, type **C:\Program Files\Microsoft Learning\2261 \Practices\Mod05**, and then click **OK**.

7. Double-click **2261_M05b_fix**.

8. In the **Success** dialog box, click **OK**.

9. Close all windows, log off, and then pause the 2261_Bonn virtual machine.

Lesson: Troubleshooting Storage Devices

- Types of Storage Devices
- What Are Basic Disks and Dynamic Disks?
- How to Convert a Basic Disk to a Dynamic Disk
- How to Import a Foreign Disk
- How to Manually Assign Drive Letters
- How to Troubleshoot Storage Devices

Introduction

A *storage device* is any device that is installed on a computer that is designed to store data. As a DST, you will encounter users with a wide variety of issues related to storage devices, and you must be able to troubleshoot these issues. This lesson describes basic disks and dynamic disks and how to perform common storage devices–related tasks, such as importing a foreign disk and assigning drive letters. Finally, this lesson provides you with general troubleshooting techniques you can use to resolve your users' issues with these devices.

Lesson objectives

After completing this lesson, you will be able to:

- Describe the various types of storage devices.
- Explain the purpose and function of basic disks and dynamic disks.
- Convert basic disks to dynamic storage.
- Import a foreign disk.
- Manually assign drive letters.
- Troubleshoot storage devices.

Types of Storage Devices

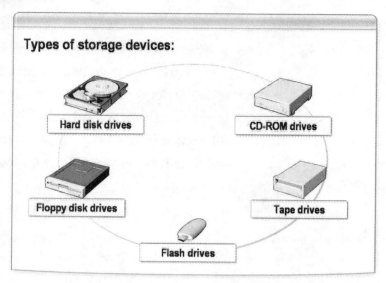

Types of storage devices:

Hard disk drives

CD-ROM drives

Floppy disk drives

Tape drives

Flash drives

Introduction

It is important to understand the categories and types of storage devices because storage device technology changes rapidly and new devices are regularly appear on the market.

Categories of storage devices

Windows XP sorts storage devices into two categories:

- Fixed storage devices. These devices cannot be removed. Hard disks are considered fixed storage devices because hard disk media cannot be removed.

- Removable storage devices. These devices or the storage media that use the devices can be removed. Most storage devices are considered removable.

Common types of storage devices

There are a variety of types of storage devices that can be installed on a computer, including:

- Hard disk drives. A *hard disk drive* is a mechanism that reads and writes data on a hard disk. There are several interface standards for passing data between a hard disk and a computer. The most common are Integrated Device Electronics (IDE) or Small Computer System Interface (SCSI) controllers. *IDE* is an interface for mass storage devices, in which the controller is integrated into the disk or CD-ROM drive. IDE is inexpensive, fast, and reliable, and therefore the most common. A *SCSI controller* is a device that controls the transfer of data from a computer to a peripheral device. SCSI controllers are more expensive than IDE, but provide better performance.

  - Portable hard disks. Portable hard disks can be connected with USB and Institute of Electrical and Electronics Engineers (IEEE) 1394 interfaces. (*IEEE* is a standard for high-speed serial devices such as digital video and digital audio editing equipment.)

  - Serial Advanced Technology Attachment (SATA). SATA is a disk drive implementation that integrates the controller on the disk drive itself. SATA is a serial link–a single cable with a minimum of four wires to create a point-to-point connection between devices. SATA cables are less bulky than IDE cables and can extend farther.

- CD-ROM/CD-RW/DVD-ROM/DVD-RW drives. CD-ROM drives are removable storage devices that use compact digital discs to store data. CD-RW and DVD-RW can copy data to the disc more than once and can be erased. These drives are typically connected to the computer with IDE or SCSI interfaces, but portable drives are available with USB and IEEE 1394 interfaces.

- Floppy disk drives and large-format removable disk drives. These disk drives are removable storage devices that are used to store smaller amounts of data. These disks are inexpensive and can be easily damaged.

- Tape drives. Tape drives are removable storage devices that use a type of cassette tape to store data. These drives are typically used to back up large amounts of data.

- CompactFlash and Smart Media cards. CompactFlash and Smart Media cards are removable storage devices typically found in digital cameras and Personal Digital Assistant (PDA) devices. This type of media is usually connected to the computer with a USB device or a USB flash card reader.

What Are Basic Disks and Dynamic Disks?

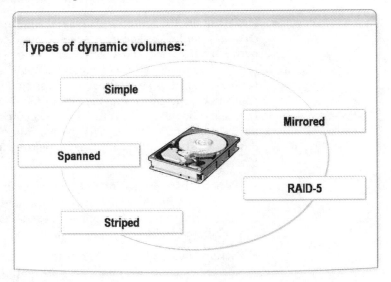

Types of dynamic volumes:

Simple

Mirrored

Spanned

RAID-5

Striped

Introduction

Windows XP Professional provides two types of disk storage: basic disk storage and dynamic disk storage. Before you can assist users in troubleshooting storage-related issues, you must understand the function of basic disks and dynamic disks.

What is a basic disk?

A *basic disk* is a physical disk that can be accessed by Microsoft MS-DOS® and all Windows-based operating systems. A *partition* is a portion of the physical disk that functions as though it were a physically separate disk. Partitions include primary partitions and logical drives. A *primary partition*, also known as a *volume*, is a type of partition that you can create on basic disks. You can create up to four primary partitions on a basic disk, or three primary partitions and an extended partition with multiple logical drives. (A *logical drive* is a volume that you create within an extended partition on a basic Master Boot Record (MBR) disk. They are similar to primary partitions, except that you can create an unlimited number of logical drives per disk.)

After you create a partition, you must format it and assign it a drive letter before you can store data on it. *Extended partitions* are useful if you want to create more than four volumes on a basic disk. Unlike primary partitions, you do not format an extended partition with a file system and then assign a drive letter to it. Instead, you create one or more logical drives within the extended partition. After you create a logical drive, you format it and assign it a drive letter. You can perform the following tasks only on a basic disk:

- Create and delete primary and extended partitions.

- Create and delete logical drives within an extended partition.

- Format a partition and mark it as active.

- Check disk properties, such as capacity, available free space, and current status.

- View volume and partition properties such as size, drive letter assignment, label, type, and file system.

- Establish drive letter assignments for volumes or partitions, optical storage devices (for example CD-ROM), and removable drives.

- Establish disk sharing and security arrangements for volumes and partitions formatted with NTFS.

- Convert a basic disk to a dynamic disk.

What is a dynamic disk?

A *dynamic disk* is a physical disk that can be accessed only by Microsoft Windows 2000 and Windows XP. Dynamic disks use a hidden database to track information about dynamic volumes on the disk and other dynamic disks in the computer. Dynamic disks provide features that basic disks do not. For example, on a dynamic disk, you can:

- Increase the size of a volume by extending the volume onto the same hard disk. This is done by using unallocated space that is not contiguous. Volumes can be extended onto other dynamic disks as well.

- Improve hard disk input/output (I/O) performance by using striped volumes.

Note   Dynamic disks are not supported in Windows XP Home Edition or on portable computers. For more information on basic disks and dynamic disks, see Microsoft Knowledge Base (KB) article 314343.

Types of dynamic volumes

There are five types of dynamic volumes:

- Simple. A simple volume consists of a single region on a hard disk or multiple regions on the same hard disk that are linked together. Simple volumes can be created on dynamic disks only. Simple volumes are not fault-tolerant, but they can be mirrored. A *mirrored volume* is a fault-tolerant volume that duplicates data on two physical disks.

- Spanned. A spanned volume consists of disk space on more than one hard disk. The size of a spanned volume can be increased by extending it onto additional dynamic disks. Spanned volumes are not fault-tolerant and cannot be mirrored.

- Striped. Striped volumes improve disk drive I/O performance by distributing I/O requests across hard disks. Striped volumes are composed of stripes of data of equal size written across each disk in the volume. They are created from equally sized, unallocated areas on two or more hard disks. Striped volumes cannot be extended and do not offer fault tolerance. If one of the hard disks containing a striped volume fails, the entire volume fails, and all data on the striped volume becomes inaccessible.

- Mirrored. A mirrored volume is a fault-tolerant volume that duplicates data on two hard disks. A mirrored volume provides data redundancy by using two identical volumes, called *mirrors*, to duplicate the information contained on the volume. A mirror is always located on a different hard disk. If one of the hard disks fails, the data on the failed hard disk becomes unavailable, but the system continues to operate in the mirror on the remaining hard disk.

- RAID-5. A redundant array of inexpensive disks (RAID)-5 volume is a fault-tolerant volume with data and parity striped intermittently across three or more hard disks. *Parity* is a calculated value that is used to reconstruct data after a failure. If a portion of a hard disk fails, Windows recreates the data that was on the failed portion from the remaining data and parity.

The benefits of dynamic disks

Dynamic disks offer greater flexibility for volume management than hard disks because they use a hidden database to track information about themselves. Because each dynamic disk contains a replica of the dynamic disk database, Windows XP Professional can repair a corrupted database on one dynamic disk by using the database on another dynamic disk.

Dynamic disk database location

The location of the database is determined by the partition style of the hard disk.

- On Master Boot Record (MBR) hard disks, the database is contained in the last 1 megabyte (MB) of the disk. The *MBR* is the first sector on a hard disk, which starts the process of starting the computer. It contains the partition table for the disk.

- On globally unique identifier (GUID) partition table (GPT) hard disks, the database is contained in a 1-MB reserved (hidden) partition known as the Logical Disk Manager (LDM) metadata partition. *GPT* is a disk-partitioning scheme that offers advantages over MBR partitioning.

How to Convert a Basic Disk to a Dynamic Disk

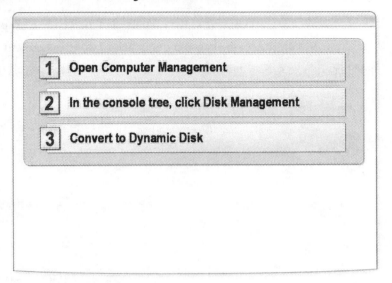

1 Open Computer Management

2 In the console tree, click Disk Management

3 Convert to Dynamic Disk

Introduction

To create partitions that span multiple disks you must convert basic disks to dynamic discs by using the Disk Management snap-in or the DiskPart command-line tool. When you convert a basic disk to dynamic, all existing basic volumes become dynamic volumes. The conversion provides increased flexibility in managing the volume in Windows XP Professional; however, the changes cannot be reversed.

Considerations when converting a basic disk to a dynamic disk

Because the changes are not easily reversed, consider the following issues before you perform a conversion:

- For the conversion to succeed, any MBR hard disk to be converted must contain at least 1 MB of space for the dynamic disk database. Windows XP Professional automatically reserves this space when creating partitions or volumes on a drive. However, hard disks with partitions or volumes created by other operating systems might not have this space available. Furthermore, this space sometimes exists even if it is not visible in Disk Management.

- When you convert a basic volume to a dynamic volume, any existing partitions or logical drives on the basic volume become simple volumes on the dynamic volume.

- Do not convert basic volumes that contain multiple installations of Windows XP Professional to dynamic volumes. When a basic volume is converted to a dynamic volume, the partition entries for all partitions on the basic volume are removed, except for the system and boot volumes of the currently running operating system. (A *boot volume* is the volume that contains the Windows operating system and its support files.)

- Converting a basic volume to dynamic does not check for other installations of Windows, and the partition entries for any other system volumes on the disk drive are deleted. In addition, the volume-related registry entries in the second installation become outdated. As a result, you can no longer start that operating system.

How to convert a basic disk to a dynamic disk

To convert a basic disk to a dynamic disk by using Disk Management:

1. In Control Panel, click **Performance and Maintenance**, click **Administrative Tools**, and then click **Computer Management**.

2. In the console tree, click **Disk Management**.

3. Right-click the volume you want to convert to a dynamic volume, and then click **Convert to Dynamic Disk**.

How to Import a Foreign Disk

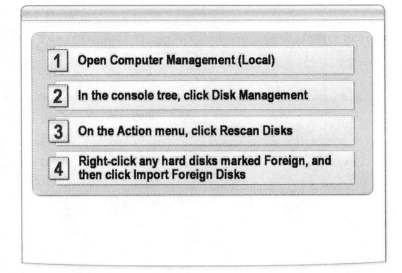

1	Open Computer Management (Local)
2	In the console tree, click Disk Management
3	On the Action menu, click Rescan Disks
4	Right-click any hard disks marked Foreign, and then click Import Foreign Disks

Introduction

From time to time, a user may install a new hard disk or move an existing hard disk from one computer to another. If you move one or more dynamic disks from a disk group (a *disk group* is a collection of dynamic disks) to another computer that has its own disk group, the dynamic disks you moved are marked as Foreign until you import the disks into the existing disk group. You must import the disks before you can access volumes on the disk. After the new hard disk has been physically installed and Windows has detected it, the user will need to run Disk Management and import the new hard disk. This process is referred to as importing a foreign disk.

How to import a foreign disk

To import a newly installed (or foreign) hard disk:

1. Open **Computer Management (Local)**.
2. In the console tree, click **Disk Management**.
3. On the **Action** menu, click **Rescan Disks**.

   If the hard disk is dynamic, Disk Management displays the **Import Foreign Disks** dialog box.

4. Right-click any hard disk marked **Foreign**, click **Import Foreign Disks**, and then follow the instructions on your screen.

Additional reading

For more information about Windows disk management, see KB articles 222189 and 329707.

How to Manually Assign Drive Letters

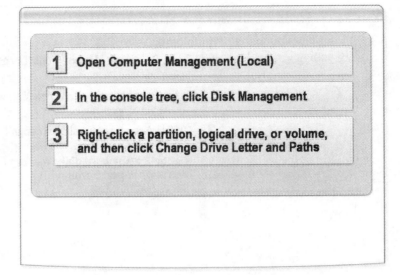

1 Open Computer Management (Local)

2 In the console tree, click Disk Management

3 Right-click a partition, logical drive, or volume, and then click Change Drive Letter and Paths

Introduction

When you add drives to your computer, or when you create new partitions, Windows automatically assigns letters to the new drives and partitions. However, this assignment might not suit your system. For example, you might have mapped a network drive to the same letter that Windows assigns to a new drive. To resolve this type of issue, Windows allows you to manually assign drive letters.

How to manually assign drive letters

To manually assign drive letters to partitions by using Disk Management:

1. Open **Computer Management (Local)**.

2. In the console tree, click **Disk Management**.

3. Right-click a partition, logical drive, or volume, and then click **Change Drive Letter and Paths**.

4. Choose an option:

    • To assign a drive letter, click **Add**, click the drive letter you want to use, and then click **OK**.

    • To modify a drive letter, click the drive letter, click **Change**, click the drive letter you want to use, and then click **OK**.

    • To remove a drive letter, select the drive letter, and then click **Remove**.

Important Be careful when making drive-letter assignments because many MS-DOS and Windows-based programs make references to specific drive letters. For example, the path environment variable shows specific drive letters in conjunction with program names.

How to Troubleshoot Storage Devices

Issue	Resolution resource
Computer does not start	• Recovery Console – Fixmbr and Fixboot • Windows XP Professional Resource Kit, Chapter 27
Stop messages displayed	• Microsoft Knowledge Base • Microsoft TechNet

Dynamic disks not accessible	• Disk Management:
	  ◦ Import Foreign Disks
	  ◦ Initialize Disk
	  ◦ Reactivate Disk
	  ◦ Rescan Disks

Flash drives not visible in My Computer	• Is the device properly connected to a USB port? • Is the USB hub overloaded?

Introduction

This section describes how to troubleshoot various issues that are related to storage devices, including hard disks, stop errors, dynamic disks, and flash drives.

How to troubleshoot issues related to hard disks

Typically, a computer has only one hard disk installed. When the disk fails or becomes corrupt, the computer will not start. If the computer cannot locate the active partition or the boot sector of the system volume, the user could receive one of the following error messages:

- Invalid partition table
- Error loading operating system
- Missing operating system

NT Loader (NTLDR) is a program that is loaded from the hard drive boot sector that displays the Microsoft Windows NT®—based system startup menu and helps Windows NT-based system load. If the computer is unable to load NTLDR, the user could receive one of these error messages:

- A disk read error occurred
- NTLDR is missing
- NTLDR is compressed

You may be able to resolve these issues by using *Recovery Console*—a command-line interface that provides a limited set of administrative commands that is useful for repairing a computer. The Recovery Console has two commands that can fix the MBR and the boot sector: Fixmbr, which rewrites the MBR, and Fixboot, which rewrites the boot sector of the system volume.

Additional reading

For more information on using the Fixmbr and Fixboot commands in Recovery Console, see KB article 314058.

For more information on startup issues that are caused by a failed or corrupted hard disk, see Chapter 27, "Troubleshooting Disks and File Systems," in the Windows XP Professional Resource Kit at http://www.microsoft.com/technet /treeview/default.asp?url=/technet/prodtechnol/winxppro/reskit /prkd_tro_gwoj.asp.

How to troubleshoot stop errors

Sometimes Windows detects an error from which it cannot recover. It reports error information in full-screen, non-window, text mode. These errors are called stop messages, stop errors, or blue screens. They provide information that is specific to the problem detected by the Windows kernel. (A *kernel* is the core of layered architecture that manages the most basic operations of the operating system and computer's processor.)

File system errors, viruses, hard disk corruption, or controller driver problems can cause stop messages. When you are troubleshooting stop errors, go to the Knowledge Base and to TechNet for information on the specific error.

How to troubleshoot issues related to dynamic disks

You can troubleshoot most issues related to dynamic disks by using Disk Management. Disk Management reports the status of a disk, and, based on that status, you should be able to resolve the issue. The following statuses indicate a problem:

■ Foreign. This status occurs when you install a dynamic disk in the local computer. You must right-click the disk and then click **Import Foreign Disks** before you can access data on the disk.

■ Missing/offline. This status occurs when a dynamic disk is not accessible. The disk might be corrupted or intermittently unavailable. The missing/offline status occurs when a dynamic disk was installed on the system but can no longer be located or identified. The missing disk might be damaged, turned off, or disconnected.

To bring an offline or missing disk online:

• Repair any hard disk, controller, or cable problems, and then confirm that the hard disk is turned on and attached to the computer.

• In Disk Management, right-click the disk, and then click **Reactivate Disk** to bring the disk back online.

If the disk status remains offline, the disk name remains missing, and you determine that the disk has a problem that cannot be repaired, you can remove the disk from the computer.

■ Not initialized. This status indicates that the disk does not contain a valid disk signature in the MBR or a valid disk GUID in the GUID partition table. To initialize the disk, right-click the disk, and then click **Initialize Disk**.

- Online (errors). This status indicates that I/O errors were detected on a region of the disk. A warning icon appears on the disk with errors. Only dynamic disks display the Online (errors) status. To attempt to return the disk to online status, right-click the disk, and then click **Reactivate Disk**.

- Unreadable. This status occurs when the disk is not accessible. The disk might not be available if it is spinning up; encountering hardware failure, corruption, or I/O errors; or the disk's copy of the dynamic disk database is corrupted. An error icon appears on disks that display the unreadable status. Try resolving this issue by rescanning the disks. To rescan the disk, in Disk Management, click **Action**, and then click **Rescan Disks**. Also try restarting the computer and see if the status changes.

How to troubleshoot issues with flash drives

These devices are typically connected with a USB interface, so if the drive does not show up in My Computer, confirm that the user has plugged the device into one of the USB ports on the computer. Even though USB can support up to 127 devices, one USB port cannot power that many devices. A USB hub may not have enough power to operate all the devices connected to it.

For example, if a user has a four-port USB hub that has a mouse, joystick, and printer already connected to it. When the user connects a digital camera to the hub, Windows cannot find the camera to install it. The resolution is either to unplug one or more devices from the hub or plug the digital camera directly into one of the USB ports on the computer instead of the hub.

Practice: Troubleshooting Storage Devices

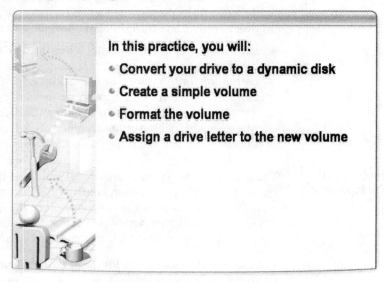

In this practice, you will:
- Convert your drive to a dynamic disk
- Create a simple volume
- Format the volume
- Assign a drive letter to the new volume

Objectives

In this practice, you will:

- Convert your drive to a dynamic disk.
- Create a simple volume.
- Format the volume.
- Assign a drive letter to the new volume.

Scenario

A user calls and says she is receiving error messages that indicate that one of her drives is running out of disk space. You decide to convert it to a dynamic disk and extend the volume to provide more space.

Practice

▶ **Create and format a simple volume on disk 1**

1. Resume the 2261_Bonn virtual machine.

2. Log on to Bonn as **Administrator** with a password of **P@ssw0rd**.

3. In Control Panel, click **Performance and Maintenance**, click **Administrative Tools**, and then double-click **Computer Management**.

4. In the **Computer Management** console tree, click **Disk Management**.

5. Right-click **New Volume (E:)** and attempt to locate **Extend Volume**. Is Extend Volume an option? Why not?

   its   not   dynamic

6. Right-click **Disk 1**, and click **Convert to Dynamic Disk**.

7. In the **Convert to Dynamic Disk** dialog box, verify that only Disk 1 is selected, and then click **OK**.

8. On the **Disks to Convert** dialog box, click **Convert**.

9. On the **Disk Management** dialog box, click **Yes**.

10. Right-click **New Volume (E:)** and click **Extend Volume**.

11. On the **Disk Management** dialog box, click **Yes**.

12. On the **Welcome to the Extend Volume Wizard** page, click **Next**.

13. On the Select Disks page, verify that Disk 1 is displayed in the **Selected** box, and then click **Next**.

14. On the Completing the Extend Volume Wizard page, click **Finish**.

Do not proceed with the next procedure until the New Volume (E:) has a status of Healthy.

▶ **Change the drive letter on the new volume**

1. In **Computer Management**, right-click **New Volume (E:)**, and then click **Change Drive Letter and paths**.

2. In the **Change Drive Letter and Paths for E: (New Volume)** dialog box, click **Change**, click the drop-down list, select **P**, and then click **OK**.

3. In the **Confirm** dialog box, click **Yes**.

4. Close all windows, log off, and then pause the 2261_Bonn virtual machine.

Lesson: Troubleshooting Display Devices

- Types of Display Devices
- What Are Display Settings?
- What Is VGA Mode?
- What Is DirectX?
- How to Troubleshoot Display Devices

Introduction

A *display device* is a visual output device, such as a monitor, that displays images, text, and menus on a screen. As a DST, you will encounter users with a wide variety of issues related to display devices, and you must be able to troubleshoot these issues. This lesson describes various types of display devices and display settings and explains the purpose and function of video graphics array (VGA) mode and Microsoft DirectX®. Finally, this lesson provides you with general troubleshooting techniques you can use to resolve your users' issues related to display devices.

Lesson objectives

After completing this lesson, you will be able to:

- Describe the types of display devices.
- Describe the purpose and function of display settings.
- Explain the purpose and function of VGA mode.
- Describe the relationship between DirectX and display devices.
- Troubleshoot display devices.

Types of Display Devices

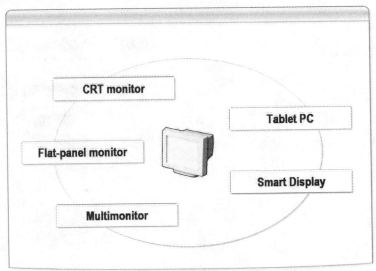

Types of display devices   Before you can troubleshoot display devices, you need to be aware of the types of display devices that exist, including:

- CRT monitor. Cathode-ray tube (CRT) monitors are based on the same technology as televisions. These devices are inexpensive and come in a wide variety of sizes and capabilities. As a result, CRT monitors are the most commonly used display devices.

- Flat-panel monitor. These devices are growing in popularity. A flat-panel monitor does not use CRT technology. Flat-panel monitors usually use liquid crystal display (LCD) or gas-discharge display (plasma) technologies. Flat-panel monitors are not as deep as CRT monitors, and so they occupy much less physical space and weigh much less than a CRT monitor with the same screen size.

- Multimonitor. Multimonitor refers to the use of multiple display devices connected to one computer. Windows XP can support up to 10 individual display devices.

- Tablet PC. Tablet PCs integrate a portable computer and a flat-panel display. Tablet PC displays are touch-sensitive, and some models feature a screen that can be rotated between portrait and landscape views.

- Windows-powered Smart Displays. A Smart Display is a wireless, touch screen monitor. Smart Displays enable you to access your computer cable-free from anywhere within the normal operating range of your wireless network.

What Are Display Settings?

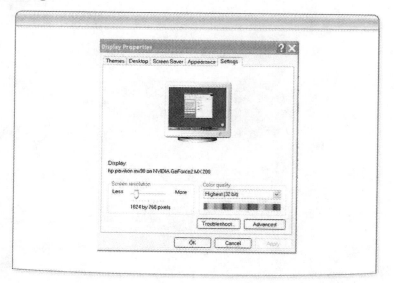

Introduction

In Windows XP Professional, the **Display Properties** dialog box lists information about the display devices that are on the computer. As a DST, you can use this information to determine the manufacturer of a device and then contact the manufacturer for device updates. You can also verify display resolution, which is useful in troubleshooting display problems. This section describes important display settings and how to access and configure these settings.

How to access the Display Properties dialog box

There are two ways to access the **Display Properties** dialog box:

- In Control Panel, click **Appearance and Themes**, and then click **Display**.
  –Or–
- Right-click on a blank portion of the desktop, and then click **Properties**.

What is screen resolution?

Screen resolution is the size of the display screen measured in pixels and the amount of colors that can be displayed on it. A typical screen resolution is 1024 × 768 pixels and true color (32-bit). That means the display device is displaying 1,024 pixels horizontally and 768 pixels vertically and millions of colors. The minimum display resolution for Windows is 640 × 480 pixels with 256 colors, but Windows can display much higher resolutions, such as 1600 × 1200 with millions of colors depending on a computer's display adapter and monitor. Certain types of monitors, such as LCD screens used for laptops, have an optimal screen resolution referred to as its *native* resolution. For the best viewing experience, configure display hardware to use its native resolution.

To change the screen resolution:

1. In Control Panel, click **Appearance and Themes**, and then click **Display**.
2. In the **Display Properties** dialog box, on the **Settings** tab, increase or decrease the screen resolution.

What is the refresh rate?

The *refresh rate* is the frequency with which the video screen is retraced to prevent the image from flickering. The entire image area of most monitors is refreshed approximately 60 times per second.

Warning A higher refresh frequency reduces flicker on the screen, but choosing a setting that is too high for a monitor can make the display unusable and can damage the hardware.

Never instruct the user to change the refresh rate unless you are confident that the refresh rate is the issue.

To change the refresh rate:

1. In Control Panel, click **Appearance and Themes**, and then click **Display**.

2. In the **Display Properties** dialog box, on the **Settings** tab, click **Advanced**.

3. On the **Monitor** tab, in the **Screen refresh rate:** list, select a new refresh rate.

How to change the display settings

Users can click on any of the tabs and change display settings to suit their preferences. Tell users they can access a short description of the function of various screen elements on each tab by right-clicking that particular setting and then clicking **What's This?**

What Is VGA Mode?

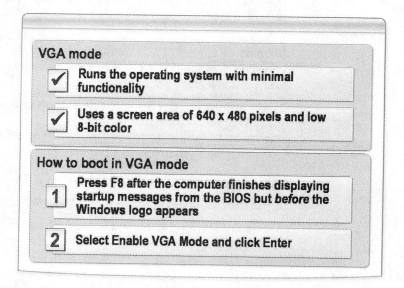

VGA mode

✓ Runs the operating system with minimal functionality

✓ Uses a screen area of 640 x 480 pixels and low 8-bit color

How to boot in VGA mode

1 Press F8 after the computer finishes displaying startup messages from the BIOS but *before* the Windows logo appears

2 Select Enable VGA Mode and click Enter

Introduction

VGA mode is a diagnostic mode in Windows XP that uses basic default settings to run the operating system with minimal functionality. This means that some hardware may not function in this mode because the drivers are not loaded. VGA mode starts a computer with a screen area of 640 × 480 pixels and low 8-bit color using the current video driver, unlike safe mode, which uses the generic Vga.sys driver.

When to use VGA mode

Use VGA mode to recover from video problems that are not caused by a faulty driver but by incorrect settings, such as an improper resolution or refresh rate.

If the operating system does not display correctly in normal mode but does display correctly in VGA mode, the problem may be that the screen resolution is configured for a setting that the monitor cannot handle. If the screen resolution is adjusted and the operating system still does not display correctly in VGA mode, the problem may be with the video driver.

How to start in VGA mode

To start in VGA mode, press F8 after your computer finishes displaying startup messages from the BIOS but before the Windows logo appears, select **Enable VGA Mode**, and then click **Enter**.

What Is DirectX?

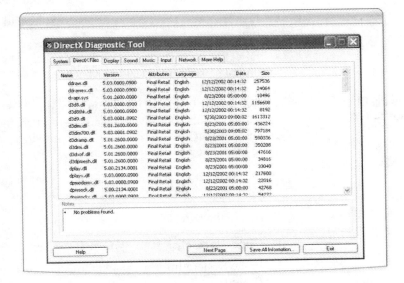

Introduction

As a DST, you might receive a support call from a user who states that an application will not install. You must understand the functionality of DirectX to troubleshoot this type of issue.

DirectX is an advanced suite of multimedia application programming interfaces (APIs) built into Windows operating systems that enhances a computer's multimedia capabilities. DirectX provides access to the capabilities of a computer's display and audio cards, which enables programs to provide realistic three-dimensional (3-D) graphics and immersive music and audio effects. DirectX enables the program to easily determine the hardware capabilities of a computer and then sets the program parameters to match. This allows multimedia software programs to run on any Windows-based computer with DirectX-compatible hardware and drivers and ensures that the multimedia programs take full advantage of high-performance hardware.

DirectX components

DirectX is made up of several different components. Each component is designed to control a different aspect of a hardware device. These components include:

- Direct3D®. Direct3D allows access to 3-D display hardware.

- DirectDraw®. DirectDraw allows access to display hardware and memory.

- DirectInput®. DirectInput allows access to various input devices, such as force-feedback joysticks, pointing devices, and keyboards.

- DirectMusic®. DirectMusic allows access to sound devices for music composition and Musical Instrument Digital Interface (MIDI) output.

■ DirectPlay®. DirectPlay allows access to network devices. DirectPlay is used in multiplayer online gaming and other networked applications.

■ DirectShow®. DirectShow allows capture and playback of streaming multimedia.

■ DirectSound®. DirectSound allows access to sound devices and allows digital sound capture and playback.

What is the DirectX Diagnostic Tool?

The Microsoft DirectX Diagnostic Tool provides information about the DirectX API components and drivers on a system. It enables you to test sound and graphics output and DirectPlay service providers. It also enables you to disable some hardware acceleration features.

During a support call, you can instruct a user to run the diagnostic tool, save the information to a text file, and then e-mail the file to you for your examination.

To access the DirectX Diagnostic Tool:

1. Click **Start**, click **Run**, type **msinfo32.exe**, and then click **OK**.

2. In the System Information window, on the **Tools** menu, click **DirectX Diagnostic Tool**.

3. If prompted to check if your drivers are digitally signed, click **Yes**.

How to Troubleshoot Display Devices

Issue	Resolution resource
Items too small to read	• Decrease the screen resolution • Increase the font DPI
DirectX does not initialize the display adapter	• Update the device driver • Adjust the screen refresh rate • Adjust the hardware acceleration
The display does not initialize at startup	Start in safe mode to: • Roll back the display adapter driver • Uninstall the display adapter driver

Introduction

This section describes how to troubleshoot various issues that are related to display devices, including screen resolution, DirectX, and display initialization issues.

How to troubleshoot screen resolution issues

For some users, the screen resolution may make items too small to view comfortably. They can decrease the screen resolution, which will solve the problem, but a better solution is to increase the font dots per inch (DPI) setting.

To change the font DPI setting:

1. In Control Panel, click **Appearance and Themes**, and then click **Display**.
2. In the **Display Properties** dialog box, on the **Settings** tab, click **Advanced**.
3. In the dialog box, on the **General** tab, in the **DPI setting** list, select the DPI setting you want to use.

   If you choose **Other** in the **DPI setting** list, you can set custom options in the **Custom DPI Setting** dialog box either by selecting one of the percentage options in the drop-down menu or by clicking the ruler and dragging the pointer to specify a setting.

4. Restart your computer when prompted.

How to troubleshoot DirectX issues

A common issue with DirectX is that it will fail to initialize the display adapter. The DirectX program will show an error relating to an inability to initialize, or the program will start and the screen will just appear black.

To resolve this issue, confirm that the user installed the correct device driver for the monitor. It is very common for the monitor to be listed as a Plug and Play Monitor or Unknown Monitor. Updating the driver and adjusting the refresh rate can resolve these issues.

This issue can also be caused by a display adapter. Try adjusting the video hardware acceleration to make the DirectX program run. *Hardware acceleration* controls the level of acceleration and performance supplied by the graphics adapter.

To adjust the hardware acceleration setting:

1. In Control Panel, click **Appearance and Themes**, and then click **Display**.

2. In the **Display Properties** dialog box, on the **Settings** tab, click **Advanced**.

3. In the dialog box, on the **Troubleshoot** tab, drag the slider one notch to the left.

4. Click **Apply**, and then click **OK**.

If this does not resolve the issue, repeat the process and adjust the setting to the most basic hardware acceleration. If reducing the hardware acceleration resolves the issue, the user should update the display adapter driver.

How to troubleshoot display initialization issues

A common display issue is the failure to initialize during startup. When the display fails to initialize, it can produce stop errors or the screen will appear blank or distorted. To troubleshoot a display initialization error, start the computer in safe mode and then roll back or uninstall the display adapter driver. Restart the computer, and the display should initialize.

Additional reading

For more information on troubleshooting display devices, see KB articles 292460 and 322205.

Lesson: Troubleshooting I/O Devices

- Types of I/O Devices
- What Is a Hardware Profile?
- How to Troubleshoot I/O Devices

Introduction

An *I/O device* is any device that can send and receive data to and from the computer. As a DST, you will encounter users with a wide variety of issues related to I/O devices, and you must be able to troubleshoot these issues. This lesson describes the types of I/O devices and how to troubleshoot users' issues related to I/O devices.

Lesson objectives

After completing this lesson, you will be able to:

- Describe the types of I/O devices.
- Explain the purpose and function of hardware profiles.
- Troubleshoot I/O device drivers.

Types of I/O Devices

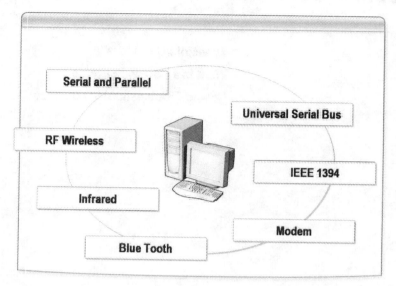

Introduction

I/O devices come in many different varieties and can serve many purposes. This section describes various types of I/O devices.

What are serial and parallel devices?

I/O devices can send and receive data either one bit at a time in a sequential fashion or they can send multiple bits of data simultaneously.

- *Serial communication* is the sequential exchange of information between computers and peripheral devices one bit at a time over a single channel. In other words, one instruction, routine, or task is executed, followed by the execution of the next in line. Serial ports are used for serial data communication and as interfaces with some peripheral devices, such as pointing devices, printers, and Pocket PC devices. Serial devices that connect to the computer through a serial port are not Plug and Play–compatible.

- *Parallel communication* sends multiple data and control bits simultaneously over wires connected in parallel. Parallel communication sends and receives data 8 bits at a time between a computer and a peripheral device such as a printer, scanner, CD-ROM, or other storage device. The parallel port uses a 25-pin connector called a DB-25 connector. Devices designed to use the parallel port and the IEEE 1284 standard are Plug and Play–compatible.

What are USB devices?

USB is an external bus that supports a Plug and Play installation. By using USB, devices can be connected to and disconnected from a computer without shutting down or restarting. A single USB port can connect up to 127 peripheral devices, including speakers, telephones, CD-ROM drives, joysticks, tape drives, mouse, or pointing devices, keyboards, scanners, and cameras. A USB port is usually located on the back of the computer near the serial port or parallel port.

There are two versions of USB: version 1.1 and version 2.0. The major difference between the versions is that version 2.0 has a higher bandwidth, which allows more data to be transferred between the computer and device. USB version 2.0 is backward-compatible with version 1.1.

What is an IEEE 1394 bus?

IEEE 1394 is an external high-speed serial bus that supports Plug and Play installation. IEEE 1394 is similar to USB in that devices can be connected and disconnected without shutting down or restarting the computer. The IEEE 1394 bus is used primarily to connect high-end digital video and digital audio devices to a computer. However, some hard disks, printers, scanners, and DVD drives can also be connected to a computer using the IEEE 1394 connector.

What is a modem?

A *modem* is a modulating and demodulating device that allows computer information to be transmitted and received over an analog telephone line. A modem can be used to connect to the Internet, make a direct connection to another computer, send and receive faxes, and log on to a network.

IR and IrDA devices

Infrared (IR) uses infrared light to transfer data. Infrared light is also used almost universally by television and VCR remote controls. In computers, IR offers an alternative to cables and floppy disks. Infrared communication provides a point-to-point, low-cost way to connect computers with each other or with devices and appliances. IR ports can be found on many printers, Pocket PCs, portable computers, cellular phones, keyboards, and mouse devices.

The Infrared Data Association (IrDA) has established the industry-wide standards that are used for IR communication.

Blue tooth

Blue tooth is the result of the result of the efforts of a number of wireless product development companies that have collaborated to develop electronic components that have the capability of communicating with each other. A blue tooth device is made up of a base-band processor, a radio, and an antenna. The base-band processor converts data into signals, which radios can decipher. The radio transmits the signals through the antenna to the antenna of another blue tooth device. The benefits of blue tooth technology include faster connectivity and speed, cost reduction, point-to-point connections, elimination of cable attachments, and secure data transmission.

What is RF Wireless?

Radio Frequency (RF) Wireless is a new standard for wireless communications. RF uses radio to connect to compatible devices. RF can currently be found in portable computers, printers, Pocket PCs, pointing devices, and cellular phones.

What Is a Hardware Profile?

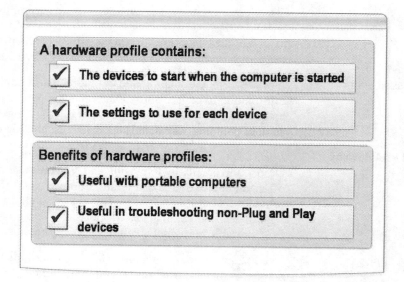

A hardware profile contains:
- ✓ The devices to start when the computer is started
- ✓ The settings to use for each device

Benefits of hardware profiles:
- ✓ Useful with portable computers
- ✓ Useful in troubleshooting non-Plug and Play devices

Introduction

A *hardware profile* is a set of instructions that tells Windows which devices to start when the computer is started, or which settings to use for each device. When first installed, Windows creates a hardware profile called Profile 1; for portable computers, the profiles are Docked Profile or Undocked Profile. By default, every device that is installed on the computer at the time of the Windows installation is enabled in the Profile 1 hardware profile.

The benefits of hardware profiles with portable computers

Hardware profiles are especially useful with portable computers. Most portable computers are used in a variety of locations, and hardware profiles enable you to change the devices the computer uses when it is moved from location to location. For example, you may have one profile named *Docking Station Configuration* for using your portable computer at a docking station with hardware components such as a CD-ROM drive and a network adapter. And you may have a second profile named *Undocked Configuration* for using your portable computer in a hotel or on an airplane, when you are not using a network adapter or a CD-ROM, but you are using a modem and a portable printer.

If there is more than one hardware profile on your computer, you can designate a default profile that is used every time you start your computer. You can also have Windows ask you which profile to use every time you start your computer.

The benefit of hardware profiles in troubleshooting

Hardware profiles are also useful in troubleshooting older hardware and non-Plug and Play devices. A new hardware profile can be created to disable devices that cause interrupt request (IRQ) or other hardware resource configuration issues. When you create a hardware profile, you can use Device Manager to disable and enable devices that are in the profile. When you disable a device in a hardware profile, the device drivers for the device are not loaded when you start your computer.

Additional reading

For more information about hardware profiles, see KB article 308577.

How to Troubleshoot I/O Devices

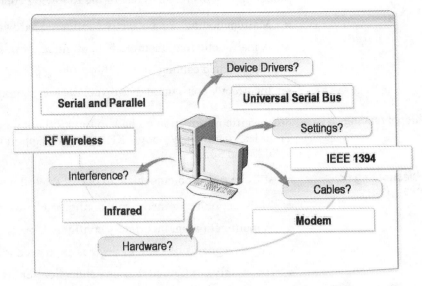

Introduction	Plug and Play devices are useful because they are automatically installed and require no configuration; however, when troubleshooting these devices, there is little manual configuration that can be done. Fortunately, these devices do not often require significant troubleshooting. This section describes the most common causes of problems related to I/O devices. When troubleshooting these issues, always eliminate a cause before troubleshooting the next.
Troubleshooting USB devices	Most USB device problems relate to one of the following conditions: ■ Malfunctioning or incorrectly configured hardware ■ A malfunctioning, incorrectly configured, or missing device driver ■ Mismatched cabling ■ Out-of-date firmware or BIOS ■ An improperly configured root hub
Additional reading	For specific information on how to troubleshoot and resolve USB problems related to each of the preceding conditions, see KB article 310575.
Troubleshooting IEEE 1394 devices	Most IEEE 1394 device problems relate to one of the following conditions: ■ Malfunctioning or incorrectly configured hardware ■ A malfunctioning, incorrectly configured, or missing device driver ■ Incorrect cabling or device placement in the chain
Additional reading	For specific information on how to troubleshoot most problems that concern IEEE 1394 devices, see KB article 314873.

Troubleshooting modem issues

Modems can vary widely in type, speed, and configurability. However, most modem problems relate to one of the following conditions:

- Malfunctioning or incorrectly configured hardware
- A malfunctioning, incorrectly configured, or missing device driver
- Mismatched cabling or a malfunctioning phone line
- Incorrectly configured dial-up connection settings

Additional reading

For specific information on how to troubleshoot modems, see "Modem Troubleshooter" in Windows XP Help and Support Center, and KB articles 308022 and 305549.

Troubleshooting IR devices

Most IR device problems relate to one of the following conditions:

- Malfunctioning or incorrectly configured hardware
- A malfunctioning, incorrectly configured, or missing device driver
- The IR signal is blocked or devices are placed too far away from each other
- Incorrectly configured dial-up connection settings

Additional reading

For specific information on how to troubleshoot infrared devices, see KB articles 305588, 313296, and 302011.

Troubleshooting RF Wireless devices

Most RF Wireless problems relate to one of the following conditions:

- Malfunctioning or incorrectly configured hardware
- A malfunctioning, incorrectly configured, or missing device driver
- A radio signal interrupted by other devices

Additional reading

For more information about troubleshooting RF Wireless devices, see KB article 811800.

Practice: Configuring Hardware Profiles

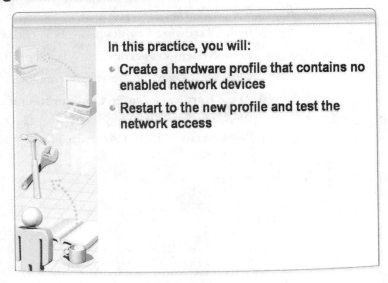

In this practice, you will:

- Create a hardware profile that contains no enabled network devices
- Restart to the new profile and test the network access

Objectives

In this practice, you will:

- Create a hardware profile that contains no enabled network devices.
- Restart to the new profile and test the network access.
- Test the new profile and then remove it.

Scenario

A user calls and says she cannot access the network. After troubleshooting, you determine the network hardware is functioning correctly. You then decide to examine the hardware profile.

Practice

▶ **Create a hardware profile**

Important You must be logged on as an administrator or a member of the Administrators group to complete this procedure. If your computer is connected to a network, network policy settings might also prevent you from completing this procedure.

1. Log on to the 2261_Bonn virtual machine as **Administrator** with a password of **P@ssw0rd**.
2. In Control Panel, click **Performance and Maintenance**, and then click **System**.
3. In the **System Properties** dialog box, click the **Hardware** tab, and then click **Hardware Profiles**.
4. In the **Hardware Profiles** dialog box, in the **Available hardware profiles** window, click **Profile 1 (Current)**, and then click **Copy**.
5. In the **Copy Profile** dialog box, in the **To:** box, type **no network** and then click **OK**.

6. In the **Hardware Profiles** dialog box, click **Properties,** select the **Always include this profile as an option when Windows starts** checkbox, and then click **OK**.

7. In the **Hardware Profiles** dialog box, click **OK**.

8. In the **System Properties** dialog box, click **OK**.

9. Close all windows and restart the computer.

10. At the **Hardware Profile/Configuration Recovery Menu** screen, select **No Network**, and then press ENTER.

11. Pause the 2261_Bonn virtual machine.

Lesson: Troubleshooting ACPI

- **What Is ACPI?**
- **What Are Power Schemes?**
- **How to Configure Power Schemes**
- **How to Troubleshoot ACPI**

Introduction

Advanced Configuration and Power Interface (ACPI) is an open industry specification that enables an operating system to control the amount of power that is given to each device that is attached to the computer. With ACPI, Windows XP can turn off peripheral devices, such as printers or the CD-ROM drive, when they are not in use. Using ACPI for this function is referred to as *power management*. ACPI also enables manufacturers to produce computers that automatically start when the keyboard is touched.

As a DST, you will encounter users with issues that are related to ACPI devices, and you must be able to troubleshoot these issues. This lesson describes power schemes, standby and hibernate, and troubleshooting techniques that you can use to resolve your users' issues related to ACPI.

Lesson objectives

After completing this lesson, you will be able to:

- Explain the purpose and function of ACPI.
- Explain the purpose and function of power schemes.
- Configure power schemes.
- Troubleshoot ACPI issues.

What Is ACPI?

Advanced Configuration and Power Interface:

- Defines a flexible and extensible hardware interface for the system board
- Enables the operating system to direct power management

Introduction

Software designers use the ACPI specification to integrate power management features throughout a computer system, including hardware, the operating system, and application software. This integration enables Windows to determine which applications are active and handles all of the power management resources for computer subsystems and peripherals.

ACPI enables the operating system to direct power management on a wide range of mobile and desktop computers, servers, and peripherals.

ACPI installation

During Windows setup, ACPI is installed only if all components present during setup support power management. Some components, especially older components, do not support power management and can cause erratic behavior with Advanced Power Management (APM) or can prevent ACPI from being installed. Examples of such components are Industry Standard Architecture (ISA) components and an out-of-date BIOS.

Additional reading

For more information about ACPI, see KB article 246236.

What Are Power Schemes?

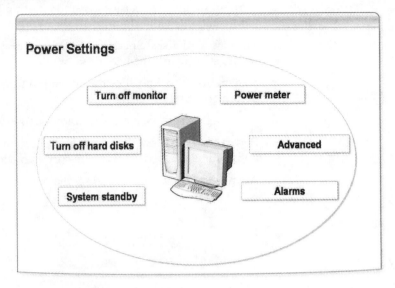

Introduction

Power Options in Control Panel enable users to reduce the power consumption of any number of devices by choosing a power scheme. A *power scheme* is a collection of power management settings that allows a user to conveniently configure power management options on a computer. Windows XP enables users to create customized power schemes and adjust the settings in a power scheme, including:

- Automatically turning off the monitor and hard disks to save power.

- Putting the computer on standby when it is idle. While on *standby*, the entire computer switches to a low-power state where devices, such as the monitor and hard disks, turn off and the computer uses less power. When the computer is needed again, it comes out of standby quickly, and the desktop is restored exactly as it was left. Standby is particularly useful for conserving battery power in portable computers. Because standby does not save desktop state to disk, a power failure while on standby can cause the loss of any unsaved information.

- Putting the computer in hibernation. The *hibernate* feature saves everything in memory on disk, turns off the monitor and hard disk, and then turns off the computer. When the computer is restarted, the desktop is restored exactly as it was left. It takes longer to bring a computer out of hibernation than out of standby.

How to configure power settings

To configure power settings:

- In Control Panel, click **Performance and Maintenance**, and then click **Power Options**.

Power Options settings   Power Options settings include the following:

- Turn off monitor. Specifies the amount of time the computer can be idle before automatically shutting off the monitor.

- Turn off hard disks. Specifies the amount of time the computer can be idle before shutting off the hard disk.

- System Standby. Specifies the amount of time the computer can be idle before going into standby mode.

- Alarms. Defines two alarms to warn the user when battery power is low.

- Power Meter. Allows the power meter icon to be displayed in the notification area and displays the current power status.

- Advanced. Allows the user to set the default options for power buttons.

How to Configure Power Schemes

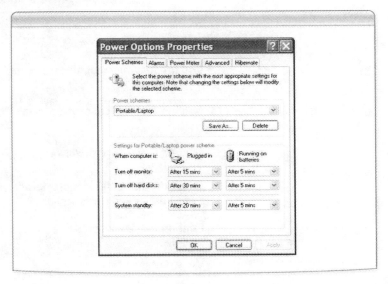

Introduction

Power Options contains default power schemes based on the specific configuration of each computer. Power Options displays only the power settings that can be configured on that computer. You can create a new power scheme that is customized to your needs and work habits.

How to create a new power scheme

To create a new power scheme:

1. In Control Panel, click **Performance and Maintenance**, and then click **Power Options**.

2. In the **Power Options Properties** dialog box, on the **Power Schemes** tab, select the appropriate time settings in the **Turn off monitor**, **Turn off hard disks**, **System standby**, and **System hibernates** lists.

3. In the **Power Schemes** area, click **Save As**, and then type a name for the power scheme. The new scheme is added to the **Power Schemes** list. Click **OK**.

How to Troubleshoot ACPI

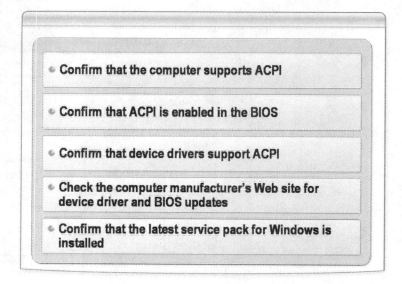

- Confirm that the computer supports ACPI
- Confirm that ACPI is enabled in the BIOS
- Confirm that device drivers support ACPI
- Check the computer manufacturer's Web site for device driver and BIOS updates
- Confirm that the latest service pack for Windows is installed

Introduction

For ACPI features to function properly, the computer must have compatible hardware and ACPI-supported device drivers, and the hardware and drivers must be correctly installed and configured. Most often, ACPI-related issues have to do with startup, shutdown, and standby and hibernation modes.

Common problems related to ACPI

Common ACPI-related problems include:

- An inability to shut down the computer.
- Standby and hibernate options not being available.
- Problems with devices after resuming from standby or hibernation.
- The computer not resuming from standby or hibernation.
- The monitor not coming back on after being powered off by ACPI.

How to troubleshoot issues with ACPI

When troubleshooting issues related to ACPI, check the following:

- Confirm that the computer supports ACPI features. If Windows did not correctly detect an ACPI-capable BIOS during setup, it will not install ACPI support. To determine whether the BIOS was detected as being ACPI-capable:

  a. In Windows Explorer, right-click **My Computer**, then click **Properties**.

  b. In the **Systems Properties** dialog box, on the **Hardware** tab, click **Device Manager**.

  c. In Device Manager, expand the entry called **Computer**.

  If the subentry is **Advanced Configuration and Power Interface (ACPI) PC**, ACPI is installed. If it says **Standard PC**, the computer BIOS was not detected as being ACPI-capable.

- Windows might have detected an ACPI-capable BIOS, but the ACPI features of the BIOS might not be enabled. Although troubleshooting steps vary between computer manufacturers, you can usually perform the following steps to confirm that ACPI is enabled in the BIOS:

    a. When the computer starts, enter the **BIOS Setup Utility**. Often you must press the F1, F2, or DELETE key when the initial BIOS information screen displays.

    b. Most BIOS setup utilities include a Power section. In the Power section, in the **Power Management** or **APM** entry, ensure the entry is set to **Enable**. If it is set to **Disable**, change it to **Enable** or **User Defined**.

- You might need to update the BIOS of the computer to enable ACPI functionality. To update the BIOS, contact the manufacturer for the latest version of BIOS and for specific instructions on updating the BIOS firmware.

- The problem might be caused by a device driver, such as a display adapter driver that does not support ACPI. If there is a problem with the monitor either not powering off or not powering back on, check for updated drivers for the video card and the monitor. Confirm that Windows is using the correct monitor driver and not the generic default monitor driver. To verify this, in Control Panel, in **Appearances and Themes**, click **Display**, and then in the **Display Properties** dialog box, on the **Settings** tab, read the information regarding the display monitor.

- Confirm that the latest service pack (SP) for Windows is installed.

Additional reading   For more information about how to troubleshoot problems related to ACPI, see KB articles 266169, 308041, and 326841.

Practice: Configuring ACPI

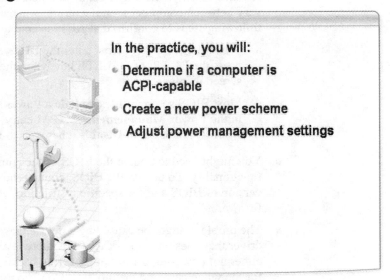

In the practice, you will:
- Determine if a computer is ACPI-capable
- Create a new power scheme
- Adjust power management settings

Objectives

In this practice, you will:

- Determine if Windows detects your computer as being ACPI-capable.
- Create a new power scheme.
- Adjust power management settings.

Scenario

A user calls and says that her laptop battery drains very quickly and that she would like to be able to use her laptop unplugged as long as possible.

Practice

▶ **Determine if Windows detects your computer as being ACPI-capable**

1. Resume the 2261_Bonn virtual machine.

2. Log on to Bonn as **Administrator** with a password of **P@ssw0rd**.

3. Click **Start**, right-click **My Computer**, and then click **Properties**.

4. From **System Properties**, click the **Hardware** tab, and then click **Device Manager**.

5. From **Device Manager**, expand **Computer**.

   Is the computer ACPI-capable?

   _____

   _____

6. Close all windows.

▶ **Configure a new power scheme**

1. In Control Panel, click **Performance and Maintenance**, and then click **Power Options**.

2. In the **Power Options Properties** dialog box, on the **Power Schemes** tab, in the **Turn off monitor** drop-down menu, click **After 1 min**.

3. Click **Save As**.

4. In the **Save Scheme** dialog box, type **my test** and then click **OK**.

5. In the **Power Options Properties** dialog box, click **Apply**.

6. In the **Power Options Properties** dialog box, click **Delete**.

7. In the **Delete Scheme** dialog box, click **Yes**, and then click **OK**.

8. On the Virtual PC window, on the **Action** menu, click **Close**, select **Turn off and delete changes**, and then click **OK**.

9. For all running and paused virtual machines, on the Virtual PC window, on the **Action** menu, click **Close**, select **Turn off and delete changes**, and then click **OK**.

Lab: Resolving Hardware Issues

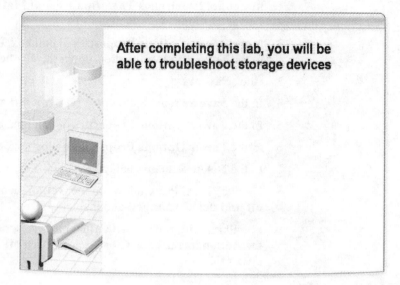

After completing this lab, you will be able to troubleshoot storage devices

Objectives	After completing this lab, you will be able to troubleshoot storage devices.
Prerequisites	Before working on this lab, you must have an understanding of how to use Microsoft Virtual PC.
Before You Begin	For each exercise in this lab, use a password of **P@ssw0rd** In Virtual PC, right-ALT+DEL is the equivalent of CTRL+ALT+DEL.
Scenario	You are a DST for Northwind Traders, a company whose workers use Windows XP Professional.
Estimated time to complete this lab: 30 minutes	

Exercise 1
Troubleshooting Storage Devices

In this exercise, you will troubleshoot issues related to store devices.

Scenario

A user calls after attempting to start his system. The boot failed with an error indicating that the hard drive could not be found.

Tasks	Guidance for completing the task
1. Start the 2261_Lab05_Ex1_Bonn virtual machine, and log on as Administrator.	▪ Use the Virtual PC console.
2. Did Bonn boot successfully?	
3. Resolve the store device issue.	▪ Refer to the How to Troubleshoot Storage Devices topic. ▪ Successful resolution of this issue will enable Bonn to start successfully.
4. Shut down Bonn, and discard changes.	

Microsoft®

Module 6: Resolving File and Folder Issues

Contents

Overview

- Managing Files and Folders
- Troubleshooting Access to Files and Folders
- Troubleshooting Access to Shared Files and Folders
- Troubleshooting Access to Offline Files

Introduction

The Microsoft® Windows® XP Professional operating system helps you, as a desktop support technician (DST), to better control how files and folders are used, and makes it easier for users to work with files and folders. By using options such as Encrypting File System (EFS), folder redirection, and offline files, you can centrally manage the use of files and folders. You can also regulate the extent to which users can modify files and folders, back up user data automatically, and give users access to their files even when they are not connected to the network. In this module, you will learn how to support your users in resolving file and folder issues both locally and across a network.

Objectives

After completing this module, you will be able to:

- Manage files and folders.
- Troubleshoot access to files and folders.
- Troubleshoot access to shared files and folders.
- Troubleshoot access to offline files.

Lesson: Managing Files and Folders

- Types of Files and Folders
- How to Filter File and Folder Events in the Security Log
- What Is File Compression?
- How to Compress and Decompress Files, Folders, and Volumes
- What Is EFS?
- How to Use EFS to Enable and Disable Encryption
- What Is an EFS Recovery Agent?
- How to Troubleshoot File and Folder Management Issues

Introduction

As a DST, you may be called on to support customers who are attempting to perform file and folder management tasks, such as compressing files, enabling and disabling encryption, verifying permissions, or specifying access to files and folders. You must be familiar with these tasks to identify potential issues and suggest solutions to your users' issues.

Lesson objectives

After completing this lesson, you will be able to:

- Explain the types of files and folders.
- Filter file and folder events in the Event Viewer security log.
- Describe the function and purpose of file compression.
- Compress files, folders, and volumes.
- Explain the purpose and function of EFS.
- Use EFS to enable and disable file encryption.
- Explain the purpose and function of EFS recovery agents.
- Troubleshoot file and folder management issues.

Types of Files and Folders

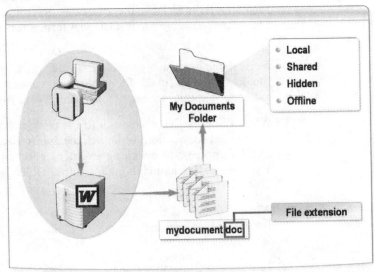

Introduction

One primary purpose of the operating system is to provide access to information that is located in files on storage devices. A *file* is a collection of data that has a name, called a *file name*. You can use the operating system to logically group files into objects called *folders*.

Types of files and folders

Windows XP provides access to the following types of files and folders:

- Local files and folders. Files and folders that are stored on the local computer.

- Shared files and folders. Files and folders that are shared between users. These files and folders may be shared from another computer or over the network.

- Default hidden files and folders. Files and folders that are assigned the Hidden attribute by default. You can choose to display hidden files and folders and to display file extensions for common file types, such as .txt or .htm.

- Offline files and folders. Files and folders from network shares that are available when you are not connected to the network. When you enable a shared file or folder for offline use, Microsoft Windows caches a copy of that file or folder on the hard disk of your local computer so that while you are disconnected from the network, you can work with the local copy exactly as though it were the original. When you reconnect to the network, Windows synchronizes your cached files with the remote counterpart, so that the file or folder is current on both the local computer and the remote network share.

What are file name extensions?

A *file name extension* is a set of characters at the end of a file name that describes the type of information that is stored in the file. For example, in the file name *Winword.exe*, the .exe extension indicates that this is an executable file. (An *executable file* is a file in a format that the computer can directly execute.)

A file name extension can also indicate which application is associated with the file. For example, in the file name *Mydocument.doc*, .doc is the extension that indicates that this is a Microsoft Office Word file.

When Windows XP accesses a file, it compares the file name extension to a list of installed applications to launch the appropriate application for viewing that file. This process of matching an extension to an application is referred to as *file association*. File association determines which application will run or open the file by default.

How to manually change a file association

When Windows is unable to associate a file with an application, or the current association for a specific extension is incorrect, you can change the file association manually.

To change a file association:

1. Click **Start**, point to **All Programs**, point to **Accessories**, and then click **Windows Explorer**.

2. On the menu bar, click **Tools**, and then click **Folder Options**.

3. In the **Folder Options** dialog box, on the **File Types** tab, in the **Registered file types** list, select the file that you want to change, and then click **Change**.

4. In the **Open With** dialog box, in the **Programs** list, choose an application to use when the file type is accessed. Click **Browse** to search the computer for other application executables that are not shown in the **Programs** list.

What is a file attribute?

A *file attribute* is information that indicates whether a file is read-only, hidden, ready for archiving (backing up), compressed, or encrypted, and whether the file contents should be indexed for fast file searching. The following list describes these attributes:

- Read-only. Files that can be read only; these files cannot be changed or deleted.

- Hidden. Files that are hidden from viewing. This protects the resource from unintended access. Windows XP hides critical system files and folders to protect them from deletion or modification. You can view hidden files and folders by selecting the option to show hidden files and folders in the **Folder Options** dialog box on the **View** tab.

- Ready for archiving. Files that have not been backed up recently. When a backup utility backs up a resource, it marks the resource as archived. If the resource changes in any way, the archived flag is removed.

- Compressed. Files that have been decreased in size, which reduces the amount of space that they use on a drive or removable storage device. Windows supports two types of compression: NTFS compression and compression using the Compressed (zipped) Folders feature.

- Encrypted. Files that have been encrypted to keep them safe from access by intruders. After a file is encrypted, you can open and change the file—it does not require decryption.

Protected folders

In addition to the hidden file attribute, Windows XP displays a warning message when the following critical files are accessed:

- System volume. The entire system volume is protected from access by users with limited rights.

- Program Files. This folder contains the majority of application-specific files on the system and is therefore protected.

- Windows. The system folder contains the operating system and is protected.

Note Any user can access hidden resources and protected folders if the appropriate steps are taken and the user is not blocked by a policy.

How to Filter File and Folder Events in the Security Log

Step	Action
1	Select the log that contains the event that you want to view
2	On the View menu, click Filter
3	Specify the filter options that you want

Only events that match your filter criteria are displayed in the details pane

Introduction

You can track Windows XP security events by *auditing*, which enables you to monitor the users that access resources on a computer. Auditing records access to files and folders in the Event Viewer security log. The security log records events such as valid and invalid logon attempts and events that are related to resource use such as creating, opening, or deleting files or other objects.

Note   For information on how to enable auditing, see How to Audit Events in Module 3, "Resolving Desktop Management Issues," in Course 2261, *Supporting Users Running the Microsoft Windows XP Operating System.*

A user with administrator permissions can specify what events are recorded in the security log. (A *permission* is a characteristic that is assigned to a folder or file resource that designates who may access that resource and describes which tasks that user might perform.) For example, when managing file and folder access, you can specify which files and folders to monitor by filtering events in the security log. As a DST, one important method for managing files and folders is to use the security log in Event Viewer.

Note   In Windows XP Home Edition, security auditing is enabled for certain events; however, because Windows XP Home Edition does not include Local Security settings, you cannot change which events are audited unless you use a tool such as Auditpol.exe, which is included in the Windows 2000 Resource Kit.

How to filter audit logs for files and folders

You can filter audit logs in the Security section of Event Viewer by event type, event source, category, event ID, user, computer, or time and date.

To filter log events:

1. In Control Panel, click **Performance and Maintenance**, click **Administrative Tools**, and then double-click **Event Viewer**.

2. In Event Viewer, in the left pane, click **Security**, and then in the right pane, select the log that contains the event that you want to view.

3. On the **View** menu, click **Filter**.

4. In the **Security Properties** dialog box, on the **Filter** tab, specify the filter options that you want, and then click **OK**.

Only the events that match your filter criteria are displayed in the details pane. To return to the log that displays all the events, on the **View** menu, click **Filter**, and then click **Restore Defaults**.

Additional reading

For more information on filtering log events, see article 308427 in the Microsoft Knowledge Base.

What Is File Compression?

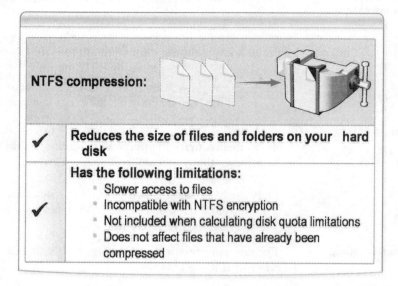

Introduction

A *file system* is the structure in which files are named, stored, and organized. The file systems that are supported by Windows includes file allocation table (FAT), FAT32, and NTFS. You can use any combination of these file systems on a hard disk, but the preferred file system for all computers running Windows XP Professional is NTFS.

NTFS compression

NTFS is an advanced file system that provides performance, security, reliability, and advanced features such as file and folder permissions, encryption, disk quotas, and file compression. *File compression* is a mathematical process that is performed by the operating system on files and folders to reduce their size. In Windows, file compression is called *NTFS compression*.

When a program opens a compressed file, NTFS decompresses only the portion of the file being read and then copies that data to memory. By leaving data in memory uncompressed, NTFS performance is not affected when it reads or modifies data in memory. NTFS compresses the modified or new data in the file when the data is later written to disk.

Considerations when using NTFS compression

You should consider the following when using NTFS compression to manage space on a hard disk:

- Before the operating system is able to gain access to a compressed file, the operating system must first decompress the file. This process can potentially result in a noticeable reduction in performance.

- NTFS compression is incompatible with NTFS encryption. A file can be compressed or encrypted, but not both.

- Reduction in file size caused by compression is not considered when disk quota limitations are calculated. For example, a 100-megabyte (MB) file that has been compressed to 80 MB is still measured as being 100 MB in size for purposes of filling a disk quota.

- NTFS compression does little to reduce the size of files that are already compressed, such as audio files, .zip format files, and compressed image files.

How to Compress and Decompress Files, Folders, and Volumes

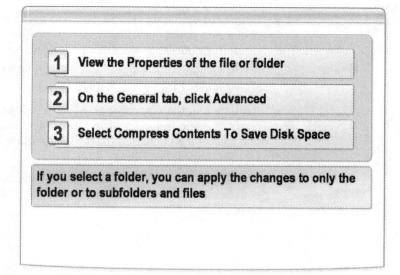

Introduction

In addition to compressing files and folders, you can compress an entire volume. This is generally applied to large data storage volumes that contain archived data. Because archived data is seldom used, compression saves space and allows for more content storage on the volume.

Note Windows XP cannot compress files that are open; verify that the files are closed before you try to compress them.

How to compress a file or folder

To compress a file or folder by using NTFS compression:

1. In Windows Explorer, right-click the file or folder you want to compress, and then click **Properties**.

2. On the **General** tab, click **Advanced**.

3. Select **Compress contents to save disk space**, and then click **OK**.

   If you select a folder, a dialog box is displayed that asks whether to apply compression to the folder or to its contents also.

How compression is applied

Consider the following when working with compressed files and folders:

- If you create a new file in a compressed folder, the new file is compressed.
- If you copy a file into a compressed folder, the file is compressed.
- If you move a file from a different NTFS volume into a compressed folder, the file is compressed.
- If you move a file into a compressed folder on the same NTFS volume, the file retains whatever compression setting it had originally and is not automatically compressed.
- If you move a compressed file into an uncompressed folder on the same NTFS volume, the file retains the compressed attribute. However, if you move a compressed file to an uncompressed folder on a different NTFS partition, the file loses the compression attribute.

How to compress a volume

To compress a volume by using NTFS compression:

1. In Windows Explorer, right-click the volume you want to compress, and then click **Properties**.

2. On the **General** tab, select **Compress drive to save disk space**.

   By default, only files in the root directory of the volume are compressed automatically.

3. To have Windows compress all folders on the drive, select **Also compress subfolders** in the message box that appears.

How to verify NTFS compression

To verify that a file or folder has been compressed:

1. Right-click the file or folder, and then click **Properties**.

2. On the **General** tab, click **Advanced**.

   If the **Compress drive to save disk space** check box is selected, the file or folder is compressed.

Windows XP displays NTFS compressed files in blue by default.

To change the color option:

1. In Windows Explorer, on the **Tools** menu, click **Folder Options**.

2. On the **View** tab, in the **Advanced Settings** list, select **Show encrypted or compressed NTFS files in color** check box.

What Is EFS?

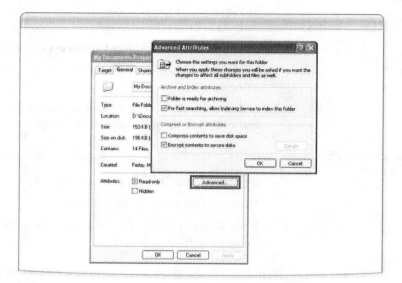

Introduction

As a DST, you will receive calls from users who are unable to access files or folders and they do not understand why. In some cases, these files or folders may be encrypted, making access impossible. In other cases, the NTFS file system may have denied the user access to the files or folders due to permission issues. This section explains encryption and provides the information that you will need to determine if a user's file and folder access issue is caused by protected files using EFS.

If you have sensitive or confidential data, you can prevent others from viewing the data by using encryption.

- *Encryption* is the process of converting data into a format that cannot be read by another user. After a user has encrypted a file, the file automatically remains encrypted whenever the file is stored on disk.

- *Decryption* is the process of converting data from encrypted format back to its original format. After a user has decrypted a file, the file remains decrypted whenever the file is stored on disk.

What is EFS?

In Windows XP Professional, you can protect files and folders by using EFS. EFS encrypts data in selected files and folders. Because EFS is integrated with the file system, it is easy to manage, difficult to attack, and transparent to the user. This is particularly useful for securing data on computers that may be vulnerable to theft, such as mobile computers.

How encryption works

The actual process of data encryption and decryption is completely transparent to the user. The user does not need to understand this process. However, understanding how data encryption and decryption works will help you to troubleshoot users' file access issues.

The most common encryption method uses two encryption keys that are mathematically related. One key is called the *private key* and is kept confidential. The other is called the *public key* and is freely given out to all potential correspondents. In a typical scenario, a sender uses the receiver's public key to encrypt a message. Only the receiver has the related private key to decrypt the message.

EFS restrictions

There are two restrictions when implementing EFS:

- You cannot use EFS on storage volumes that are not formatted with NTFS.
- You cannot use EFS to encrypt a file that has been compressed with NTFS compression.

Note EFS is not available in Windows XP Home Edition.

EFS versus NTFS

Although NTFS manages access to file system resources in Windows or on an internal network, when you have a dual-boot configuration, NTFS permissions can be circumvented by the second operating system. This issue is especially pertinent to portable computers because they can easily be moved or stolen, which would enable a second installation of Windows to be installed as a dual boot. The protected NTFS files would then be accessible on the second installation of Windows. EFS addresses this security gap by requiring you to enter your user account and password information before it will encrypt a file. In a dual-boot environment, the EFS protected files would still be inaccessible.

How to verify that a file or folder is encrypted by using EFS

Windows XP displays the names of encrypted files in green by default, but you can change this setting. To verify that a folder or file is encrypted:

1. Right-click the file or folder, and then click **Properties**.

2. On the **General** tab, click **Advanced**.

   If the **Encrypt contents to secure data** check box is selected, the file or folder is encrypted.

Troubleshooting tip

When an unauthorized user attempts to access a resource that is encrypted by using EFS, the user receives an "access denied" message. This message is similar to what a user experiences when he attempts to access an NTFS resource that he does not have permission to access.

How to Use EFS to Enable and Disable Encryption

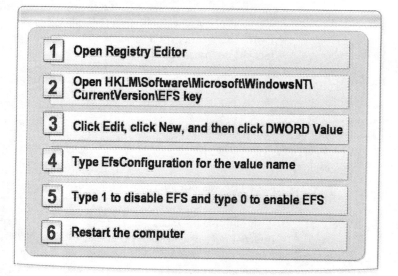

1	Open Registry Editor
2	Open HKLM\Software\Microsoft\WindowsNT\CurrentVersion\EFS key
3	Click Edit, click New, and then click DWORD Value
4	Type EfsConfiguration for the value name
5	Type 1 to disable EFS and type 0 to enable EFS
6	Restart the computer

Introduction

You encrypt or decrypt a folder or file by setting the encryption property for folders and files just as you set any other attribute such as read-only, compressed, or hidden. If you encrypt a folder, all files and subfolders created in the encrypted folder are automatically encrypted. This section describes how to encrypt and decrypt a file or folder and how to perform this task on a local computer and as part of a domain.

How to encrypt or decrypt a file or folder

In Windows XP, you can use Windows Explorer to encrypt individual files or folders.

To encrypt or decrypt a file or folder:

1. In Windows Explorer, right-click the file or folder, and then click **Properties**.

2. On the **General** tab, click **Advanced**.

3. In the **Advanced Attributes** dialog box, select the **Encrypt contents to secure data** check box, and then click **OK** twice.

   To decrypt a file or folder, in the **Advanced Attributes** dialog box, clear the **Encrypt contents to secure data** check box.

Note   If you receive an error message when you attempt to encrypt or access an encrypted file or folder, it may indicate that EFS has been disabled on your computer.

If the file or folder contains any files or subfolders, the operating system displays a confirmation message asking if you want to apply the changes to the folder only or also to subfolders and files. If you select **Apply changes to this folder only** option, the operating system will not encrypt any of the files that are in the folder. However, any new files that you create in the folder, including files that you copy or move to the folder, will be encrypted.

Tip It is a best practice to encrypt folders rather than individual files. Encrypting files without encrypting the folder weakens EFS security. For example, when you open a document in an unencrypted folder for editing in certain applications, the application creates a copy of the original document. When you save the document after you edit it, the application saves the copy, which is not encrypted, and deletes the original, encrypted document. If the entire folder is encrypted, the new copy of the file will also be encrypted.

How to enable or disable EFS locally

You can disable or enable EFS on a particular computer.

To enable or disable EFS locally:

1. Click **Start**, and then click **Run**.

2. In the **Run** dialog box, type **cmd** to open a command prompt.

3. Type **regedit** to open the Registry Editor.

4. Open the HKLM\Software\Microsoft\Windows NT \CurrentVersion\EFS key.

5. Click **Edit**, click **New**, and then click **DWORD Value**.

6. Type **EfsConfiguration** as the name for the new value.

7. Double-click the new value, and change its value to 1 to disable EFS or 0 to enable EFS.

8. Restart the computer.

EFS on a domain

You can also enable or disable EFS on the Microsoft Windows Server™ 2003 Active Directory® directory service by using Group Policy. For the detailed steps in this process, see article 222022 in the Microsoft Knowledge Base.

What Is an EFS Recovery Agent?

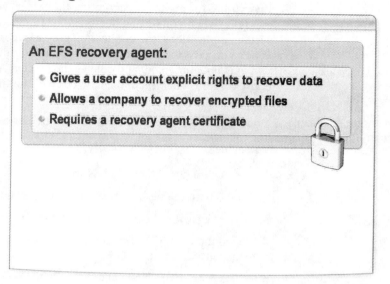

An EFS recovery agent:

- Gives a user account explicit rights to recover data
- Allows a company to recover encrypted files
- Requires a recovery agent certificate

What Is an EFS recovery agent?

An EFS *recovery agent* is a user account that is explicitly granted rights to recover encrypted data. The purpose of a recovery agent is to allow a company to recover encrypted files on a company resource at any time.

Recovery agent certificates

To grant a user account recovery agent rights, an administrator must first generate a *recovery agent certificate*. This certificate grants permission to the user account to access encrypted resources. After the recovery agent rights are granted, the certificate should be removed from the computer or domain and stored in a safe place.

You must create a recovery agent certificate before a resource is encrypted to allow the user account to access this resource. Files and folders that are encrypted *before* a recovery agent certificate has been created cannot be accessed by that recovery agent certificate.

How to generate a recovery agent certificate

If your computer is not part of a domain, there is no default recovery agent and you should create one. To create a data recovery agent, you must first create a data recovery agent certificate and then designate a user to be the data recovery agent.

To generate a recovery agent certificate:

1. Log on as Administrator.
2. Open a command prompt and type **cipher /r:** *filename* where *filename* is the name of the recovery agent certificate.
3. When prompted, type a password that will be used to protect the recovery agent certificate.

When you create the recovery agent certificate, it creates both a .pfx file and a .cer file with the file name that you specify. You can designate any user account as a data recovery agent, but do not designate the account that encrypts the files as a recovery agent. Doing so provides little or no protection of the files. If the current user profile is damaged or deleted, you will lose all the keys that allow decryption of the files.

How to designate an EFS recovery agent

To designate an EFS recovery agent:

1. Log on to the account that you want to designate as a data recovery agent.

2. Click **Start**, click **Run**, type **certmgr.msc** and then click **OK**.

3. In Certificates, under **Certificates - Current User**, expand **Personal**, and then click **Certificates**.

4. On the **Action** menu, click **All Tasks**, click **Import** to launch the **Certificate Import Wizard**, and then click **Next**.

5. On the **File To Import** page, enter the path and file name of the encryption certificate (a .pfx file) that you exported, and then click **Next**. If you click **Browse**, in the **Files of type** box, you must select **Personal Information Exchange** to see .pfx files, and then click **Next**.

6. Enter the password for this certificate, select **Mark This Key As Exportable**, and then click **Next**.

7. Select **Automatically select the certificate store based on the type of certificate**, click **Next**, and then click **Finish**.

8. Click **Start**, click **Run**, type **secpol.msc** and then click **OK**.

9. In Local Security Settings, under Security Settings, expand **Public Key Policies**, and then click **Encrypting File System**.

10. On the **Action** menu, click **Add Data Recovery Agent**, and then click **Next**.

11. On the **Select Recovery Agents** page, click **Browse Folders**, and then navigate to the folder that contains the .cer file that you created.

12. Select the file, and then click **Open**.

13. The **Select Recovery Agents** page now shows the new agent as USER_UNKNOWN. This is normal because the name is not stored in the file.

14. Click **Next**, and then click **Finish**.

The current user is now the recovery agent for all encrypted files on this computer.

EFS data loss risks

All encrypted files and folders will be inaccessible if you reinstall the operating system. For this reason, make a copy of your personal encryption certificate and, if possible, the recovery agent certificate on a disk. Store the disk in a safe place.

Additional reading

For more information about EFS best practices, see article 223316 in the Microsoft Knowledge Base.

How to Troubleshoot File and Folder Management Issues

> **General file and folder troubleshooting questions:**
>
> - What was the task when the error occurred?
> - Whose resources were used?
> - Where are the resources located?
> - When and how were the resources created?
> - How were the resources accessed?

Introduction

Although there are many issues that may occur when managing files and folders, most issues occur when users try to access and configure files and folders that are corrupt or that have been encrypted.

Troubleshooting questions

When troubleshooting file and folder management, you can begin to develop a general idea of the problem and possible solutions by asking the user the following questions:

- What was the task when the error occurred?
- Whose resources were used?
- Where are the resources located?
- When and how were the resources created?
- How were the resources accessed?

Troubleshooting compression issues

Compression issues are usually related to disk space issues, moving files, and conflicts with open files. To troubleshoot compression issues, remember the following:

- Encrypted resources cannot be compressed.
- Open files that are currently being accessed by applications or the operating system cannot be compressed.
- Compressed resources, when uncompressed, may exceed the available space on the storage volume. This problem can also occur when a compressed resource is moved to another volume. To resolve this issue, the amount of empty drive space must be increased or portions of the compressed data must be moved separately.

- Performance issues may be related to disk compression. High-performance areas of a volume, such as system folders, databases, and video game directories, should not be compressed. If the user has compressed the entire volume, recommend that she undo the compression and recompress files and folders on a case-by-case basis.

- You can enable color coding of compressed and encrypted files for easy identification.

Troubleshooting EFS issues

EFS issues are generally caused by conflicts with domain policies, lost certificates, or operating system reinstallations. To troubleshoot EFS issues, remember the following:

- NTFS compressed resources cannot be encrypted.

- Only the user who encrypted the resource or a user account equipped with a recovery agent certificate *at the time the resource was encrypted* can access the resource. If a copy of one of the certificates can be obtained and copied to the computer, access can be reestablished; otherwise, the resource is lost.

- EFS can be disabled, preventing the encryption of new files and access to old files. Re-enable EFS in the system registry.

- There may be domain policies preventing the implementation of auditing on a local computer.

Troubleshooting corruption issues

To verify that files are not corrupt:

- Run Chkdsk on the volume to verify its integrity.

- Try to copy or move the affected resources to another location or volume.

- Attempt to access the resource with an application, such as Microsoft Windows Notepad.

- Check for viruses with a third-party virus scanner.

- If you feel that the issue is one of data loss caused by the operating system or other product, escalate the issue.

Troubleshooting auditing issues

If you have set up auditing to help users find issues with their files and folders, and no data is appearing in the event log, it is generally the result of auditing configuration errors. To troubleshoot auditing issues, remember the following:

- For auditing to work properly, it must be enabled correctly in Policy Editor. In most cases in which audit events are not being displayed inside Event Viewer, incorrect Policy Editor settings are the cause.

- Ensure that the security log's filter settings in Event Viewer are properly configured.

- The volume being audited must be NTFS.

- There may be domain policies preventing the implementation of auditing on a local computer.

Additional reading

For more information about troubleshooting file and folder issues, see articles 228002, 251186, and 314958 in the Microsoft Knowledge Base.

Practice: Configuring Files and Folders

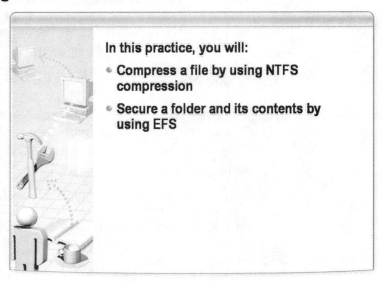

Objectives

In this practice, you will:

- Compress a file by using NTFS compression.
- Secure a folder and its contents by using EFS.

Scenario

A user calls and states that they have sensitive files on their system and want to protect them from being read by unauthorized individuals. Specifically, this user uses a portable computer and is concerned that if the computer was stolen, someone could reinstall the operating system, make himself or herself an administrator, and gain access to all the files on the computer. If possible, she would also like to make more disk space available on her computer.

Practice

▶ **Compress a file**

1. Start the 2261_Bonn virtual machine.
2. Log on to Bonn as Administrator with a password of **P@ssw0rd**.
3. Click **Start**, click **Run**, in the **Open** box, type **C:\Program Files \Microsoft Learning\2261\Practices\Mod06**, and then click **OK**.
4. In the Mod06 window, right-click **Compression**, and then click **Properties**.
5. What is the size/size on disk for the Compression file?

_____

6. In the **Compression Properties** dialog box, on the **General** tab, click **Advanced**.
7. In the **Advanced Attributes** dialog box, select **Compress contents to save disk space**, and then click **OK**.
8. In the **Compression Properties** dialog box, click **OK**.
9. In the Mod06 window, right-click **Compression**, and then click **Properties**.

10. What is the size/size on disk for the Compression file?

_____

11. Close the **Compression Properties** dialog box.

▶ **Secure a file**

1. In the Mod06 window, right-click the **Encryption** folder, and then click **Properties**.

2. On the **General** tab, click **Advanced**.

3. In the **Advanced Attributes** dialog box, select **Encrypt contents to secure data**, and then click **OK**.

4. In the **Encryption Properties** dialog box, click **OK**.

5. In the **Confirm Attribute Changes** dialog box, verify **Apply changes to this folder, subfolders, and files** is selected, and then click **OK**.

6. In the Mod06 window, double-click the **Encryption** folder to open it.

   Notice that the Encryption file has been encrypted.

Note   Encryption.doc is an alternate color to indicate that it is an encrypted file.

---

7. Close all windows and log off.

▶ **Test the encrypted folder**

1. Log on to Bonn as Frank Lee with a password of **P@ssw0rd**.

2. Click **Start**, and then click **Run**.

3. In the Open box, type **C:\Program Files\Microsoft Learning\2261 \Practices\Mod06\Encryption**, and then click **OK**.

4. In the Encryption window, double-click the **Encryption** file.

5. In the **WordPad** warning message box, click **OK**.

   An error message is displayed stating access was denied.

6. Close all windows and log off.

7. Pause Bonn.

Lesson: Troubleshooting Access to Files and Folders

* **What Are NTFS File and Folder Permissions?**
* **How to Verify and Modify NTFS File and Folder Permissions**
* **What Are Effective Permissions?**
* **How to Modify Inherited Permissions**
* **How to Troubleshoot Access to Files and Folders**

Introduction

One of the benefits of using Windows XP is the ability to use permissions to control which users and groups have access to the files or folders on a computer. However, file and folder permissions require the use of the NTFS file system because file and folder permissions are not available on FAT partitions. When you assign or modify NTFS permissions for files and folders, problems can arise. Troubleshooting these problems is important to keep resources available to users. This lesson describes some common permission-related problems and their solutions.

Lesson objectives

After completing this lesson, you will be able to:

* Explain the purpose and function of NTFS file and folder permissions.
* Verify and modify NTFS file and folder permissions.
* Explain the purpose and function of effective permissions.
* Determine effective file permissions.
* Troubleshoot access to files and folders.

What Are NTFS File and Folder Permissions?

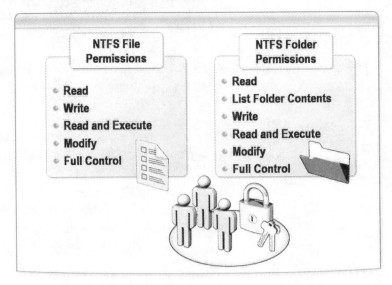

Introduction

One of the primary benefits of the NTFS file system is the ability to control access to specific files and folders through the use of permissions. NTFS permissions provide security for both local and network access to the file system. NTFS permissions differ from shared folder permissions in that shared folder permissions are applied only to folders and only secure network access to the file system. The specific NTFS permission settings that are available depend on whether the resource is a file or a folder.

NTFS permission information is independent of the operating system. If the operating system is reinstalled, the NTFS permissions that are assigned to volume resources are not affected.

NTFS file permissions

The following table describes available NTFS file permissions:

Permission	Enables the user to
Read	Open the file and view its permissions, attributes, and ownership.
Write	Modify the file and its attributes, and view its permissions, attributes, and ownership.
Read and Execute	Delete the file and do everything that the Read permission allows.
Modify	Delete the file and do everything that the Read and Execute and the Write permissions allow.
Full Control	Take ownership, modify permissions, and do everything that the Modify permission allows.

NTFS folder permissions   The following table describes available NTFS folder permissions.

Permission	Enables the user to
Read	View contents of the folder and view its permissions, attributes, and ownership.
List Folder Contents	List and traverse the folder, view file properties on any file in the folder even if file permissions prevent them from seeing the contents of the file.
Write	Create new files and folders in the folder, modify the folder's attributes, and view its permissions, attributes, and ownership.
Read and Execute	View subfolders within the folder and do everything that the Read and the List Folder Contents permissions allow.
Modify	Delete the folder and do everything that the Read and Execute and the Write permissions allow.
Full Control	Take ownership, modify permissions, and do everything that the Modify permission allows.

Ownership of files and folders   The user account that creates a file or folder is the *owner* of that file or folder. By default, that account has complete control over the resource, including the rights to assign permissions to the resource.

To apply permissions to an NTFS file or folder, the user account must be the owner of the resource, have full control of the resource, or be a member of the local Administrators group.

Any user account that is granted the permission to take ownership of files and other objects might assume ownership of a volume resource and then change the permissions on the resource.

Note   To learn more about the differences between permission states and to test your knowledge, see the activity *Permission States*. To start the activity, open the Web page on the Student Materials compact disc, click **Multimedia**, and then click the title of the activity. Do not start this activity unless you are instructed to do so by the instructor.

How to Verify and Modify NTFS File and Folder Permissions

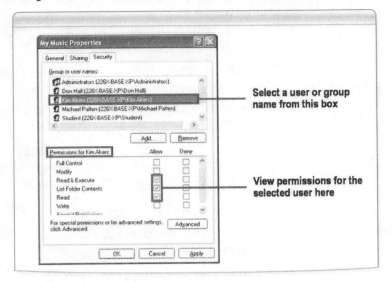

Select a user or group name from this box

View permissions for the selected user here

Introduction

When a user calls with a file or folder access issue, recommend that they view the NTFS permissions on the file or folder to determine if the problem is caused by insufficient permissions.

How to verify and modify permissions in a domain environment

To view, set, change, or remove file and folder permissions in a domain environment:

1. In Windows Explorer, right-click the file or folder for which you want to set permissions, and then click **Properties**.

2. On the **Security** tab, in the **Group or user names** box, select a group or user. To set permissions for a group or user that does not appear in the **Group or user names** box, click **Add**, type the name of the group or user for whom you want to set permissions, and then click **OK**.

   Note   If the **Security** tab is not available, the file or folder is either not on an NTFS volume or simple file sharing is enabled.

3. To allow or deny a permission, select either the **Allow** or **Deny** check box in the **Permissions for** *user_or_group* box (where *user_or_group* is the name of the currently selected user or group).

4. To remove all permissions for a user or group, remove the user or group by selecting the group or user from the **Group or user names** box, and then click **Remove**.

How to use simple file sharing in a non-domain environment

By default, computers running Windows XP Professional that are not in a domain and computers running Windows XP Home Edition do not use full NTFS permissions to control other users' access to local files and folders that have been shared on the network. Instead, they use a simplified method for controlling access to shared resources called *simple file sharing*.

Simple file sharing provides fewer, simpler options for sharing files and folders that make it easy to set up common security arrangements. When simple file sharing is enabled, in the **Properties** dialog box, the **Security** tab is hidden to prevent users from changing NTFS permissions directly. To disable simple file sharing:

1. In Control Panel, click **Appearance and Themes**, and then click **Folder Options**.

2. On the **View** tab, in the **Advanced settings** box, deselect the **Use simple file sharing [Recommended]** check box.

Note   In Windows XP Home Edition, you must start the computer in safe mode and log on as Administrator or an administrative user to access permissions settings.

Key points

The following list describes key points to remember when troubleshooting permission issues:

- You can set permissions only on drives that are formatted to use NTFS.

- To change permissions, you must be the owner or have been granted permissions by the owner.

- Groups or users who are granted Full Control for a folder can delete files and subfolders in that folder, regardless of the permissions that protect the files and subfolders in the folder.

- If the check boxes in the **Permissions for user or group** box are unavailable or if the **Remove** button is unavailable, the file or folder has inherited permissions from the parent folder. For more information about how inheritance affects files and folders, see Windows Help.

- When you add a new user or group, by default the user or group has Read and Execute, List Folder Contents, and Read permissions.

Additional reading

For more information on working with NTFS file and folder permissions, see article 308421 in the Microsoft Knowledge Base.

What Are Effective Permissions?

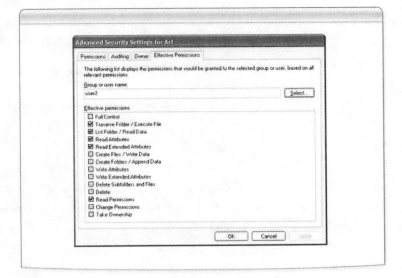

Introduction

Determining which permissions users have may be confusing because multiple permissions can be assigned to users and groups for the same files and folders.

What are effective permissions?

Effective permissions are the combined permissions for a user who is accessing files and folders through a shared folder or disk. For example, if a user has Read and Execute permissions on a folder, but the user is also a member of a group that has been assigned Write permissions to that folder, the user's effective permissions for that folder are Read, Execute, and Write.

How to determine effective permissions

To troubleshoot issues, you might need to determine the effective permissions that are applied to a resource. To determine effective permissions on files and folders in Windows XP:

1. In Windows Explorer, right-click the file or folder on which you want to view effective permissions, and then click **Properties**.

2. On the **Security** tab, click **Advanced**.

3. In the **Advanced Security Settings for** *Folder name* dialog box, on the **Effective Permissions** tab, click **Select**.

4. In the **Enter the object name to select** box, type the name of a user or group, and then click **OK**.

   The check boxes that are selected indicate the effective permissions of the user or group for that file or folder.

How to Modify Inherited Permissions

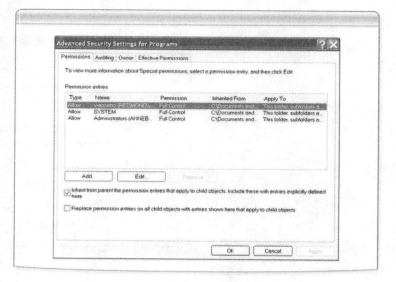

Introduction

NTFS permissions follow rules of inheritance. This means that when you apply specific permissions to one folder, the permissions automatically apply to all the files and folders that are stored in that folder. Any new files and subfolders that you create in this folder inherit these permissions. This section describes how to modify inherited permissions.

How to prevent inherited permissions

To prevent specific files or subfolders from inheriting permissions:

1. Right-click the file or subfolder, and then click **Properties**.

2. On the **Security** tab, click **Advanced**.

3. In the **Advanced Security Settings** dialog box, clear the **Inherit from parent the permission entries that apply to child objects. Include these with entries explicitly defined here** check box.

How to change inherited permissions

If the check boxes in the **Advanced Security Settings** dialog box are not available, the file or folder has inherited permissions from the parent folder. There are three ways to change inherited permissions:

1. Make the changes to the parent folder so that the file or folder inherits the permissions.

2. Select the opposite permission (Allow or Deny) to override the inherited permission.

3. Clear the **Inherit from parent the permission entries that apply to child objects. Include these with entries explicitly defined here** check box.

   When you clear this check box, you can make changes to the permissions or remove the user or group from the permissions list. However, the file or folder does not inherit permissions from the parent folder.

How to use Allow and Deny permissions

In most cases, the Deny permission overrides the Allow permission unless a folder inherits conflicting settings from different parent folders. When this occurs, precedence is given to the setting that is inherited from the parent closest to the object in the subtree.

When you use the Deny and Allow settings, note the following:

- Allow permissions are cumulative, so a user's permissions are determined by the cumulative effect of all of the groups to which the user belongs.

- Deny permissions override Allow permissions. Use caution when you apply Deny permissions.

When you grant permissions to a parent object, you can decide whether folders or subfolders can inherit permissions with the **Apply onto** setting.

How to Troubleshoot Access to Files and Folders

Common file and folder actions that create issues

- Copying a file or folder to an NTFS drive
- Moving a file or folder within a single NTFS drive
- Moving a file or folder from one NTFS drive to another
- Copying or moving a file or folder from a FAT32 drive to an NTFS drive
- Copying or moving a file or folder from an NTFS drive to a FAT32 drive

Introduction

Many issues that involve file and folder access and permissions occur when users move or copy files or folders from one location to another and the file and folder permissions change during the move.

Consequences of moving and copying files and folders

The following table lists the actions and describes the consequences of moving or copying files or folders:

Action	Consequence
Copying a file or folder to an NTFS drive.	The new copy of the file or folder inherits the permissions of the destination folder, and the original object retains its permissions. This is true regardless of whether the destination is on the same NTFS drive as the original file or on a separate NTFS drive. The user account that created the copy becomes the Creator Owner of the new file or folder, which means that this user account can change the permissions of the copy.
Moving a file or folder within a single NTFS drive.	The moved folder or file retains its original permissions, and the account that moved the file or folder becomes the Creator Owner.
Moving a file or folder from one NTFS drive to another.	The moved folder or file inherits the permissions of the destination folder, and the account that moved the file or folder becomes the Creator Owner.
Copying or moving a file or folder from a FAT32 drive to an NTFS drive.	The newly created folder or file inherits the permissions of the destination folder, and the account that copied the file or folder becomes the Creator Owner.
Copying or moving a file or folder from an NTFS drive to a FAT32 drive.	The moved or copied folder or file in the new destination loses all permission settings because the FAT32 file system is incapable of storing these details.

Common file and folder access issues and solutions

When troubleshooting file and folder access, you may encounter certain issues more frequently than others. Some of these common issues and their solutions are:

- A user or group cannot access a file or folder.

  - Verify the permissions that are granted to the user or group. Permissions may not be granted for the selected resource, or permission could be denied. Remember that the permissions could have been changed if the file or folder was copied or moved.

  - Review inherited permissions. Look in the **Advanced Security Settings** dialog box, and pay particular attention to the **Inherited From** column in the **Permission Entries** list. The data here will often show you the exact source of an unexpected permissions problem.

  - See if the file or folder was encrypted with EFS by another user. Remember that by default, Windows XP displays the names of encrypted files in green.

- The Administrator grants permissions to a group for a selected file or folder, but a user in that group still cannot access the file or folder.

  - Ask the user to log off and then log back on. When the user logs back on, the user's NTFS permissions are updated to include the new group to which he or she was added. Another way to update a user's permissions is to ask the user to disconnect the network drive on which the file or folder resides and then reconnect it. This forces the permissions to update on the reconnect of the network drive.

- A user with Full Control to a folder accidentally deletes files in the folder, and you want to prevent the user from doing it again.

  - In the Properties window of the folder, on the **Security** tab, click **Advanced** to view the **Permission Entry** box for that folder. Select the user from the list of entries, and then click **Edit**. Clear the **Delete Subfolders and Files** check box.

- A user is logged on as Administrator and must access a file or folder that was created by another user, but the first user is denied access.

  - If the files have not been encrypted by the other user, you can assist the user to take ownership of the files to gain access. For more information on this issue, see article 308421 in the Microsoft Knowledge Base.

Common file and folder permission issues

You may encounter some of the following issues when you attempt to change file or folder permissions:

- You made changes to the permissions of a file or folder, but the check marks do not appear. If you apply permissions to anything other than the default location—**This Folder, Subfolder, And Files**—Windows adds a check mark in the **Special Permissions** box. To see this box, you must scroll to the bottom of the **Permissions** list.

- Permission settings are unavailable. Check your user account rights. You must be logged on as a member of the Administrators group or be the owner of an object to set its permissions. Permission settings will also be unavailable if the selected object inherits its permissions from a parent folder.

Practice: Troubleshooting File and Folder Access

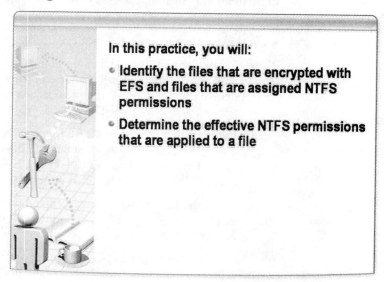

Objectives

In this practice, you will:

- Identify files that are encrypted with EFS and files that are assigned NTFS permissions.

- Determine the effective NTFS permissions that are applied to a file.

Scenario

A user calls and says he is having trouble accessing certain files after he changed the NTFS permissions and encrypted the files. He is uncertain which files he encrypted and what NTFS permissions were actually applied to the files.

Practice

▶ **Identify files that are encrypted with EFS and files that are assigned NTFS permissions**

1. Resume Bonn.

2. Log on to Bonn as Samantha Smith with a password of **P@ssw0rd**.

3. Click **Start**, and then click **Run**.

4. In the Open box, type **C:\Program Files\Microsoft Learning\2261 \Practices\Mod06**, and then click **OK**.

5. In the Mod06 window, double-click **AccessDenied1**.

   Why did you not have access to the file, because of encryption or NTFS permissions?

6. In the WordPad warning window, click **OK**.

7. From the Mod06 window, double-click **AccessDenied2**.

Why did you not have access to the file, because of encryption or NTFS permissions?

_____

8. In the WordPad warning window, click **OK**.

Class Discussion

How did you come up with your answers?

_____

9. Close all windows and log off.

▶ **Determine the effective permissions applied to a file**

1. Log on to Bonn as Administrator with a password of **P@ssw0rd**.

2. Click **Start**, and then click **Run**.

3. In the Open box, type **C:\Program Files\Microsoft Learning\2261 \Practices\Mod06**, and then click **OK**.

4. In the Mod06 window, right-click **AccessDenied2**, and then click **Properties**.

5. In the **AccessDenied2 Properties** dialog box, click the **Security** tab, and then click **Advanced**.

6. In the **Advanced Security Settings for AccessDenied2** dialog box, click the **Effective Permissions** tab.

7. Click **Select**.

8. In the **Select User or Group** dialog box, in the **Enter the object name to select** box, type **Administrator** and then click **OK**.

What are the Administrator's effective permissions for the file AccessDenied2?

_____

_____

9. In the **Advanced Security Settings for AccessDenied2** dialog box, click **Select**.

10. In the **Select User or Group** dialog box, in the **Enter the object name to select** box, type **samantha smith** and then click **OK**.

What are Samantha Smith's effective permissions for the file AccessDenied2?

_____

11. On the Advanced Security Settings for AccessDenied2 dialog box, click **OK**.

12. In the **AccessDenied2 Properties** dialog box, click **OK**.

13. Close the 2261_Bonn virtual machine without saving changes.

Lesson: Troubleshooting Access to Shared Files and Folders

- What Is File and Folder Sharing?
- How to Share Files and Folders
- How to Determine Effective Share Permissions
- How to Map a Network Drive
- How to Troubleshoot Access to Shared Files and Folders

Introduction

One benefit of a networked environment is the ability to access files and folders that are on other computers. In Windows XP, a resource must be shared before it can be accessed on the network.

A *shared folder* is a folder on another computer that has been made available for other users on the network. After the resource is shared, users can connect to the folder over the network and gain access to its contents. Shared folder permissions allow you to control which users or groups can gain access to the contents of a shared folder. This lesson describes how to use shared folder permissions to determine who can gain access to resources on remote computers so that you can troubleshoot users' issues regarding access to shared files and folders.

Lesson objectives

After completing this lesson, you will be able to:

- Explain the function and purpose of file and folder sharing.
- Share files and folders.
- Determine effective share permissions.
- Map a network drive.
- Troubleshoot access to shared files and folders.

What Is File and Folder Sharing?

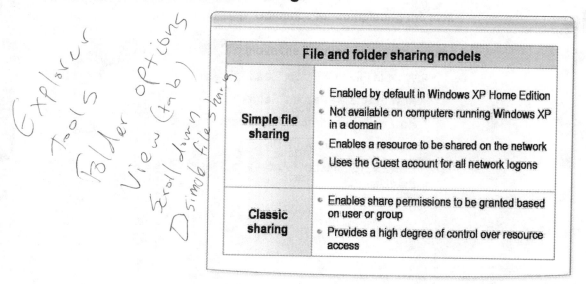

Handwritten notes in left margin:
Explorer
Tools
Folder options
View (tab)
Scroll down file sharing
☐ simple file sharing

File and folder sharing models

Simple file sharing	• Enabled by default in Windows XP Home Edition • Not available on computers running Windows XP in a domain • Enables a resource to be shared on the network • Uses the Guest account for all network logons
Classic sharing	• Enables share permissions to be granted based on user or group • Provides a high degree of control over resource access

Introduction

Only drive and folder resources can be shared. When a resource is shared, sharing not only makes the resource available on the network, but sharing grants *share permissions* that define who can and cannot have access to the resource over the network. Share permissions are distinctly different from NTFS file permissions, which define the level and type of control that is granted to user accounts.

To access a shared drive or folder across a network, a user account must have both the share permissions and the NTFS permissions (if the file system is NTFS).

Types of file and folder sharing models

Windows XP provides the following methods for sharing resources on the network:

- Simple file sharing. Enables you to share a resource on the network by selecting a single check box. Through the Guest account, Windows XP automatically makes the resource available to everyone and sets the appropriate share and NTFS permissions on the object.

- Classic sharing. Enables you to grant the share permissions based on the user or group. This provides a high degree of control over who has access to the resource.

Note   Simple file sharing is enabled by default in Windows XP Home Edition and Windows XP Professional. It is not available to any computer running Windows XP in a domain.

Shared resource permissions

A shared resource provides access to applications, data, or a user's personal data. You can grant or deny permission for each shared resource. In general, it is best to set permissions using the NTFS file system or access control. The more restrictive permissions will always apply. Shared resource permissions:

- Apply only to users who gain access to the resource over the network. They do not apply to users who gain access to the resource at the computer where the resource is stored.

- Apply to all files and folders within the shared resource. For this reason, shared resource permissions provide less detailed security than NTFS permissions.

- Are the only way to secure network resources on FAT and FAT32 volumes because NTFS permissions are not available on FAT or FAT32 volumes.

- Specify the maximum user access allowed over the network for users who access the resource through the share. This is in addition to the security provided by the NTFS file system.

Types of shared folder permissions

The following table describes the types of shared folder permissions.

Permission	Enables user to
Read	Display folder and file names, display file data and attributes, run program files and scripts, and change folders within the shared folder.
Write	Create folders, add files to folders, change data in files, append data to files, change file attributes, delete folders and files, and perform all tasks permitted by the Read permission.
Full Control	Change file permissions, take ownership of files, and perform all tasks permitted by the Change permission.

What is automatic search?

By default, Windows XP automatically searches the local network for available, shared resources and lists those resources in Windows Explorer. Automatic search enables users to easily locate network resources on their local computers. To control the shared drives and folders that users are able to view, disable the automatic search feature. For more information on disabling the automatic search feature, see article 320138 in the Microsoft Knowledge Base.

Note Automatic search is automatically disabled when a computer joins a domain.

How to Share Files and Folders

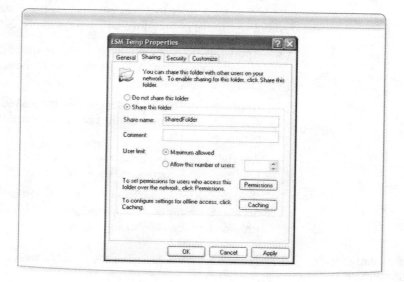

Introduction	Sharing folders and drive resources allows users to exchange information and to access the same central resources. Individual files cannot be shared directly; instead, you must share the folder that contains the files you want to share.
	Note To share resources in Windows XP, you must be logged on as a member of the Administrators or Power Users groups. You also must have the File and Printer Sharing for Microsoft Networks network service enabled on your local network connection.
How to share a folder or drive	To share a folder or drive: 1. In Windows Explorer, right-click the folder or drive that you want to share, and then select **Sharing And Security**. 2. Select the **Share This Folder** option, accept or change the proposed share name, and then click **Apply**. 3. If you want to share this same folder or drive multiple times under different names, click the **New Share** button, and then type a different share name. 4. Creating multiple shares for the same resource allows you to grant different share permissions. 5. When finished creating shares for the folder or drive, click **OK**.
What is a share name?	The *share name* is the name that other users will see and use to access the resource from their computers. A share name can be hidden by appending a dollar sign character ($) to the end of the share name. This allows you to share resources and tell particular users about those resources, but still hide those resources from general viewing on the network.

Each local storage volume also has a default administrative share whose share name consists of the drive letter and a dollar sign, for example, C$. This share name is not visible to others, and you cannot set permissions for the default share. The purpose of this share is to provide a network administrator with full access to the resources on each volume at any time. For security reasons, Windows XP Home Edition does not create these shares.

Number of users permitted to access one resource

By default, Windows XP limits the number of concurrent user connections to any one shared resource to 10. If you must provide access to more than 10 concurrent users to your shared resources, you must use a computer running Windows Server 2003.

How to Determine Effective Share Permissions

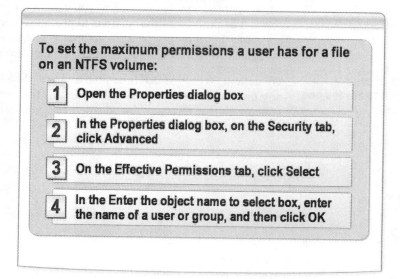

To set the maximum permissions a user has for a file on an NTFS volume:

1 Open the Properties dialog box

2 In the Properties dialog box, on the Security tab, click Advanced

3 On the Effective Permissions tab, click Select

4 In the Enter the object name to select box, enter the name of a user or group, and then click OK

Introduction

When a folder is shared on a network, each user or group that attempts to connect to the share is subject to the permissions that are granted to that share. These permissions are applied in addition to any local NTFS permissions that are applied to the folder and file contents of that share.

How to determine effective share permissions

To determine the effective permissions that a user or group has when accessing a shared folder over the network, you must combine the share permissions with the NTFS permissions. When combining permissions, the more restrictive permission always takes precedence. For example, if the share permission is Everyone = Read and the NTFS permission allows users to make changes to a shared file, the share permission applies, and the user is allowed only to read and cannot change the file. You must have access to the local computer where the share resides to access the required information.

To determine effective share permissions:

1. Determine the maximum local NTFS permissions that are assigned to the share for the user or group desired.

2. Determine the maximum shared permissions that are assigned to the share for the user or group. To determine the maximum permissions a user has for a shared folder:

   a. Open the **Properties** dialog box for the shared folder.

   b. Find the maximum permissions the user has to the share by determining which groups the user belongs to.

3. Determine the total effective permissions for the share:

   a. Compare the maximum NTFS permissions with the maximum shared folder permissions.

   b. The most restrictive permission for the user between the maximum NTFS and shared folder permissions is the effective permissions.

How to Map a Network Drive

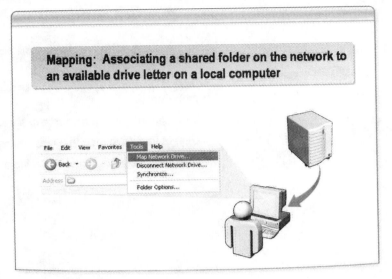

Mapping: Associating a shared folder on the network to an available drive letter on a local computer

Introduction

Some users must access the same shared drives and folders frequently. Although the shared drive or folder can be easily accessed by browsing for it in My Network Places, this task may become unnecessarily repetitive for connecting to common shares.

What is a network drive?

To simplify the process of browsing for shared folders and drives, you can make a semi-permanent connection to a shared resource by *mapping* it in Windows Explorer. This mapped resource is referred to as a *mapped drive* or a *network drive*. After you map a resource, you can access it as you would a local volume.

How to map a network drive

To map a network drive:

1. In Windows Explorer, click **Tools**, and then click **Map Network Drive**.

2. Choose an available drive letter to assign to the share, and in the **Folder** box, enter the path to the shared folder (for example, \\london\users).

3. Specify any required credentials that are necessary to gain access to the shared folder.

Limitations of network drives

Although a mapped network drive appears in Windows Explorer the same way as any other local storage volume, it is subject to a few restrictions:

- You may be restricted by the share permissions and NTFS permissions that are applied to the share by its owner.

- You cannot access the network drive if the computer on which the share resides is not present on the network. This may cause extended delays when starting your local computer as it attempts to reconnect to the shared resources that are not currently present on the network.

- Because the data stored in the share is located across the network, opening shared files and saving changes to those files may be considerably slower than if the files were located on your local computer.

How to Troubleshoot Access to Shared Files and Folders

Common shared file and folder issues

- User is unable to specify who can access a shared resource
- User cannot see the resource in My Network Places
- User is unable to map to a network resource
- User has accidentally deleted a file on a share

Introduction

As a DST, you may receive calls from customers who are having difficulties sharing, locating, or gaining access to shared resources. The first step in troubleshooting these issues is to determine whether the issue is a sharing or connectivity issue and then to identify the user's effective NTFS permissions.

To immediately rule out connectivity as the issue, perform connectivity diagnostics, such as verifying whether the user's computer can access the Internet and whether the user receives responses from other network computers using the Ping command-line utility. The **Ping** command-line utility is the primary command-line utility used to troubleshoot network connectivity issues.

Common shared file and folder issues and solutions

When troubleshooting access to shared files and folders, you may encounter certain issues more frequently than others. Some of these common issues, and their solutions, are:

- The user does not have a **Sharing** tab when he accesses a drive's or folder's properties. Ensure that the user has the correct permissions to share a folder or drive. The user must be a member of the local Administrators, Power Users, or Server Operators group. Also, ensure that File and Printer Sharing for Microsoft Networks network service is installed on the local network connection.

- The user is unable to specify who can access a shared resource because simple file sharing is enabled. Help the user to disable simple file sharing.

- The user shared a resource, but others cannot see the resource in My Network Places on their computers. Verify that the Server service is enabled on the user's computer using the **Services** console. To open the **Services** console, in the **run as** command, type **services.msc**. Locate the Server service in the list. The Server service is enabled by default, but if it is stopped, start the service by clicking it, and then click the **Start Service** button on the toolbar.

- The user has set up a shared resource and granted everyone the Full Control permission, but other users are not able to access the shared resource. This is most likely an NTFS permissions issue. Determine the NTFS permissions and ensure that there are no restrictions in these permissions that are overriding the permissions on the shared resource. Ensure that the Windows XP Windows Firewall is not enabled. If the firewall is enabled, disable it for local network connections.

- The user is unable to map to a network resource. Ensure that the path specified to the resource is correct and that the user has the appropriate credentials to access the shared resource.

- A remote user has accidentally deleted a file on a shared resource. Tell the user that shared resources do not have a recycle bin, so deleted files cannot be restored. However, if the remote user has not done *anything* on her computer since accidentally deleting the file, the remote user can attempt to undo the file delete by pressing CTRL+Z. If the remote shared resource resides on a computer running Windows Server 2003, find out whether shadow copy is enabled. If so, the user can either contact an administrator to restore the file, or the user can download and install the shadow copy client and restore the file. The only remaining alternative is to see whether the administrator performs routine backups of shared resources and obtain the last backed-up copy.

Common remote file and folder issues

When troubleshooting access to remote shared resources, you might encounter certain issues more frequently than others. Some of these common issues and their solutions are:

- A mapped network drive is no longer available. The most likely cause is that the shared resource is no longer available. Attempt to access the shared resource directly from the command line. You might need to delete the old mapping and create a new one. If the user belongs to a domain and is dialing in remotely, creating a new mapping to *any* shared resource will restore all network drives (delete the new mapping after performing this task).

- In a workgroup, the user is being prompted to provide credentials to a shared resource. In workgroup scenarios in which local computer security is the rule, this is normal behavior. An account must be provided for the user on the remote computer to access the resource or the user must contact the shared resource owner to obtain the appropriate credentials.

- In a domain, the user is being prompted to provide credentials to access a network shared folder or drive. The shared resource does not provide permissions to the user's domain account for accessing the shared resource, so the remote computer is prompting for credentials. The domain user account must be added to the shared resource's permissions or the user must obtain the appropriate credentials from the shared resource owner to connect.

- A user is attempting to access a shared folder or drive from a home computer and cannot find it. This is because shared resources are not available across the Internet. The user must be able to connect to the remote network with a secure connection and then browse and connect to remote resources.

Practice: Troubleshooting Shared Files and Folders

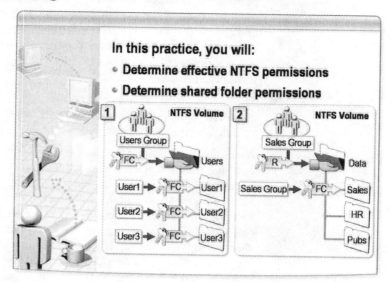

Objectives

In this practice, you will:

- Determine the effective NTFS permissions that are applied to a file.
- Use shadow copy to recover a previous version of a document.

Class discussion

The graphic on this page illustrates two shared folders that contain folders or files that have been assigned NTFS permissions. In the graphic, *FC* stands for *Full Control* and *R* stands for *Read*. Look at each example and determine a user's effective permissions.

1. In the first example, the Users folder has been shared, and the Users group has the shared folder permission Full Control. User1, User2, and User3 have been granted the NTFS permission Full Control to *only* their folder. These users are all members of the Users group.

   Do members of the Users group have Full Control to *all* home folders in the Users folder once they connect to the Users shared folder?

   _____

   _____

2. In the second example, the Data folder has been shared. The Sales group has been granted the shared folder permission Read for the Data shared folder and the NTFS permission Full Control for the Sales folder.

What are the Sales group's effective permissions when they access the Sales folder by connecting to the Data shared folder?

_____

_____

▶ **Use shadow copy to recover a previous version of a document**

1. Start the 2261_London virtual machine.

2. Wait until London has completely booted, then start the 2261_Acapulco virtual machine.

3. On Acapulco, log on to the domain as **Samantha**.

4. Using London, log on to the domain as **Administrator** with the password **P@ssw0rd**

5. On Acapulco click **Start**, click **Run**, type **\\london\rahelp** in the **Open** box, and then click **OK**.

6. In the RAHelp on London window, on the File menu, point to New and then click **Text document**.

7. Name the text file **Recover**.

8. Open the Recover text file, type **Original text** save the document and close Notepad.

▶ **To create a shadow copy**

1. Using London, in My Computer, right-click **Local Disk (C:)**, and then click **Properties**.

2. In the Local Disk (C:) Properties window, on the **Shadow Copies** tab, click **Create Now**.

   Under Shadow copies of selected volume section verify another entry showing the current time and date is displayed.

3. Using Acapulco, in the RAHelp on London window, double-click **Recover**.

4. In Notepad, on a new line, type **New text** save the document, and then close Notepad.

5. On London, in the Local Disk (C:) Properties window, on the **Shadow Copies** tab, click **Create Now** and then click **OK**.

   Under Shadow copies of selected volume section verify another entry showing the current time and date is displayed.

6. On Acapulco, in the RAHelp on London window, right-click **Recover**, and click **Properties**.

7. On the **Previous Versions** tab, click **Restore**.

8. In the **Previous Versions** dialog box, click **Yes**, and then click **OK**.

9. To close the **Recover Properties** dialog box, click **OK**.

10. In the RAHelp on London window, double-click **Recover**.

    Notice that the document has been restored to the version that it was before you added **new text** to the document.

11. On Acapulco, close all windows, log off, and pause Acapulco.

12. On London, close all windows, log off, and pause London.

Lesson: Troubleshooting Access to Offline Files

- **What Are Offline Files?**
- **How to Configure Offline File Settings**
- **What Is Synchronization of Offline Files?**
- **What Is File Caching?**
- **How to Define Cache Settings for Shared Folders**
- **What Is the Folder Redirection Process?**
- **How to Troubleshoot Access to Offline Files**

Introduction

Offline files provide access to network files and folders from a local disk when the network is unavailable. This feature is particularly useful when access to information is critical, when network connections are unstable, or when using mobile computers. This lesson describes offline files, how to specify when and how they are synchronized, how to use file caching, and how to combine folder redirection with offline folders. These tasks and some common troubleshooting scenarios are addressed in this lesson.

Lesson objectives

After completing this lesson, you will be able to:

- Explain offline files.
- Configure offline file settings.
- Explain file caching.
- Explain cache settings for shared folders.
- Describe the folder redirection process.

What Are Offline Files?

Offline files are files that allow you to take your computer off the network and still have access to shared files

For more information, see Knowledge Base article 312221

Introduction

Offline files in Windows XP Professional enable mobile users to download and use shared files on their local computer when they are not connected to the network. These benefits are also useful to onsite workers who might temporarily lose network connectivity due to server maintenance or technical problems.

Note   To use offline files, Fast User Switching must be disabled on the computer.

How offline files work

When you designate a shared file for offline use, your local computer downloads and caches a local copy of the file. You can then continue to work on this file, even if you are not connected to the network. When you connect to the network again, the operating system automatically compares any changes that you made to the offline file with the original copy and attempts to resolve any differences. This means that you do not need to manually update copies of offline files every time you reconnect to the network—the operating system does this for you.

Offline files are primarily used by people who work on portable computers and require sporadic access to network files.

Where are offline files stored?

When a user implements offline files, Windows XP Professional creates a new hidden system folder named CSC within the operating system directory to cache files that have been made available offline on the local computer. The CSC folder is transparent to the user of offline files. The user continues to access these shared resources as if they were still on the network, from within Windows Explorer or My Network Places.

Network resources that are designated for offline use are marked with an offline folder icon. When working offline, even though the user is accessing local cached copies of the network shared files, the files and folders appear to be in the same location as when accessing them online.

Encrypting offline files

In Windows XP Professional, you can encrypt offline files to secure private information or data. When you encrypt offline files, only your user account can access the cached data.

Note   For detailed instructions on how to encrypt offline files, see article 312221 in the Microsoft Knowledge Base.

How to Configure Offline File Settings

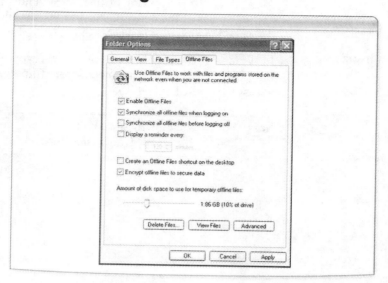

Introduction	Before you can use the offline files feature, you must enable it.
How to configure offline files	To configure offline files:

1. Click **Start**, and then click **My Computer**.

2. On the **Tools** menu, click **Folder Options**.

3. On the **Offline Files** tab, select the **Enable Offline Files** check box, and then click **OK**.

How to make shared files available offline

After you enable offline files, you can specify which files you want to make available when you are not connected to the network.

To make shared network files or folders available when you are offline:

1. Right-click the file or folder, and on the context menu, click **Make Available Offline**.

2. In the Offline Files Wizard, click **Next**.

3. Select the **Automatically synchronize Offline Files when I log on and log off my computer** check box, and then click **Next**.

4. If you want to create a shortcut to the files on your desktop, select the **Create a shortcut to the Offline Files folder on my desktop** check box.

5. Click **Finish**.

The files are copied to your computer.

How to adjust offline file settings

To adjust offline file settings:

- In Windows Explorer, on the **Tools** menu, click **Folder Options**, and then click the **Offline Files** tab.

Use the **Offline Files** tab to change any or all of the following settings:

- When the computer synchronizes offline files.

- Whether to enable reminders, which causes a notification balloon to appear over the system tray when a computer goes offline. If you select this option, you can also specify how often the reminder balloon is displayed after the computer goes offline.

- Whether to create a shortcut icon for the offline files folder on the desktop.

- Whether to encrypt offline files as an extra security precaution for sensitive data.

- The amount of disk space that is allocated for storing offline files that are automatically cached. This does not affect the files that the user makes available offline.

The **Offline Files** tab also displays three buttons:

- Delete Files. Allows you to remove selected offline files from the local computer. This does not delete the files from the network location.

- View Files. Allows you to view the contents of the offline files folder, which shows all files made available offline, along with their type, synchronization information, availability, access, location, size in the Knowledge Base when last modified, and the status of the server.

- Advanced. Allows you to specify what happens if you are connected to the network and the connection is lost. For example, you can configure the operating system to notify you that you are offline and allow you to continue working with network resources offline.

How to enable remote sharing while offline

For Windows XP to make network shares available offline, the computer that is sharing those files must have caching enabled in the properties of that share.

When creating a new share, offline caching is enabled by default. Share owners can prevent a share's contents from being available for offline use by other computers. If you are unable to configure shared resources to be available offline, caching may have been disabled on the computer on which the share resides.

What Is Synchronization of Offline Files?

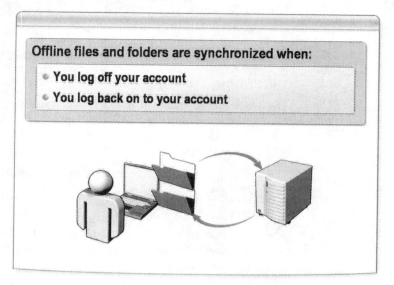

> **Offline files and folders are synchronized when:**
> - You log off your account
> - You log back on to your account

Introduction

To ensure that users are always working with the most current version of a file, offline files implement synchronization.

What is synchronization?

Synchronization is the process of ensuring that shared content on the network and its offline copy are the same. Synchronization takes place when a computer containing offline content logs on or off the network. When a computer logs on to the network, synchronization occurs with the offline resource. When a computer logs off of the network, synchronization occurs with the shared resource.

Note   Users may have issues with synchronization if the shared resource changes while the computer containing the offline content is disconnected from the network.

How synchronization works

When synchronization takes place between a shared resource and its offline copy, the operating system compares the two copies and performs the following tasks, depending on the state of the two copies since the last synchronization:

- If the content of the offline file has changed and the content of the shared copy has not changed, the operating system updates the shared copy with the offline copy.

- If the content of the offline file has not changed and the content of the shared copy has changed, the operating system updates the offline copy to reflect the changes.

- If both the shared copy and the offline copy have changed, the user can keep the offline version, the original shared version, or both.

- If either the offline copy or the shared copy of a file is deleted, the file on the other computer is deleted as well, as long as the offline copy was not changed since the last synchronization.

- If the shared copy has been deleted and the offline copy was changed, a dialog box is presented to the user with the offline copy. The user has the option of saving the offline file on the share on which it originated or deleting the offline copy.

- If the offline copy has been deleted and the shared copy has been changed, the user can delete the shared copy or replace the offline copy with the shared copy.

- If a new file has been added on the share to a folder that the user has marked for offline availability, the new file is copied to the user's cache of the computer on which the offline copy resides.

How to customize synchronization settings

In addition to the default logoff and logon synchronization scheme, you can instruct the operating system to synchronize at other times. To customize synchronization settings, in Windows Explorer, on the **Tools** menu, select **Synchronize**.

The Synchronization Manager provides a central location where you can view and synchronize all the shared files that you have made available offline. You may specify when the synchronization process occurs. For example, you can synchronize:

- Every time you log on to your computer, every time you log off, or both.

- At specific intervals while your computer is idle.

- At scheduled times.

- Any combination of these options. These options can be specified for each offline resource.

Note   If you attempt to synchronize offline files while you are still offline, or if you configure synchronization at specific intervals or times, the operating system will attempt to connect to the network using available dial-up and virtual private network (VPN) connections.

What Is File Caching?

File caching:

- Helps eliminate unnecessary network traffic when remote computers log on to a shared network resource
- Creates a temporary copy of data

Pinning:

- When you make a file available offline, you pin that file to your local file cache
- The total number of files that you can pin, or make available offline, is limited by your cache size limits

---

Introduction

File caching is a feature designed to help eliminate unnecessary network traffic when remote computers log on to a network shared resource. Caching creates a more localized, temporary copy of data to improve speed and reduce communications time. The concept is applied across a wide variety of computer-based technologies and is not limited in scope to file sharing.

Offline files are one form of file caching used by computers running Windows XP.

What is pinning a file?

To *pin a file* means to make a network file available for offline use. When enabling caching of shared files, you enable remote computers to pin local, cached copies of your shared resources to the local computer. On a client computer, the total number of files that you can pin is determined by your cache size limits.

What is the default cache size?

By default, Windows XP prevents the cache size of a computer from exceeding 10 percent of the size of the partition on which Windows is installed.

Warning When you reach the limit of your cache size, Windows begins to discard older files from the cache and replace them with newer files.

How to increase or decrease the cache size

To increase or decrease the cache size:

1. Click **Start**, and then click **My Computer**.

2. On the **Tools** menu, click **Folder Options**, and then click the **Offline Files** tab.

3. Move the **Amount of disk space to use for temporary offline files** slider to the appropriate position.

Note You cannot move or extend the cache to another partition. .

How to Define Cache Settings for Shared Folders

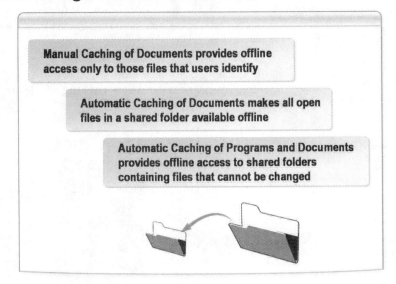

Manual Caching of Documents provides offline access only to those files that users identify

Automatic Caching of Documents makes all open files in a shared folder available offline

Automatic Caching of Programs and Documents provides offline access to shared folders containing files that cannot be changed

Introduction

When a shared resource is made available on a network, you can control the cache settings for that shared resource. This allows you to determine how files inside each of your shares are accessed by remote users.

The cache settings defined on the computer on which the shared resource resides dictate the caching behavior of the client computers that connect to the shared resource, not the computer on which the share resides.

How to define cache settings

To define cache settings for shared folders:

1. Right-click a shared folder, and then click **Properties**.

2. Click the **Sharing** tab, and then click **Caching**.

3. In the Caching Settings window, make the appropriate selection in the **Settings** list, and then click **OK** twice. This list contains the available cache settings:

   - Manual Caching of Documents. Provides caching only to those files that users specifically identify for offline use. This caching option is ideal for a shared folder containing files that several people will access and modify when not on the network. Manual caching is the default option when you create a new share.

   - Automatic Caching of Documents. Makes every file in a shared folder cache to a local computer automatically when the computer first accesses the share. When you open a cached document from a client computer, the cached copy is used, but the original document on the share is also opened to prevent other people from changing the file while you have it open.

- Automatic Caching of Programs and Documents. Provides automatic, read-only caching of files from the share. This is ideal for shares containing static configuration files for network-based applications and for providing access to documents that are not intended for editing by others.

In the Caching Settings window, you can also disable caching for a shared resource by clearing the **Allow caching of files in this shared folder** check box.

What Is the Folder Redirection Process?

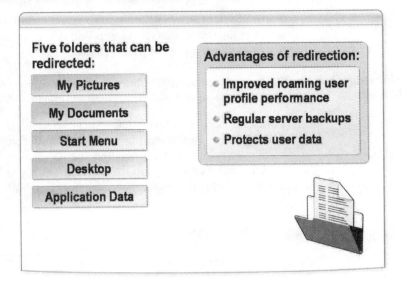

Introduction

Folder redirection allows network administrators to change the path of a folder on a user's computer to point to a different location. This new location can be another folder on the user's local computer or a network share. This feature helps information technology (IT) departments to reduce the administrative costs of managing large numbers of users and all of the data that those users generate and require access to.

Folders that can be redirected

Redirection is implemented by an extension to Group Policy. Only five folders can be redirected on a computer running Windows XP:

- My Documents
- My Pictures
- Application Data
- Desktop
- Start Menu

A user can determine where a folder is redirected by right-clicking the folder and clicking **Properties**. The **Target folder location** field specifies where the folder is currently redirected.

Advantages of folder redirection

Folder redirection provides a number of advantages to network administrators:

- Improved roaming user profile performance. With folder redirection properly configured, not all of the data in the user profile is transferred to the desktop each time the user logs on—only the data the user requires.
- Data stored on a shared network server can be backed up as part of routine system administration. This is safer and it requires no action on the part of the user.
- Data specific to a user can be redirected to a different hard disk on the user's local computer from the hard disk holding the operating system files. This protects the user's data if the operating system must be reinstalled.

- When the user logs on to different computers, folder redirection can make the same documents available to the user from any computer on the network.

- Administrators can use Group Policy to set disk quotas, limiting the amount of space taken up by users' folders.

Combining redirection and offline files

Folder redirection and offline files can be effectively combined to improve the availability and reliability of redirected files.

For example, if a company has a sales associate who often travels with her portable computer, an administrator can configure the sales associate's My Documents folder to be redirected to a server share, which simplifies data backup, and then configure Automatic Caching of Documents for that share to ensure that she always has access to her files while away from the office.

How to Troubleshoot Access to Offline Files

Common support issues with offline files

- Not compatible with Fast User Switching
- Cannot be enabled for offline use
- Cannot be synchronized
- Unable to make encrypted files available offline
- Cannot browse to offline files combined with folder redirection

Introduction

When troubleshooting access to offline files, you should first determine if an offline files issue is a caching issue or a share permissions issue. If you believe it to be a share permissions issue, see the topic How to Troubleshoot Access to Shared Files and Folders in this module.

Note Windows XP Home Edition does not provide the offline files feature.

Common offline file configuration issues and solutions

When troubleshooting offline files, you may encounter issues relating to offline files configuration. Some of these issues and their solutions are:

- The user cannot enable offline files. Ensure that Fast User Switching is disabled. Offline files are not compatible with Fast User Switching.

- The user is unable to make certain files available for offline use. Some types of files cannot be synchronized for offline use, including Microsoft Outlook® Personal Folders files (.pst) and files with the .dbf extension, which may be database files or Microsoft Outlook Express folders.

- If shared files are open when the user synchronizes, that is, in use by someone else or by another running process, the user cannot make these files available offline. Instruct the user to ensure that the shared resources are not in use by another user. It might be helpful for the user to restart the computer and try to make the shared resource available offline again.

- The user is unable to make encrypted files available offline. This can happen for several reasons:

  - The user is not an administrator on the local computer.

  - The local volume is not formatted as NTFS.

  - A system administrator has implemented an encryption policy for offline caching.

  - The user's computer is running Windows XP Home Edition. Offline files are not available in Windows XP Home Edition.

Caution   When users select encrypted files for offline access, the local cached copies will be *unencrypted*. Working offline with decrypted files can be dangerous, especially when using a portable computer, because portable computers have a high rate of theft and intrusion. Encourage users not to work offline with decrypted files.

Common offline synchronization issues and solutions

When troubleshooting offline files, you might encounter issues relating to synchronization. Some of these issues and their solutions are:

- The user is prompted to keep the original copy, the offline copy, or both. This indicates that the original shared copy has been changed in the user's absence. Always instruct the user to keep both copies and to check with the network administrator regarding how to merge the offline file changes into the shared copy.

- The user has deleted an offline file but the shared copy of the file is still on the network share. This is expected behavior. It indicates that another user has made a change to the shared file because the user last synchronized the shared file to the offline file. Instruct the user to either ignore the file or determine who changed the network copy of the file.

- The user is receiving synchronization errors at various times when away from the network. Whenever the user's computer connects to *any* network, Windows will attempt to resynchronize offline files. The user can either safely ignore these messages or attempt to reconfigure the synchronization and caching settings in the **Advanced** dialog box of the **Offline Files** tab of the **Windows Explorer Tools** menu.

Common folder redirection issues and solutions

If a user is unable to browse to the My Documents folder from within Windows Explorer, check the redirection setting of the My Documents folder. It has most likely been redirected to a network share. This behavior is expected, and the user should access the My Documents folder directly from the My Documents desktop shortcut instead of Windows Explorer.

Practice: Troubleshooting Access to Offline Folders

In this practice, you will:

- Configure a shared folder and its contents to be available offline
- Configure offline settings for the shared folder
- Determine if a folder is being redirected to the server

Objectives

In this practice, you will:

- Configure a shared folder and its contents to be available offline.
- Configure offline settings for the shared folder.
- Determine if a folder is being redirected to the server.

Scenario

A user calls and says she would like to have access to the departmental folders when she is away from the office. When she is away from the office, she is rarely connected to the Internet and does not want to manage the process of copying files from the server to her laptop because in the past this process has caused version control problems with documents. Additionally, she does not always know which documents she'll need when she's away from the office.

Practice

▶ **Configure a shared folder and its contents to be available offline using offline files**

1. Resume the 2261_Acapulco and 2261_London virtual machine.

2. On Acapulco, log on to the domain as **Samantha** with a password of **P@ssw0rd**

3. Click **Start**, click **Run**, type **\\London** in the **Open** box, and then click **OK**.

4. In the London window, right-click **RAHelp**, and then click **Make Available Offline**.

5. On the **Welcome to the Offline Files Wizard** page, click **Next**.

6. Select the **Automatically synchronize Offline Files when I log on and log off my computer** check box, and then click **Next**.

7. Click **Finish**.

8. Close all windows and log off Acapulco.

▶ **Configure offline settings for the shared folder**

1. Log on locally to Acapulco as Administrator with a password of **P@ssw0rd**

2. Click **Start**, and then click **My Computer**.

3. In the My Computer window, click **Tools**, and then click **Folder Options**.

4. On the **Offline Files** tab, on the slide bar labeled **Amount of disk space to use for temporary offline files**, decrease the amount of disk space to use for temporary offline files to five percent of the drive.

5. Select the **Encrypt offline files to secure data** check box.

6. Click **View Files**.

7. Close the Offline Files Folder window.

8. In the Folder Options window, click **OK**.

9. Close all windows.

▶ **Determine if a folder is being redirected to the server**

1. Click **Start**, right-click **My Documents**, and then click **Properties**.

   Has your My Documents folder been redirected or is it local?

   _____

2. Close the My Documents Properties window.

3. Log off Acapulco.

▶ **To enable redirection**

1. On London, log on as **Administrator** with the password **P@ssw0rd**

2. Click **Start**, point to **Administrative Tools**, and then click **Active Directory Users and Computers**.

3. In **Active Directory Users and Computers**, right-click **nwtraders.msft**, and then click **Properties**.

4. On the **Group Policy** tab, click **UserFolderRedirect**, and then click **Options**.

5. Clear the **Disabled** checkbox, and then click **OK**.

6. In the **nwtraders.msft Properties** dialog box, click **OK**.

▶ **Determine if a folder is being redirected to the server again**

1. On Acapulco, log on to the domain as **Samantha** with the password **P@ssw0rd**.

2. Click **Start**, and then click **Run**.

3. In the **Open** box, type **gpupdate /force** and then click **OK**.

4. At the command prompt, type **y** and then press ENTER.

5. On Acapulco, log back on to the domain as **Samantha** with the password **P@ssw0rd**.

6. Click **Start**, right-click **My Documents**, and then click **Properties**.

   What is listed in the **Target** box of the **My Document Properties** dialog box?

   _____

   Has your My Documents folder been redirected or is it local?

   _____

7. For all running and paused virtual machines, on the Virtual PC window, on the **Action** menu, click **Close**, select **Turn off and delete changes**, and then click **OK**.

Lab: Resolving File and Folder Issues

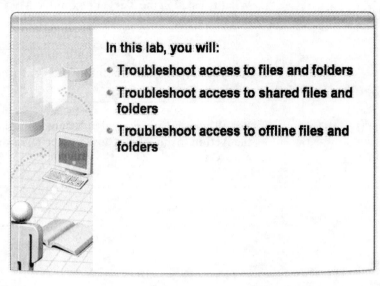

Objectives

After completing this lab, you will be able to:

- Troubleshoot access to files and folders.
- Troubleshoot access to shared files and folders.
- Troubleshoot access to offline files and folders.

Prerequisites

Before working on this lab, you must have an understanding of how to use Microsoft Virtual PC.

Before You Begin

For each exercise in this lab, use a password of **P@ssw0rd**.

In Virtual PC, <right>ALT+DEL is the equivalent of CTRL+ALT+DEL.

Scenario

You are a DST for Northwind Traders, a company whose workers use Microsoft Windows XP Professional.

Estimated time to complete this lab: 60 minutes

Exercise 1
Troubleshooting File and Folder Issues

In this exercise, you will troubleshoot issues related to files and folders.

Scenario

A user calls and says he cannot access a folder. He was very concerned about security, so he used the Security tab to modify permissions and also encrypted the file. Now he can access it from other user accounts and the Administrator account, but he cannot access it when logged on as Acapulco\Frank Lee.

Tasks	Guidance for completing the task
1. Start the 2261_Acapulco virtual machine, and using Acapulco log on locally as \Administrator.	■ Use the Virtual PC console.
2. Using Acapulco, navigate to C:\Program Files \Microsoft Learning\2261 \Labfiles\Lab06\ and run 2261_Lab06_Ex1.	■ This step introduces the problem.
3. Log off Acapulco and back on as Frank Lee	
Navigate to C:\Program Files \Microsoft Learning\2261 \Labfiles\Lab06\Exercise_1.	*denied*
4. Were you able to successfully view the contents of the folder?	*no*
5. Resolve the inaccessible folder issue.	■ Refer to the How to Troubleshoot File and Folder Management Issues topic in this module. ■ Successful resolution of this issue will result in the Frank Lee account having Full Control of the Exercise_1 folder.
6. Close all windows and log off Acapulco.	

Exercise 2
Troubleshooting Access to Shared Files and Folders

In this exercise, you will troubleshoot issues related to shared files and folders.

Scenario

A user calls and says he is unable to access a file on the network.

Tasks	Guidance for completing the task
1. Start the 2261_London virtual machine and log on as Administrator.	▪ Use the Virtual PC console.
2. On London, navigate to C:\Program Files \Microsoft Learning\2261 \Labfiles\Lab06\ and run 2261_Lab06_Ex2	▪ This step introduces the problem.
3. On Acapulco, log on as NWTRADERS\Samantha.	
On Acapulco, navigate to \\London\Exercise_2.	
4. Were you able to successfully view the contents of the folder?	
5. Were you able to successfully open the Ex2.txt file?	
6. Resolve the inaccessible folder issue.	▪ Refer to the How to Troubleshoot Access to Shared Files and Folders topic in this module. ▪ Successful resolution of this issue will result in the Samantha account having Full Control of the Exercise_2 folder and the ability to open, edit, and save the Ex2.txt file.

Exercise 3
Troubleshooting Offline Access to Files and Folders

In this exercise, you will troubleshoot issues related to access to files and folders.

Scenario

A user calls and says he created a file named London.txt and that it must have been deleted because when he opens the network folder, it is not there. He is surprised by this because he recently configured that folder to be available offline.

Tasks	Guidance for completing the task
1. Log on to Acapulco as NWTRADERS \AcapulcoAdmin with a password of **P@ssword**	■ Use the Virtual PC console. ■ London should still be running.
2. Using Acapulco, configure \\london\OfflineFolder\ to be available offline.	
On Acapulco, configure Disable the Local Area Connection.	
On Acapulco, navigate to \\london\OfflineFolder and create a file named Acapulco.txt.	
On London, navigate to C:\Program Files\Microsoft Learning\2261\Labfiles\Lab 06\OfflineFolder.	
3. Is Acapulco.txt listed in the Offline folder? Why not?	
4. On London, in the C:\Program Files\Microsoft Learning\2261\Labfiles\Lab 06\OfflineFolder directory, create London.txt.	
On London, edit Ex3.txt, save and close it.	
On Acapulco, navigate to \\London\OfflineFolder and locate London.txt.	
5. Is London.txt listed in the Offline folder? Why not?	

(*continued*)

Tasks	Guidance for completing the task
6. On Acapulco, navigate to \\London\OfflineFolder and edit the Ex3.txt file.	▪ Insert some text into the Ex3.txt file, then save and close it.
7. On Acapulco, enable the Local Area Connection and synchronize files.	
8. Did the file synchronization complete successfully?	
9. Are you able to locate the London.txt file? Why or why not?	
10. Resolve the synchronization issue.	▪ Refer to the How to Configure Offline File Settings topic in this module. ▪ A successful resolution to this exercise results in the same set of files being available offline and online.

Course Evaluation

Your evaluation of this course will help Microsoft understand the quality of your learning experience.

At a convenient time before the end of the course, please complete a course evaluation, which is available at http://www.CourseSurvey.com.

Microsoft will keep your evaluation strictly confidential and will use your responses to improve your future learning experience.

Module 7: Resolving Printer Issues

Contents

Overview

- **Installing Local and Network Printers**
- **Troubleshooting Printer Drivers**
- **Troubleshooting Printers and Print Jobs**

Introduction

Users can connect a printer directly to a local computer and print documents from that computer, or they can share the local printer with other users on the network. A user on a network might also connect to a shared network printer that is attached to another computer on the network, or even attached directly to the network itself. Microsoft® Windows® XP Professional and Microsoft Windows XP Home Edition offer many advanced options for implementing printers locally or on a network, including the ability to operate printers in groups so that print jobs from different network locations can be routed to an available printer for faster printing.

As a desktop support technician (DST), you must understand how to install a local printer and share it with the network. You must also know how to access a shared printer, control access to printers, configure printers, and manage documents that are waiting to be printed.

Objectives

After completing this module, students will be able to:

- Install local and network printers.
- Troubleshoot issues with printer drivers.
- Troubleshoot issues with printers and print jobs.

Lesson: Installing Local and Network Printers

- Understanding Printer Terminology
- How to Install and Uninstall Local Printers
- How to Install and Uninstall Network Printers
- How to Troubleshoot Printer Installations

Introduction

Installing printers is a basic function that all DSTs and most users should be able to perform. Many printers support automatic Plug and Play detection, and Windows XP automatically starts the installation process when the printer first connects to the computer. If a printer is not Plug and Play compliant, the printer may require manual installation. The steps that are involved in installing a printer depend on whether the printer is connected directly to a computer or if it is connected to another computer that is available on a network. As a DST, you must be able to assist users in installing, configuring, and troubleshooting both local and network printers.

Lesson objectives

After completing this lesson, you will be able to:

- Understand common printer terminology.
- Install and uninstall local printers.
- Install and uninstall network printers.

Understanding Printer Terminology

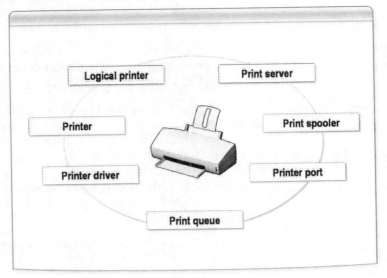

Introduction

To successfully resolve printer issues, you must first understand the printing concepts and terminology that are used in a Microsoft environment. This section describes important printer terminology.

Logical printer

A *logical printer* is the software configuration that is created in Windows XP and represented by an icon in the Printers and Faxes window. The logical printer controls the printer's configuration and the way in which Windows sends documents to the printer.

Note In previous versions of Windows, Microsoft made an important distinction using the terms *printer* and *print device*. Prior to Windows XP, a *printer* was the software on the computer that controlled printing and a *print device* referred to the actual hardware device. The two terms were not used interchangeably. In Windows XP, the terminology has changed. The Windows XP documentation generally defines the *printer* as "a device that puts text or images on paper or other print media" and the *logical printer* as the "collection of software components that interface between the operating system and the printer."

Printer

A *printer* is the actual physical device that performs the printing. This is usually a printer but could also be a fax device or a plotter.

Printer driver

A *printer driver* is a software program that enables other programs to communicate with a particular printer. To assure users that they are using the highest quality drivers, Microsoft digitally signs the printer drivers that pass the Windows Hardware Quality Lab (WHQL) tests. This digital signature is associated with individual driver packages and is recognized natively by Windows.

Print queue

A *print queue* is a buffer for documents and images that are waiting to be printed.

Print server

A *print server* is a computer or other network device that has a printer physically attached to it and shares that printer with the network. When a user's computer running Windows XP is sharing a locally attached printer with the network, the user's computer is referred to as the *print server*.

Print spooler

A *print spooler* is a software program that intercepts a print job on its way to the printer and sends it to disk or memory instead, where the print job is held until the printer is ready for it. In other words, the print spooler receives, processes, schedules, and distributes documents for printing.

The process of *print spooling* increases user productivity because after the job has been spooled, the application is released, and the user can continue working while the printing process continues in the background. Print spooling also ensures that print jobs will be saved in the event of a computer, application, or printer failure. In addition, when a client is printing to a printer on the network, print spooling also manages the routing of the print job from the client to the appropriate print server.

Printer port

A *printer port* is the means through which a printer is connected to a computer. The most common types of ports used for printing are:

- Parallel port. Sends and receives data 8 bits at a time, in parallel, using a 25-pin connector called a *DB-25 connector*. In the past, printers were usually connected through the parallel port, which is typically identified in the operating system by the logical device name LPT. The term printer port is often used synonymously with parallel port.

- Universal Serial Bus (USB) port. Connects up to 127 peripherals, such as external CD-ROM drives, printers, modems, pointing devices, and keyboards, to the system through a single, general-purpose port. A USB port is designed to automatically add and configure new devices and add devices without having to shut down and restart the system.

- Institute of Electrical and Electronics Engineers (IEEE) 1394 port. Uses a high-speed, serial bus input/output (I/O) standard and a 4- or 6-pin connector. The IEEE 1394 bus is used primarily to connect digital video and audio devices, but some new printers support this type of port. Most printers use USB connections.

- Infrared ports. Optical ports on printers that interface with infrared-capable devices. Infrared ports use infrared light to wirelessly transfer information between a computer and another computer, or device such as a printer.

- Virtual network printing ports. Software-based instead of using a physical connector on the computer. Communication with the printer is accomplished by using standard networking protocols over a network.

Note   To learn more about printing terminology and to test your knowledge, see the activity *Printing Terminology*. To start the activity, open the Web page on the Student Materials compact disc, click **Multimedia**, and then click the title of the activity. Do not start this activity unless you are instructed to do so by the instructor.

How to Install and Uninstall Local Printers

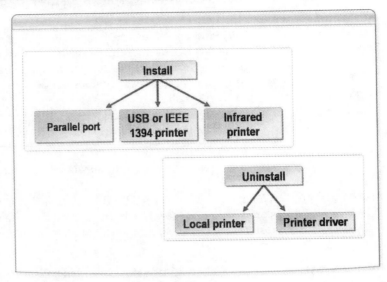

What is a local printer?	A *local printer* is a printer that is attached directly to a computer. Printers typically come with an installation CD that is provided by the manufacturer that includes a custom wizard to install the necessary drivers and to configure printer settings automatically. The best method for installing a new printer is to use this CD and follow the manufacturer's setup instructions.
	If, however, the manufacturer's installation CD is not available, connect the printer to the appropriate port on the computer, and ensure that the printer is turned on and that it indicates that it is ready to print. Although most new printers support Plug and Play, and Windows automatically detects and installs most printers, additional input may be required to complete the installation.
	If a printer is not Plug and Play compliant, you must use the Add Printer Wizard to install it. The Add Printer Wizard is located in the Printers and Faxes folder, which is accessible from the Start menu or Control Panel.
How to install a local printer connected to a parallel port	Printers are generally connected to a parallel port (also called an LPT port). A *parallel port* is an I/O connector for a parallel interface device. (A *parallel interface device* uses a parallel connection to simultaneously transmit both data and control bits over wires connected in parallel.)
	To install a local printer that is connected to a parallel port:

1. Attach the parallel cable to the printer and the computer, and turn on the printer.
2. Click **Start**, and then click **Printers and Faxes**.
3. In the **Printers and Faxes** dialog box, in the left pane, under **Printer Tasks**, click **Add a printer**.
4. In the Add Printer Wizard, click **Next**.

5. Click **Local Printer attached to this computer**, verify that the **Automatically detect and install my Plug and Play printer** check box is selected, and then click **Next**.

   If Windows XP detects a printer, depending on the printer you are installing, a Found New Hardware message or the Found New Hardware Wizard appears to notify you that the printer has been detected and that installation has begun. If Windows XP does not detect a printer, you must install the printer manually.

   Note The procedure for installing a printer manually is described below.

6. Follow the instructions in the wizard to complete the printer installation.

How to install a USB or IEEE 1394 printer

When Windows detects a USB or IEEE 1394 printer, Windows automatically starts the Found New Hardware Wizard. You do not need to shut down or restart the computer; simply follow the instructions on the screen to finish the setup.

How to install a printer that uses infrared communication

Windows automatically detects and installs printers that use infrared light to communicate with computers. To establish a wireless infrared connection, ensure that the infrared-enabled computer and the printer are turned on, and then position the computer and printer within approximately one meter of each other. After several seconds, the computer recognizes the printer, and the appropriate drivers are installed on the computer.

How to manually install a printer

If Windows does not automatically detect a printer, you must install the printer manually.

To manually install a printer:

1. In Printers and Faxes, click **Add a printer** to start the Add Printer Wizard, and then click **Next**.

2. Select **Local printer**, clear the **Automatically detect and install my Plug and Play printer** check box, and then click **Next**.

3. To complete setup, follow the instructions in the wizard to select a printer port, select the manufacturer and model of the printer, and type a name for the printer.

   Note If a particular printer driver is not included with Windows, Windows prompts you to insert a manufacturer's disk that contains the driver.

To connect to a shared printer, install the printer as a local printer and then configure a Transmission Control Protocol/Internet Protocol (TCP/IP) port, which acts like a virtual printer port. You must know the Internet Protocol (IP) address of the printer and the type of network interface that the printer uses.

How to uninstall a local printer

The best method for uninstalling a local printer is to use the custom uninstall program that is provided by the manufacturer. If a custom uninstall program is unavailable, you must remove the printer manually.

To manually uninstall a local printer:

1. Shut down the computer and physically remove the printer connection.

2. Restart the computer.

3. In Printers and Faxes, right-click the icon of the printer you want to uninstall, and then click **Delete**.

Note Uninstalling a local printer deletes the printer device only—it does not delete the printer driver.

---

4. On the **File** menu, click **Server Properties**.

5. On the **Drivers** tab, click the name of the driver for the printer that you deleted, click **Remove**, click **Yes**, and then click **Close**.

Note Windows XP Professional users must be members of the Administrators or Power Users groups to install a printer. Windows XP Home Edition users must have a user account of the Computer Administrator type to install a printer. For more information about user access issues, see Module 3, "Resolving Desktop Management Issues" and Module 6, "File and Folder Issues" of this course.

How to Install and Uninstall Network Printers

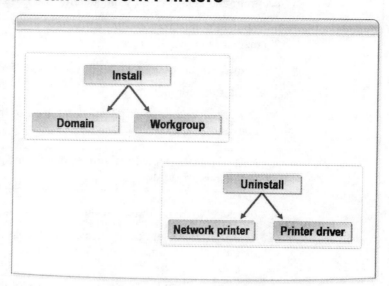

Introduction

In a network environment, you can make printers available to other network users by sharing the printer. When a printer is shared, a user can install the printer through the network. Using a network printer requires an appropriate printer driver and access rights to the printer.

How to install a network printer

To install a network printer:

1. In Printers and Faxes, in the left pane, under Printer Tasks, click **Add a printer**.

2. In the Add Printer Wizard, click **Next**.

3. Click **A network printer, or a printer attached to another computer**, and then click **Next**.

   At this point, the procedure for installing a network printer differs slightly depending on whether you are in a workgroup or a domain.

   If you are in a domain:

   a. Click **Find a printer in the directory**, and then click **Next**.

      You can search for printers that are available to you by domain, printer name, location, and model.

   b. Define your search parameters, and then click **Find Now**. A list of available printers that match your search criteria is displayed.

   c. Select the printer that you want to install, and then click **OK**.

If you are in a workgroup:

a. Click **Connect to this printer** (or to browse for a printer, select this option and click **Next**), and then in the Name field, type the Universal Naming Convention (UNC) name of the printer as *\\server\printer*, where *server* is the name of the network computer that you want to connect to, and *printer* is the name of the shared printer. (*UNC* is a format for specifying the location of resources on a local area network, or LAN).

Tip   You can also leave the Name field blank and click **Next** to browse for a shared printer.

b. Browse through the list of shared printers, select the printer you want to install, and then click **Next**.

When you select a printer to install, the computer that is sharing the printer automatically downloads the necessary drivers for that printer.

Note   Products in the Microsoft Windows Server™ 2003 family support several advanced printer features. One of these features enables Windows XP users to use a printer without installing the device driver. The driver is downloaded automatically when the client connects to a print server computer running the Windows Server 2003 family operating system.

How to uninstall a network printer

To uninstall a network printer:

1. Right-click the icon for the printer that you want to uninstall, and then click **Delete**.

Note   Uninstalling a network printer deletes only the printer device; the printer driver is not deleted.

2. On the **File** menu, click **Server Properties**.

3. On the **Drivers** tab, click the name of the driver for the printer that you deleted, click **Remove**, click **Yes**, and then click **Close**.

How to Troubleshoot Printer Installations

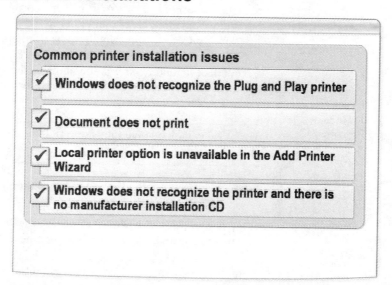

Common printer installation issues

✓ Windows does not recognize the Plug and Play printer

✓ Document does not print

✓ Local printer option is unavailable in the Add Printer Wizard

✓ Windows does not recognize the printer and there is no manufacturer installation CD

Introduction

As a DST, there are some basic troubleshooting techniques that you can use to troubleshoot printer installation issues. This section describes common printer issues and their solutions.

Common printer installation issues

Although most problems that are associated with printer installations involve printer drivers, which are covered in the next lesson, there are issues that you may encounter that are not driver related. Some common issues and their solutions are:

- A user says that Windows does not recognize the Plug and Play printer.

  Begin troubleshooting by asking the most basic questions, such as "Is there power connected to the printer?" and "Is the printer turned on?" After you troubleshoot the most basic issues, begin troubleshooting more complex issues, such as verifying that the cables are properly connected, and determining the type of connection to the computer.

- A user installed a printer with the Add Printer Wizard and everything seemed to work, but when the user sends a file to the printer, he receives a message that the document did not print.

  Verify that the user selected the correct port. The wizard defaults to the parallel port, which is LPT1, but the printer may be attached to a different port, such as a serial port or COM port (communication port). (A *COM port* is a port on a computer that allows *asynchronous communication* or data transmission in which information is sent at irregular intervals one byte at a time.)

- A user attempts to install a local printer, but the local printer option in the Add Printer Wizard is unavailable.

  Verify that the user has the correct local privileges on that computer to install a printer.

- A user has a printer from a lesser-known manufacturer or a manufacturer who is no longer in business. Windows is unable to recognize the printer and an installation CD is not available from the manufacturer.

  Research whether the printer emulates a well-known printer. Some printers are clones of models that are produced by other manufacturers. You can attempt to use the driver for the better-known printer.

Tools for troubleshooting printer installations

Windows XP includes a wizard to help troubleshoot printing issues. To access the Microsoft Windows XP Printing Troubleshooter:

- In Printers and Faxes, in the left pane, click **Troubleshoot printing**.

  – Or –

- Double-click the printer's icon, and then on the **Help** menu, click **Troubleshooter**.

Verify that a printer is correctly installed

After you determine the problem with the printer, you can use the following methods to verify that the printer is correctly installed:

- Print a test page.
- On non-PostScript printers, print from the command line. Open a command prompt, and then type **Dir > LPT1**.
- To determine if the printing issue lies with the printer or with the application from which the user is printing, print from a different application such as Notepad. Open Notepad, type some text, and then attempt to print the file. If a user can print from Notepad, the correct printer driver is installed, and the problem lies with the application. If a user cannot print from Notepad, the problem lies with the printer driver.

Additional reading

For more information on troubleshooting printer installations, see article 308028 in the Microsoft Knowledge Base (KB).

Practice: Installing and Creating a Local Printer

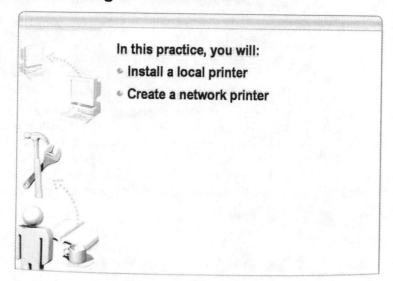

In this practice, you will:
* Install a local printer
* Create a network printer

Objectives

In this practice, you will install a local printer and create a network printer.

Practice

▶ **Install a local printer**

1. Start the 2261_London virtual machine.

2. After the Windows log in screen is displayed on London, start the 2261_Acapulco virtual machine.

3. Using Acapulco, log on to the NWTRADERS domain as **AcapulcoAdmin** with a password of **P@ssw0rd**.

4. Click **Start**, and then click **Printers and Faxes**.

5. On the Printers and Faxes page, in the Printer Tasks pane, click **Add a printer**.

6. On the Welcome page, click **Next**.

7. Click **Local printer attached to this computer**, clear the **Automatically detect and install my Plug and Play printer** check box, and then click **Next**.

8. On the Select a Printer Port page, click **Next**.

9. In the Manufacturer list, click **HP**, and in the Printers list, click **HP LaserJet 5**, and then click **Next**.

10. On the Name Your Printer page, in the **Printer name** box, type **Acapulco HP LaserJet 5** and then click **Next**.

11. On the Printer Sharing page, click **Next**.

12. On the Print Test Page page, click **No**, click **Next**, and then click **Finish**.

13. If you are prompted for a file, in the **Copy files from** box, type **c:\winxp** and then click **OK**.

▶ **Create a network printer**

1. Using Acapulco, on the Printers and Faxes page, click **Add a Printer**.

2. On the Welcome page, click **Next**.

3. On the Local or Network Printer page, click **A network printer, or a printer attached to another computer**, and then click **Next**.

4. On the Specify a Printer page, click **Find a printer in the directory**, and then click **Next**.

5. In the **Find Printers** dialog box, leave the criteria blank, click **Find Now**, click **HP Laser Jet 5**, and then click **OK**.

6. Click **Next**, and then click **Finish**.

7. On Acapulco, close all windows and log off.

8. Pause the 2261_London and 2261_Acapulco virtual machines.

Lesson: Troubleshooting Printer Drivers

- What Is a Printer Driver?
- How to Install Printer Drivers
- How to Update Printer Drivers
- How to Troubleshoot Printer Drivers

Introduction

Choosing the correct printer driver is critical to proper printer operation. If you choose an incorrect driver, one of two things is likely to happen: not all features of the printer will be available or the printer output will be incorrect. This section describes how to install, update, and troubleshoot printer drivers.

Lesson objectives

After completing this lesson, you will be able to:

- Explain the purpose and function of printer drivers.
- Install a printer driver.
- Update printer drivers.
- Troubleshoot printer drivers.

What Is a Printer Driver?

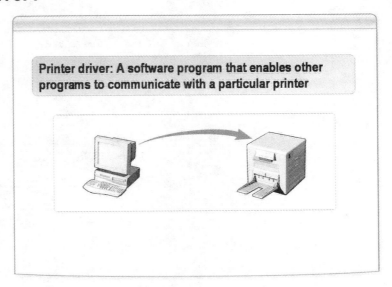

Printer driver: A software program that enables other programs to communicate with a particular printer

What is a printer driver?

A *printer driver* is a software program that enables other programs to communicate with a particular printer. Many printing issues are the result of improperly installing and configuring the printer driver or using the wrong driver.

Windows automatically installs or updates drivers from the Drivers.cab file. Drivers.cab contains thousands of commonly used files, including printer drivers. Drivers.cab is installed as part of the Windows XP Professional operating system installation.

What are printer driver files?

Printer drivers are normally composed of several files. A typical driver contains a configuration file (.ini), a driver file (.dll), a data file (.ppd), a Help file (.hlp), and one or more dependent files (.ntf).

Where are printer driver files located?

Windows XP stores printer driver files in the %systemroot%\System32\spool\ Drivers\W32X86\3 folder. You may need to access this folder if, for example, a printer driver file becomes corrupt and you need to manually delete the file from the W32X86\3 folder.

How to Install Printer Drivers

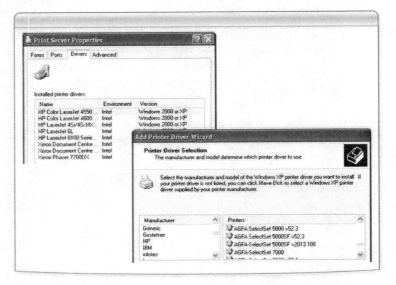

Introduction

The best method for installing a printer driver is to use the installation CD that is provided by the printer manufacturer. Most printer manufacturers include a custom wizard on the CD to install the necessary drivers and to automatically configure printer settings.

Users can also manually install printer drivers for a particular printer by using the Add Printer Wizard. When you use the wizard, the printer does not have to be attached to the computer. However, to use the Add Printer Wizard, you must specify:

- How the printer is attached to the computer; that is, whether it is a local or network printer.

- The port that the printer uses.

- The name of the printer.

How to install a printer driver

To install a printer driver by using the Add Printer Driver Wizard:

1. In Printers and Faxes, on the **File** menu, click **Server Properties**.

2. In the **Print Server Properties** dialog box, on the **Drivers** tab, click **Add**.

3. In the Add Printer Driver Wizard, click **Next**.

4. On the Printer Driver Selection page, select the manufacturer and model of the Windows XP printer driver you want to install, and then click **Next**.

5. On the Environment and Operating System Selection page, select the environment and operating system of all computers that will be using the driver you selected in the previous step, click **Next**, and then click **Finish**.

   When you complete the wizard, the printer driver is installed and the driver name appears in the list of installed drivers.

Note   After a user installs a printer driver, an icon representing the printer appears in the **Printers and Faxes** dialog box, and the user can use the printer.

How to Update Printer Drivers

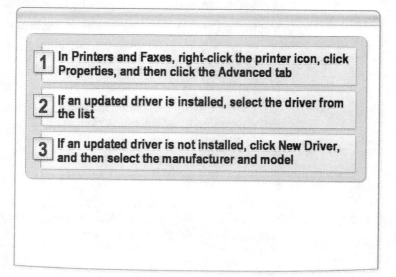

1	In Printers and Faxes, right-click the printer icon, click Properties, and then click the Advanced tab
2	If an updated driver is installed, select the driver from the list
3	If an updated driver is not installed, click New Driver, and then select the manufacturer and model

Introduction

When updating printer drivers, it is best to obtain the newest driver from the printer manufacturer and follow the recommended procedure for installing the update. Most printer manufacturers provide customized tools that automatically install the updated driver.

However, there are times when a printer driver must be manually updated. For example, if a printer is from a company that has gone out of business and the current driver is unavailable, sometimes a driver for a different type of printer can be used; however, it may require trying a number of drivers before you find one that works.

How to update a printer driver

To update a printer driver:

1. In Printers and Faxes, right-click the printer icon, and then click **Properties**.

2. In the **Properties** dialog box, on the **Advanced** tab, if an updated driver is installed, select it from the **Driver** list, click **OK**, and then complete the steps in the wizard.

3. If an updated driver is not installed:

    a. Click **New Driver** to start the Add Printer Driver Wizard.

    b. In the Add Printer Driver Wizard, select the manufacturer and model, or click **Have Disk** if you know the location of the driver files, and complete the steps in the wizard.

    Clicking **Have Disk** enables users to browse to the location where the driver files are stored, whether on the hard disk, a floppy disk, a compact disc, or a network location. After completing the wizard, the printer driver is installed and is automatically selected as the current printer.

How to Troubleshoot Printer Drivers

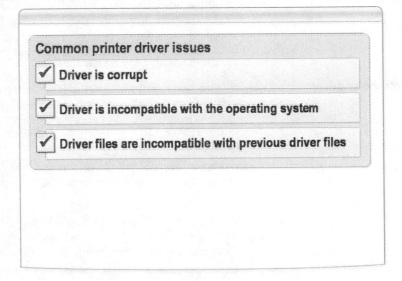

Common printer driver issues

- ✓ Driver is corrupt
- ✓ Driver is incompatible with the operating system
- ✓ Driver files are incompatible with previous driver files

Troubleshooting tips

If a user is unable to print, you can easily determine if the driver is the problem by having the user attempt to print from Notepad. If the user can print from Notepad, the printer driver is functioning correctly and the problem lies with the application. If the user cannot print from Notepad, the problem lies with the printer driver.

Another method for troubleshooting printer driver issues is to install a different printer driver, and then attempt to print a file. If the problem does not recur, the problem lies with the printer driver, and the user needs to reinstall or update the original printer driver.

Use one of the following methods to locate updated printer drivers:

- Check the printer manufacturer's Web site.
- Go to Windows Update to automatically scan the computer for new and updated printer drivers.
- Access a third-party source for printer drivers.

Choosing compatible and incompatible drivers

If you choose a compatible but incorrect driver, you will be able to use whatever features of the printer that the selected driver allows. For example, if you choose an HP LaserJet 4 driver for use with an HP LaserJet 5si printer, you would get basic printer functionality, but the enhanced font and paper-handling capabilities of the LaserJet 5si would be unavailable because the driver does not support them.

If you choose an incompatible printer driver, the printer's output will be significantly affected and, in most cases, unrecognizable. A common symptom of an incompatible driver is that the printer will produce a given character, or a line of characters, on a page for a significant period of time (potentially hundreds or thousands of pages). If this condition occurs, turn off the printer to clear its memory, delete the print job from the print queue if it is still there, and then install an appropriate driver.

> **Note** If Windows XP does not support a printer and you do not have drivers from the manufacturer, try using the driver for a similar or older printer from the same manufacturer. You will often get partial functionality until you can get the appropriate drivers for the printer. You should also check the printer's user manual for compatibility with other printers that have a Windows XP driver.

Common printer driver issues

Most problems associated with printer installations involve printer drivers. Some common issues and their solutions are:

- A user receives an error message and is unable to print because of a corrupted printer driver.

  Remove and then reinstall the driver. If during the removal process the user is prompted to remove extra files on the system, instruct the user to click **Yes**.

- When a user clicks **Finish** in the Add Printer Driver Wizard, she receives an error message indicating that the printer driver was not installed and the operation could not be completed. When this occurs:

  - The user installed a Windows 95–based, Windows 98–based, or Windows Millennium Edition–based printer driver on Windows XP. Windows 95–based and Windows 98–based printer drivers are not compatible with Windows XP.

  - Use a Windows XP–based printer driver that ships with Windows XP, or a driver from the printer manufacturer. If a Windows XP–based printer driver is unavailable, try a Windows 2000 Professional–based printer driver.

- A user's printer driver is functioning properly, and he uses System Restore to create a checkpoint to preserve the current configuration. (A *checkpoint* is a representation of a stored state of a computer.) The user then upgrades or installs a new driver with files that are shared with the currently installed driver. After the installation, the user cannot print because one of the printer driver files is incompatible with the other printer driver files that are installed on the computer. The user then restores the computer to the checkpoint that he created before using System Restore, but the printer still does not work.

  To resolve this problem, in Printers and Faxes, right-click the printer icon, click **Properties**, and then on the **Advanced** tab, in the Drivers list, select the last driver installed.

Practice: Installing Printer Drivers

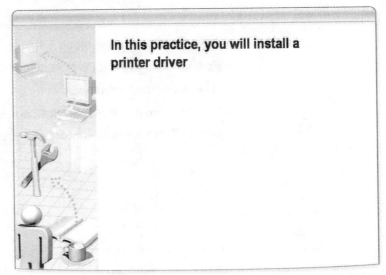

Objective

In this practice, you will install a printer driver to enable a user to print from a computer running Windows 98 to a computer running Windows XP.

Practice

▶ **To install a Windows 98 printer driver**

1. Resume the 2261_Acapulco virtual machine.

2. Using Acapulco, log on locally to Acapulco as **Administrator** with a password of **P@ssw0rd**.

3. Click **Start**, and then click **Printers and Faxes**.

4. On the **File** menu, click **Server Properties**.

5. In the **Print Server Properties** dialog box, on the **Drivers** tab, click **Add**.

6. On the **Add Printer Driver Wizard** welcome page, click **Next**.

7. On the **Printer Driver Selection** page, in the **Manufacturer** box, select **HP**, and in the **Printers** box, select **HP LaserJet 5MP,** and then click **Next**.

8. On the **Environment and Operating System Selection** page, select the **Intel, Windows 95, 98, and Me** version check box, and then click **Next**.

9. On the **Completing the Add Printer Driver Wizard** page, click **Finish**.

10. If you are prompted for a file, in the **Copy files from** box, type in **c:\winxp** and click **OK**.

11. If you are prompted to insert the Windows XP CD-ROM, click **OK**, and in the **Copy files from** box, type **c:\winxp** and then click **OK**.

12. In the **Windows 95, 98, and Me Printer Drivers** dialog box, type **c:\windows\sytstem32\drivers\lj388**, and then click **OK**.

13. In the **Select Device** dialog box, click **HP LaserJet 5P/5MP**, and then click **OK**.

14. To close the Print Server Properties window, click **Close**.

15. On Acapulco, close all windows, log off and pause the virtual machine.

Lesson: Troubleshooting Printers and Print Jobs

- **What Are Print Permissions?**
- **How to Manage Print Permissions**
- **How to Redirect Print Jobs**
- **How to Move and Reset a Print Spooler**
- **How to Troubleshoot Printers and Print Jobs**

Introduction	A *print job* is simply a document waiting in a printer queue to be printed. As a DST, you must know how to control access to printers by using permissions and you must know how to redirect print jobs and move and reset print spoolers.
Lesson objectives	After completing this lesson, you will be able to:

- Explain the purpose and function of print permissions.
- Manage print permissions.
- Redirect print jobs.
- Move and reset a print spooler.
- Troubleshoot printers and print jobs.

What Are Print Permissions?

Print Permission	Description
Print	Allows the user to connect to the printer, print documents, and manage their own documents
Manage Documents	Allows the user to connect to the printer, manage all documents, and control print settings for all documents
Manage Printers	Allows the user to perform all the tasks included in the Print and Manage Documents permissions

What are print permissions?

Print permissions specify the type of access that a user or group has to a printer. Using and modifying specific print permissions is important in a corporate environment where printers are shared from servers and controlled by an administrator. In most corporate network environments, users are not allowed to share printers from their local computers. However, in a home network environment, specific permissions are not as important and default permissions are suitable.

You can assign printer permissions to printers in Windows XP Professional. Windows XP Home Edition does not support printer permissions. In Windows XP Professional, there is only one set of permissions that apply to printers, and these permissions are in effect when a printer is accessed both locally and remotely.

Note   You cannot assign specific permissions if simple file sharing is enabled in Windows XP Professional or in Windows XP Home Edition. For more information about simple file sharing, see "How to Verify and Modify NTFS File and Folder Permissions" in Module 6, "Resolving File and Folder Issues," in Course 2261, *Supporting Users Running the Microsoft Windows XP Operating System.*

Managing print permissions

When a printer is installed on a network, default printer permissions are assigned that allow all users to print and that allow select groups to manage the printer, the documents sent to it, or both. Because the printer is available to all users on the network, you might want to limit access for some users by assigning specific printer permissions.

For example, all non-administrative users in a department could have the Print permission, while all managers have the Print and Manage Documents permission. That way, all users and managers can print documents, but managers can also change the print status of any document sent to the printer.

Basic printer permissions

For each user account or group, you can assign the following basic printer permissions: Print, Manage Documents, Manage Printers, and Deny. When multiple permissions are assigned to a group of users, the least restrictive permissions apply. However, when Deny is applied, it takes precedence over any other permission. The following table lists and describes the basic printer permissions.

Printer permission	Description
Print	Allows users or groups to connect to a printer, print documents, and manage their own documents in the print queue. Managing a document includes the ability to pause, resume, restart, and cancel the document.
Manage Documents	Allows users to connect to the printer, manage all documents in the print queue, and control print settings for all documents. This permission does not include the ability to print documents.
Manage Printers	Allows the user to perform all the tasks included in the Print and Manage Documents permissions. In addition, the user can pause and resume the printer, take the printer offline, share the printer, change printer properties, delete a printer, and change printer permissions.

Advanced printer permissions

You can control most printer security requirements by using basic permissions, but sometimes you might need to use advanced permissions. Advanced printer permissions include Read Permissions, Change Permissions, and Take Ownership.

To access advanced permission, on the printer properties page, on the **Security** tab, click Advanced. Using the Advanced Security Settings for *printer* (where *printer* is the name of your printer), you can apply printer permissions in a more granular manner. You can specify one type of permission for documents only, for the printer only, or for both the printer and documents.

Printing permissions assigned to groups

Windows assigns printer permissions to six groups of users. By default, each group is assigned a combination of the Print, Manage Documents, and Manage Printers permissions as shown in the following table.

Group	Print	Manage Documents	Manage Printers
Administrators	X	X	X
Creator Owner		X	
Everyone	X		
Power Users	X	X	X
Print Operators	X	X	X
Server Operators	X	X	X

Note   The Print Operators and Server Operators groups are located only on domain controllers. Also, by default, members of the Administrators and Power Users groups have full access, which means that these users are assigned the Print, Manage Documents, and Manage Printers permissions.

Level of access associated with print permissions

Each permission consists of a group of special rights that allows the user to perform specific tasks. The following table summarizes the level of access that is associated with each of the printing security permissions.

Task permitted	Print	Manage Documents	Manage Printers
Print	X		X
Manage Documents		X	
Manage Printers			X
Read Permissions	X	X	X
Change Permissions		X	X
Take Ownership		X	X

How to Manage Print Permissions

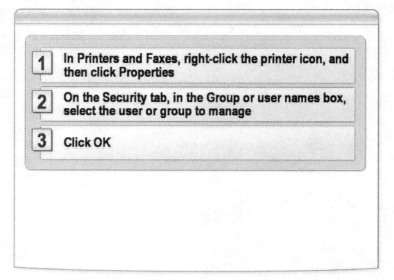

Introduction

You add, edit, and remove printer permissions on the **Security** tab of the printer's Properties page.

How to manage print permissions

To manage print permissions:

1. In Printers and Faxes, right-click a printer icon, and then click **Properties**.

2. In the **Properties** dialog box, on the **Security** tab, in the **Group or user names** box, select the user or group you want to manage:

    *   To add a user or group, click **Add**.

    *   To remove a user or group, click **Remove**.

    *   To edit a user's or group's permissions, select the group or user name you want to edit, and then in the **Permissions for** *group or user name* box, select or clear the appropriate check boxes.

    Note   To manage print permissions, you must have the Administrator permissions. To view or change the Print, Manage Printers, and Manage Documents print permissions, in Printers and Faxes, right-click the printer icon, click **Properties**, and then in the **Properties** dialog box, click the **Advanced** tab.

    ---

3. Click **OK** to close the **Properties** dialog box.

How to Redirect Print Jobs

1	In Printers and Faxes, click Add a printer
2	In the Add a Printer Wizard, click Next
3	Click Local printer attached to this computer, and click Next
4	Clear the Automatically detect and install my Plug and Play printer check box, and click Next
5	Click Create a new port
6	In the Type box, click Local Port, and then click Next
7	In the Enter a port name box, type the share name, and complete steps in the wizard

What is redirection?

Redirection makes it possible to send print jobs that are waiting in the queue of one printer to another printer, as long as the printers are the same or they use compatible drivers. For example, if a printer stops working and you still have print jobs pending for that printer, you can redirect those print jobs to another printer.

How to install a printer with a redirected local port

When you redirect a printer, you configure the printer to print to a local port that is configured to send print jobs to another shared printer on the network.

To install a printer with a redirected local port:

1. In Printers and Faxes, click **Add a printer**.
2. In the Add a Printer Wizard, click **Next**.
3. Click **Local printer attached to this computer**, and then click **Next**.
4. Clear the **Automatically detect and install my Plug and Play printer** check box, and then click **Next**.
5. Click **Create a new port**.
6. In the **Type** box, click **Local Port**, and then click **Next**.
7. In the **Enter a port name** box, type the share name *PrintServer\Sharename*, where *PrintServer* is the name of the computer with the print share, and *Sharename* is the share name of the printer, and then complete the steps in the wizard.

How to redirect documents from a failed printer to a different printer

To modify the port settings of a failed printer:

1. In Printers and Faxes, right-click the printer icon, and then click **Properties**.
2. In the **Properties** dialog box, on the **Ports** tab, click **Add Port**.
3. In the **Printer Ports** dialog box, click **Local Port**, and then click **New Port**.
4. In the **Port name** box, type the share name (*PrintServer\Sharename*), and then click **OK**.

How to Move and Reset a Print Spooler

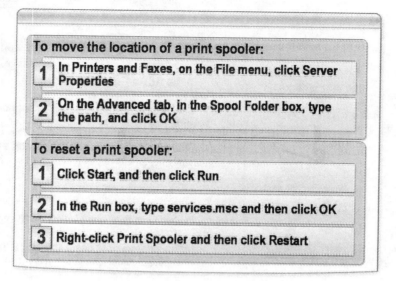

To move the location of a print spooler:

1. In Printers and Faxes, on the File menu, click Server Properties
2. On the Advanced tab, in the Spool Folder box, type the path, and click OK

To reset a print spooler:

1. Click Start, and then click Run
2. In the Run box, type services.msc and then click OK
3. Right-click Print Spooler and then click Restart

Introduction

In Windows, a print spooler controls the print spooling process.

How to move the location of the print spooler

There may be instances, such as a lack of sufficient storage space on drive C, when it is desirable to move the spooler location. The default spooler location is C:\Windows\System32\spool\Printers.

To move the location of the print spooler:

1. In Printers and Faxes, on the **File** menu, click **Server Properties**.
2. In the **Print Server Properties** dialog box, on the **Advanced** tab, in the **Spool Folder** box, type the path that you want to use, and then click **OK**.

How to reset a print spooler

At times, it may be necessary to reset the print spooler. For example, if a document becomes stuck in the queue and you are unable to delete it or cancel printing, you may need to reset the spooler.

To reset the spooler:

1. Click **Start**, and then click **Run**.
2. In the **Run** box, type **services.msc** and then click **OK**.
3. In the **Services** dialog box, right-click **Print Spooler**, and then click **Restart**.

How to Troubleshoot Printers and Print Jobs

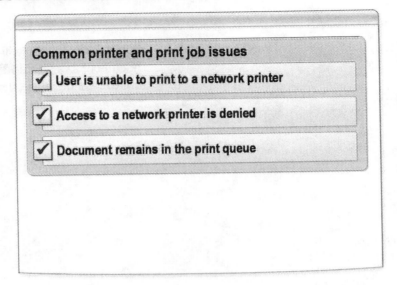

Common printer and print job issues

✓ User is unable to print to a network printer

✓ Access to a network printer is denied

✓ Document remains in the print queue

Introduction

Printing problems can be related to print permissions or to the print jobs themselves.

Issues with network printers

If a user is unable to print to a network printer, verify that the user can connect to other network resources. For example, if the user can access network shares, the problem is most likely not related to the network connection.

If a user attempts to print to a network printer and receives an error message stating that access is denied, the problem could be with the permissions that are granted to or denied that user. If the problem is caused by a permission issue, you should escalate the issue to a system administrator who can grant the proper permissions. If the user is the administrator, such as in a home network, have the user check the permission settings on the computer where the error message was received.

Issues with the print queue

Many printers display a message in the print queue when a printing problem occurs, such as being out of paper. If a user is unable to print, have the user double-click the printer's icon to view documents that are waiting in the queue. Problems with the document are listed in the Status column.

If a document that is sent to a local printer does not print and it remains in the print queue where it cannot be deleted, have the user stop and restart the Print Spooler service in the Services snap-in (services.msc).

Practice: Troubleshooting Printers and Print Jobs

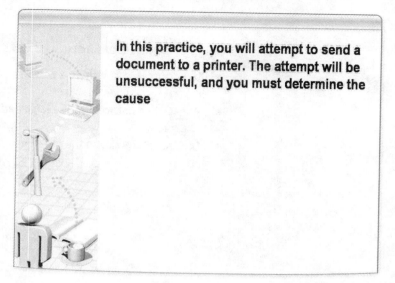

In this practice, you will attempt to send a document to a printer. The attempt will be unsuccessful, and you must determine the cause

Objective

In this practice, you will modify printer permissions to send a document to a printer. The attempt will be unsuccessful, and you must determine the cause.

Practice

▶ **Print a document**

1. Resume the 2261_London and 2261_Acapulco virtual machines.

2. On London, log on to the domain as Administrator with a password of **P@ssw0rd**.

3. Click **Start**, and then click **Printers and Faxes**.

4. Right-click the **HP LaserJet 5** printer, and then click **Properties**.

5. On the **Security** tab, click **Everyone**, in the Permissions for Everyone box select **Deny** for the **Print** permissions.

6. Click **OK**.

7. In the Security warning dialog box, click **Yes**.

8. Using Acapulco, log on to the domain as **AcapulcoAdmin** with a password of **P@ssw0rd**.

9. Click **Start**, and then click **Run**.

10. In the **Open** box, type **notepad**, and then click **OK**.

11. In Notepad, type **Hello World**, click **File**, and then click **Print**.

12. Confirm that **HP LaserJet 5 on London** is selected, and then click **Print**.

Note If HPLaserJet 5 is not listed among the available printers, click **Add Printer** and follow the steps in the "Installing and Creating a Local Printer" practice.

What error did you receive? Why?

_____

_____

_____

13. In the **Notepad** message box, click **OK**.

14. Close the Untitled Notepad window, and then click **No**.

15. For all running and paused virtual machines, on the **Action** menu, click **Close**, select **Turn off and delete changes**, and then click **OK**.

Lab: Resolving Printer Issues

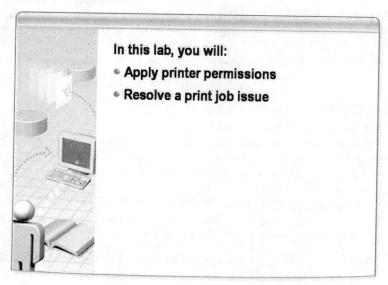

In this lab, you will:
- Apply printer permissions
- Resolve a print job issue

Objectives

After completing this lab, you will be able to:

- Apply printer permissions to solve printer problems.
- Resolve a print job problem by redirecting it to another printer.

Prerequisites

Before working on this lab, you must have an understanding of how to use Microsoft Virtual PC.

Before You Begin

For each exercise in this lab, use a password of **P@ssw0rd**.

In Virtual PC, right-ALT+DEL is the equivalent of CTRL+ALT+DEL.

Estimated time to complete this lab: 30 minutes

Exercise 1
Applying Printer Permissions

In this exercise, you will troubleshoot a situation in which two groups of users require different access to the same physical printer.

Scenario

Northwind Traders has both full-time employees and contract staff. Only full-time employees should be able to print to the color laser printer after business hours. You have been asked to solve this problem by installing two software printers that print to the same physical printer connected to London. On the software printer designated for contractors, you will limit hours of availability and enable contractors to print to it. The other software printer will have no time restrictions, however, only Northwind Traders full-time employees will be allowed to print to it.

Tasks	Guidance for completing the task
1. Start the London and Acapulco virtual machines, and using London, log on to the NWTRADERS domain as Administrator with a password of **P@ssw0rd**	▪ Use the Virtual PC console.
2. Using London, install and share two HP Color LaserJet 4500 printers.	▪ Use the Printers and Faxes window. ▪ Name the printers HP Color Internal and HP Color External. ▪ Both software printers will print to the same physical printer on port LPT1. ▪ If prompted for Windows XP source files use C:\Win2k3\i386 as source file directory.
3. Apply appropriate permissions to each printer.	▪ Two Domain local groups have been created for your use: Northwind FTEs, Northwind Contractors
4. Verify that permissions are set correctly.	▪ The issue is considered resolved when the contract staff are unable to print to the color laser printer after business hours. ▪ Leave both virtual machines running for the next exercise.

Exercise 2
Troubleshooting Print Job Issues

In this exercise, you will troubleshoot a print job problem.

Scenario

You receive a call from a customer who says, "My printer stopped working. I tried turning it off and back on again but nothing happens. I share this printer with 15 other people in the processing department, and all their print jobs are still in the queue. Everyone is yelling at me. A coworker in the sales group has the same printer and he is sharing his also, so can I tell everyone to print to that one instead? And what should I do about all the jobs already in the queue? Can I take my PC down to his office and plug into his printer and still get the jobs to print? I really do not want to have to do that. Do you know of a better way?"

Tasks	Guidance for completing the task
1. Using London, set Generic1 to work offline.	▪ Setting Generic1 to work offline simulates a non-working printer in our scenario.
2. Using Acapulco, log on to the domain as Administrator and print a document to the Generic1 printer.	▪ Use notepad to create and print a text file.
3. Resolve the issue.	▪ Refer to the How to Redirect Print Jobs topic. ▪ The issue is considered resolved when you are able to redirect the existing document in the Generic1 queue and have it processed by Generic2.
4. Close both virtual machines without saving changes.	

Microsoft®

Module 8: Resolving Installation Issues

Contents

Overview

- Pre-Installation Tasks
- Troubleshooting an Attended Installation
- Troubleshooting an Upgrade
- Troubleshooting an Unattended Installation
- Troubleshooting the Boot Process

Introduction

As a desktop support technician (DST), you may be called on to support users who are attempting to install Microsoft® Windows® XP Professional and Microsoft Windows XP Home Edition. Before you can support users who are installing Windows XP, you need to understand the tasks that must be performed prior to installing the operating system. In this module, you will learn how to support users as they prepare for and perform successful installations of Windows XP.

Objectives

After completing this module, you will be able to:

- Describe the tasks that must be performed on a computer before installing an operating system.
- Troubleshoot an attended installation.
- Troubleshoot an upgrade to an existing operating system.
- Troubleshoot an unattended installation.
- Troubleshoot the boot process.

Lesson: Pre–Installation Tasks

- Verify System Requirements and Hardware Compatibility
- Choose a Disk Partition or File System
- How to Use WPA to Activate Windows XP
- How to Install Updates

Introduction

Installing Windows XP is not difficult; however, there are a number of important tasks that you must perform prior to installation. For example, you must ensure that the minimum hardware and software requirements are met and that your hardware and software are compatible. After you have done this, you must choose a file system on the disk drive so that the operating system can write information to it.

After you complete these tasks, you must activate Windows XP and then update any necessary applications or devices. Finally, if you are upgrading from an older version of the operating system, you will need to move your files and settings to Windows XP. This lesson describes these pre-installation tasks.

Lesson objectives

After completing this lesson, you will be able to:

- Verify system requirements and hardware compatibility.
- Choose the appropriate file system.
- Use Windows Product Activation (WPA) to activate Windows XP.
- Install updates, including Windows Update, Automatic Update, and Dynamic Update.

Verify System Requirements and Hardware Compatibility

- **Verify hardware meets minimum system requirements**
    - 233-MHz processor from Pentium/Celeron family or AMD K6/Athlon/Duron family
    - 64 MB of RAM
    - 1.5 GB of spare disk space
    - Video adapter capable of Super VGA (800x600) resolution
    - CD-ROM or DVD drive
    - Keyboard and mouse or other compatible pointing device
- **Check hardware and software compatibility**
    - Windows Catalog: http://www.microsoft.com/windows/catalog/

Introduction

Many hardware and software devices originally written or designed for Windows 95, Windows 98, or Windows Millennium Edition are incompatible with Windows XP and will not run properly on the operating system. To ensure that Windows XP successfully installs, you should advise users to verify that their hardware meets the minimum system requirements, and ensure hardware and software compatibility.

Verify system requirements

Microsoft recommends the following system requirements for Windows XP:

- Minimum system requirements:
    - 233-megahertz (MHz) processor from the Pentium/Celeron family or from the AMD K6/Athlon/Duron family
    - 64 megabytes (MB) of RAM
    - 1.5 gigabytes (GB) of spare disk space
    - Video graphics adapter (VGA) capable of Super VGA (800×600) resolution
    - CD-ROM or DVD drive
    - Keyboard and mouse or compatible pointing device
- Recommended system requirements:
    - 300-MHz central processing unit (CPU)
    - 128 MB of RAM

Check system compatibility

The following resource is useful for ensuring hardware and software compatibility:

Windows Catalog. The Windows Catalog includes information about products that are specifically designed for Windows XP and products that are compatible with Windows hardware and software. You can access the Windows Catalog at http://www.microsoft.com/windows/catalog/.

Tip   Recommend that users run the Windows XP Upgrade Advisor and Windows XP Professional Setup in the Check Upgrade Only mode before installing Windows XP. The Upgrade Advisor is a utility that examines the current system and produces a report that lists problems that you might encounter during the upgrade process, including hardware and software incompatibilities. You can download the Upgrade Advisor in an executable form at http://www.microsoft.com/windowsxp/home/upgrading/advisor.mspx.

The Check Upgrade Only mode tests the upgrade process and gives you a report that shows potential problems before you actually install Windows XP. The report lists hardware and software compatibility issues, such as unsupported Plug and Play hardware, unsupported software, and software that should be reinstalled after the upgrade. To run Windows XP Professional Setup in Check Upgrade Only mode, run Winnt32.exe from the i386 folder with the command-line switch checkupgradeonly.

Choose a Disk Partition or File System

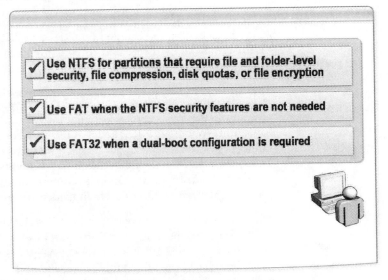

Introduction	The most important disk decision a user must make when installing Windows XP is determining which file system to choose for each drive or volume. The user must determine:

- How many disk partitions to create.
- Whether to combine space from multiple physical disks into a single volume.
- Which file system to use to format drives.

Before you help a user answer these questions, you must understand the function of disk partitions and the types of file systems that are used by Windows XP. This section explains the function of disk partitions and FAT, FAT32, and NTFS and then explains when to use each file system.

What is a hard disk?	A *hard disk* is a physical disk drive that is installed in a computer. The computer's first hard disk is identified as Disk 0; additional hard disks are identified as Disk 1, Disk 2, and so on. Windows XP Professional allows you to define two types of hard disks:

- Basic disks. A hard disk that can be accessed by all MS-DOS®-based and Windows-based operating systems.
- Dynamic disks. A hard disk that can be accessed only by Windows 2000 and Windows XP.

What is a disk partition?	A *disk partition* is a portion of a hard disk that functions as though it is a physically separate disk. After you create a partition, you must format it and assign a drive letter to it before you can save data on it. On basic disks, partitions are known as *basic volumes,* which include primary partitions and logical drives. On dynamic disks, partitions are known as *dynamic volumes,* which include simple, striped, spanned, mirrored, and a redundant array of independent disks (RAID)-5 volumes.

What appears in My Computer as one hard disk drive might actually correlate to more than one physical device. A single physical device can be subdivided into partitions, volumes, or logical drives—each appearing in My Computer as a separate drive letter. In Windows XP Professional, you can combine storage space from several physical devices so that it appears as a single drive letter.

Types of disks partitions

There are three critical types of partitions:

The *active partition* is the partition that contains the hardware-specific files required for x86-based computers to start up. The active partition must be a primary partition. If you use Windows exclusively, the active partition can be the same as the system volume.

The *system partition* is the partition that contains the hardware-specific files needed to load Windows. On most computers, the system partition is the first primary partition on Disk 0, which is identified as drive C.

The *boot partition* is the partition that contains the Windows operating system files (located in the Windows folder) and its support files (located in the Windows\system32 folder). On most systems, the boot partition is the same as the system partition. On a multiboot system, if drive C contains files from an earlier Windows version and you have installed Windows XP to drive D or drive E, then the boot partition is identified as such in the Disk Management window. On dynamic disks, the boot partition is known as the boot volume.

Note   For additional information about disk storage in Windows XP, see article 314343 in the Microsoft Knowledge Base.

What are FAT, FAT32, and NTFS?

A file system is the overall structure in which files are named, stored, and organized. Windows XP uses the following types of file systems:

- *FAT* is a table that the operating system uses to locate files on a disk. Due to fragmentation, a file may be divided into many sections that are scattered around the disk, and FAT keeps track of these pieces.

- *FAT32* is a derivative of the FAT file system. FAT32 supports smaller cluster sizes and larger volumes than FAT, which results in more efficient space allocation on FAT32 volumes.

- *NTFS* is an advanced file system that provides performance, security, reliability, and advanced features that are not found in any version of FAT. If a system fails, NTFS uses its log file and checkpoint information to restore the consistency of the file system.

The main features of FAT, FAT32, and NTFS

The following table summarizes the main features of the three file systems.

Feature	FAT	FAT32	NTFS
Maximum partition size	7.8 GB	32 GB	16 exabytes
Sector size	16 kilobytes (KB) to 64 KB	As low as 4 KB	As low as 4 KB
Security	File attributes	File attributes	File, folder, and encryption
Compression	None	None	Files, folders, and drives

When to choose a file system

With a clean installation, users must choose a file system during Windows Setup. When upgrading from Windows 98 or Windows Millennium Edition, users can choose whether to convert their current file system to a different file system. When repartitioning an existing drive or adding additional drives to an existing system, users must choose a file system again.

When to use NTFS

NTFS is the recommended file system for Windows XP Professional because it provides a higher level of security and enables file compression. Use NTFS for partitions that require:

- File- and folder-level security to control access to files and folders.
- File compression to create more storage space.
- Disk quotas to control disk usage on a per-user basis.
- File encryption to transparently encrypt file data.

If you plan to access files that are on a local Windows XP Professional partition with the Windows 95 or Windows 98 operating systems, you should format the partition with a FAT or FAT32 file system.

When to use FAT or FAT32

Usually, you would not use FAT to format the partition on which Windows XP Professional resides because it does not provide the file- and folder-level security that NTFS provides. However, if you do not require the security and compression features that are available with NTFS, or if you require a dual-boot configuration to run applications that are not compatible with Windows XP Professional, you might need to use FAT32.

FAT and FAT32 do not provide file- and folder-level security, and FAT does not support partitions larger than 7.8 GB. If you attempt to use FAT to format a partition larger than 7.8 GB, you must perform an unattended installation using oemextend parameter.

Note   When you upgrade an operating system on an existing FAT or FAT32 partition to Windows XP Professional, you have the option to use NTFS or FAT32. If you choose NTFS, you can convert the partition to NTFS or format the partition using NTFS. If the partition contains data that you want to keep after the installation, do *not* format the partition. Instead, choose to convert the partition to NTFS to preserve the data.

Important   Some operating systems, such as MS-DOS 6.22 or earlier and Windows 95, do not recognize partitions that are formatted with FAT32 or the NTFS file system.

How to Use WPA to Activate Windows XP

Windows Product Activation:

- Enforces license restrictions
- Disables users from using the same CD and product key on multiple computers

Introduction

Before you can install Windows XP, you must activate it. This section describes how to use Windows Product Activation (WPA) to activate Windows XP.

What is WPA?

WPA is a Windows XP antipiracy feature that uses license restrictions to prevent the most common form of software piracy, casual copying. *Casual copying* is the sharing and installation of software that is not in compliance with the software's End-User License Agreement (EULA). A Windows XP license usually entitles a user to install the operating system software on one computer. If a user attempts to use the same CD and product key to install Windows XP on a second computer, the software will fail to activate.

WPA also requires users to activate Windows XP within 30 days of installing the operating system. Users can do this either by connecting to a Microsoft activation server over the Internet or by calling a toll-free number and speaking with a user service representative at a WPA clearinghouse.

How to use WPA

Using WPA to activate Windows XP is a simple process that entails:

1. Selecting an activation method (over the Internet or using a modem connected to a phone line).

2. Microsoft verifying the license.

3. Confirming the license and activating the product.

Note Activation is not registration. The activation process is completely anonymous and does not require you to divulge personal information. If you choose to register your copy of Windows XP, this is a completely separate and optional process.

Common user issues with WPA

The following list describes the most common issues users have with using WPA:

- The user cannot locate WPA. The icon for WPA is located in the Notification area on the desktop and may not be obvious. Direct the user to locate the icon on the lower right side of the desktop or click **Start**, and then click **Activation** or click **All Programs**, click **Accessories**, click **System Tools**, and then click **Activate Windows**.

- The Windows XP has been activated but the user cannot locate online help. After the operating system has been activated, the icon for WPA is removed from the Notification area on the desktop. Direct the user to access WPA by using Help and Support.

- The user did not activate Windows XP and now they cannot log on. After the 30-day grace period, WPA prevents interactive logon. Direct the user to boot into safe mode to activate, upgrade, and retrieve data.

Reinstalling and reactivating Windows XP

You can reinstall Windows an unlimited number of times on the same hardware. During the activation process, Windows XP transmits an encrypted file that registers key components on your computer. If you reinstall Windows XP on the same hardware, the activation server checks the key components against the database. If the key components match, activation is enabled.

If you upgrade your hardware, you might need to reactivate Windows XP. Call a user service representative to assist you with the reactivation process.

If you want to move a retail copy of Windows XP from one computer to another, you must first completely uninstall Windows XP from the first computer. When you install Windows XP on the second computer and attempt to activate Windows, it will fail because the hardware is different. The activation wizard will supply you with a toll-free number to call a user service representative. Explain to the representative that you want to move your copy of Windows XP to another computer, and the user service representative will provide a 42-digit confirmation ID.

When WPA requirements are exempt

WPA requirements may be exempt for users who buy:

- Copies of Windows XP sold with new computers. If you purchase a new computer with Windows XP preinstalled on it, the activation process may have been completed. Further, you can reinstall Windows XP an unlimited number of times, regardless of how many upgrades you make, as long as you do not change the basic input/output system (BIOS). (*BIOS* is the set of essential software routines that test hardware at startup, start the operating system, and support the transfer of data.) In fact, you can replace the motherboard on a system activated with WPA as long as the new part is from the same manufacturer and uses the same BIOS identifier. However, you may be prohibited by the license agreement from transferring that copy of Windows to another computer.

- Copies of Windows XP through a volume licensing (VL) program. Some corporations are exempt from WPA requirements even if they purchase as few as five copies of Windows XP if the software is bought through a Microsoft VL program. These corporations receive VL media and product keys that do not require activation. Under the terms of a volume license agreement, each computer with a copy of Windows XP must have a valid license.

How to Install Updates

- **Windows Update**
  - Includes minor changes and critical updates
  - Repairs issues that:
    - Affect system performance
    - Compromise security
    - Cause system crashes
- **Automatic Update**
  - Enables operating system to automatically check for critical updates on a regular basis

---

Introduction

After you install the operating system, you must ensure that the latest critical security and compatibility updates are installed on the system. This section describes how to use Windows Update and Automatic Update to obtain the most recent updates and fixes and to protect your computer and keep it running smoothly.

What are service packs?

Microsoft publishes changes to Windows. Some changes are minor additions to the Windows feature set. Other changes are designated as critical updates. Critical updates (hotfixes) repair bugs that can hamper system performance, compromise security, or cause system crashes. At regular intervals, Microsoft gathers these updates into collections called *service packs* and makes them available for download. Applying a service pack to your computer is functionally equivalent to—and much simpler than—individually installing all the updates.

What is Windows Update?

Windows Update is an online extension of Windows that helps you keep your computer up to date. It provides access to the entire collection of newly released updates for the Windows operating system, software, and hardware. The list of available updates includes service packs, updated device drivers, and security updates.

How to run Windows Update

You can run Windows Update from a variety of locations.

To run Windows Update:

- Click **Start**, click **Help and Support**, and then under **Pick a task**, click **Keep your computer up-to-date with Windows Update**.

  -or-

- Click **Start**, click **All Programs**, and then click **Windows Update**.

  -or-

- Click **Start**, click **Run**, and then at the command prompt, type **wupdmgr**.

  -or-

- In Microsoft Internet Explorer, on the **Tools** menu, click **Windows Update**.

  -or-

- In Internet Explorer, navigate to http://v5.windowsupdate.microsoft.com/v5consumer/default.aspx?ln=en-us.

Windows Update categories

The following table lists the categories for the Windows operating system updates.

Update	Includes
Critical Updates	Security fixes and other important updates to keep a computer current and the network secure
Recommended Downloads	The latest Windows and Internet Explorer service packs and other important updates
Windows Tools	Utilities and other tools to enhance performance, facilitate upgrades, and ease the burden on system administrators
Internet and Multimedia Updates	The latest Internet Explorer releases, upgrades to Microsoft Windows Media® Player, and other media-related features
Additional Windows Downloads	Upgrades for desktop settings and other Windows features
Multi-Language Features	Menus and dialog boxes, language support, and Input Method Editors for a variety of languages

What is Windows Update Catalog?

Windows Update Catalog is intended for advanced users and network administrators who want to download updates for other computers and distribute them over a corporate network. The list of available updates includes Windows updates, fixes, enhancements, and Designed for Windows Logo device drivers.

What is Automatic Update?

Windows XP includes a feature named Automatic Update. When Automatic Update is enabled, the operating system automatically checks for critical updates on a regular basis. Using the preferences you define, Automatic Update checks for new critical updates, downloads them in the background using a small segment of your available Internet connection bandwidth, and installs them automatically.

**How to configure
Automatic Update**

To configure Automatic Update:

1. In Control Panel, click **Performance and Maintenance**, and then click **System**.

2. In the **System Properties** dialog box, on the **Automatic Updates** tab, select one of the following three options:

   - **Automatic (recommended)**

     Choose this option if you want Windows Update to automatically download and install critical updates for you. The default time is 3:00 A.M. every day.

   - **Download updates for me, but let me chose when to install them**

     This option is most appropriate for users with a high-speed, constant Internet connection, such as a cable modem or a Digital Subscriber Line (DSL). An icon in the notification area alerts you when a download is available. You can accept or reject any download. If you reject an update that has been downloaded, Windows deletes the downloaded files from your computer.

   - **Notify me but don't automatically download or install them**

     Choose this option if you do not want to tie up your dial-up Internet connection while downloading updates. An icon in the notification area alerts you when a download is available. You can accept or reject any update.

   Important   Automatic Update retrieves only *critical* updates. To view, download, and install other Windows updates and newly released drivers, you must visit the Windows Update Web site at http://v5.windowsupdate.microsoft.com/v5consumer/default.aspx?ln=en-us.

**What is Dynamic
Update?**

Dynamic Update enables Windows XP Setup to check the Windows Update Web site for new Setup files, including drivers and other files, while Windows XP is being installed.

Dynamic Update decreases the need to apply patches to recently installed systems, and makes it easier to run Setup with hardware that requires a driver that was recently added or updated on Windows Update. For example, if a new video adapter requires a driver that was recently added to Windows Update, with Dynamic Update, the video adapter is recognized and supported during Setup.

How to run Dynamic Update

To run Dynamic Update:

1. From Windows Update Catalog, click **Find updates for Microsoft Windows operating systems**.

2. Under **Operating system**, select **Windows XP Home Edition or Windows XP Professional**.

3. Click **Advanced search options** to display additional search criteria.

4. Under **Update types**, select the **Service Packs and Recommended Downloads** check box, clear all other check boxes, and then click **Search**.

5. Under **Your search returned *n* results**, click **Service Packs and Recommended Downloads**.

6. Under **Dynamic Setup Updates**, click **Add**, and then click **Go to Download Basket**.

7. Type the path to the network share where you want to copy the Dynamic Update package, and then click **Download Now**.

Lesson: Troubleshooting an Attended Installation

- How to Create Setup Boot Disks
- How to Boot When the CD-ROM Drive Is Unavailable
- How to Start Setup from MS-DOS
- How to Configure a Computer to Run Multiple Operating Systems
- How to Repair an Installation
- How to Troubleshoot an Attended Installation

Introduction

An attended installation refers to a manual installation that requires user input. There are many different ways to perform an attended installation; you can do a clean install on a new computer, a clean install from another version of Windows, or upgrade from another version of Windows. Regardless of how an attended installation is performed, users who perform this type of installation will likely require your assistance. This lesson describes issues you can expect users to encounter when attempting to perform an attended installation and provides procedures for solving these issues.

Lesson objectives

After completing this lesson, you will be able to:

- Create setup boot disks.
- Explain how to boot a computer when the CD-ROM drive is unavailable.
- Start Setup from MS-DOS.
- Explain how to configure a computer to run multiple operating systems.
- Repair an installation.
- Troubleshoot an attended installation.

How to Create Setup Boot Disks

* Use Windows XP startup disks to perform new installation on computers without a bootable CD-ROM

* Download Windows XP startup disks from Microsoft

To create the setup boot disks for Microsoft Windows XP, you need six blank, formatted, high-density disks

---

Introduction

Windows XP Setup is designed to run directly from a CD-ROM. However, if a computer does not support this function, you can run Setup by using setup boot disks. This section describes how to create setup boot disks.

What are setup boot disks?

Setup boot disks are used to load the drivers that are required to access a CD-ROM drive. The CD-ROM drive is then used to start Setup. You do not perform an installation or upgrade by using Windows XP setup boot disks.

Note Future products will not support installation using setup boot disks. Installing future Microsoft operating systems will require booting from a CD or performing a Pre-Boot execution Environment (PXE) boot from a network. *PXE boot instructions* can direct controlled devices to boot using a virtual floppy disk, to boot and run the Deployment Agent, or to boot and run the operating system image installed on the hard disk. For more information about using setup boot disks, see http://www.microsoft.com/downloads/details.aspx?FamilyID=e8fe6868-6e4f-471c-b455-bd5afee126d8&displaylang=en.

Note Windows XP Home Edition startup disks will not work for Windows XP Professional installations, and Windows XP Professional startup disks will not work for Windows XP Home Edition installations.

How to create the setup boot disks

Setup boot disks are downloaded from Microsoft in one large program file. When you run the downloaded file, it extracts the files you need to create the setup boot disks. The high-level process for creating setup boot disks is as follows:

1. Run the downloaded file. The following message is displayed:

   "This program creates the setup boot disks for Windows XP. To create these disks, you need to provide six blank, formatted, high-density disks."

2. Type the drive letter for the disk drive, which is typically drive A. After you click **OK**, the following message is displayed:

   "Insert one of these disks into drive *drive letter*. This disk will become the Windows XP setup boot disk. Press any key when you are ready."

3. When you press a key, the downloaded file starts extracting and copying the files.

4. Continue inserting the blank disks as you are prompted until all six disks are created. If the process is interrupted, you must run the downloaded program file again to create all six disks.

Note   Setup boot disks for Windows XP Setup are available only from Microsoft.

How to Boot When the CD-ROM Drive Is Unavailable

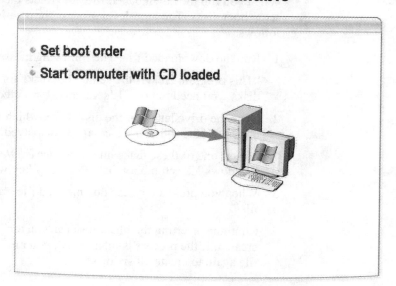

- **Set boot order**
- **Start computer with CD loaded**

Introduction

Most computers that meet the minimum requirements for Windows XP include the capability to boot from a CD-ROM drive. However, in some configurations, this option is not available. This section describes how to boot when the CD-ROM drive is unavailable.

Why this issue occurs

An unavailable CD drive occurs most frequently when the CD-ROM is connected to a SCSI adapter that does not allow booting from a CD or if the user is trying to install Windows XP on a portable computer that does not include an integrated CD drive.

Set the boot order to solve this issue

For a bootable CD to work properly, set the boot order in the BIOS so that the CD drive appears ahead of the hard disk drive and any other bootable media. The boot options available are different for every computer, as is the technique for accessing the BIOS setup program.

During boot, watch for a message that tells which key to press for setup. Often the BIOS setup program includes a **Boot** tab in which you can specify the order of boot devices. If this option is not immediately apparent, look for a page named Advanced CMOS Settings or something similar.

How to Start Setup from MS-DOS

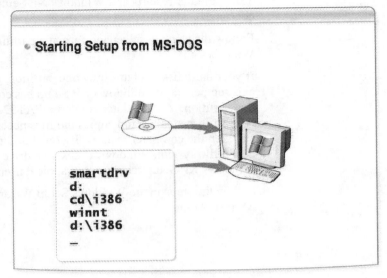

• Starting Setup from MS-DOS

```
smartdrv
d:
cd\i386
winnt
d:\i386
_
```

Introduction

When you cannot (or do not want to) use setup boot disks, you can start Setup from the MS-DOS prompt. This section describes this procedure.

Procedure

To start Setup from the MS-DOS prompt:

1. Insert the Windows XP CD-ROM in the CD-ROM or DVD-ROM drive.

2. Start the computer to an MS-DOS prompt with CD-ROM support. For CD-ROM support, you will need real-mode MS-DOS drivers.

   Note If the computer does not have MS-DOS installed, or it does not allow you to choose to start to an MS-DOS prompt in the **Boot** menu, see Microsoft Knowledge Base article 187632.

3. Start SMARTDrive if it is not already started. (*SMARTDrive* is a disk caching system that provides faster access to data on a hard disk.) To start SMARTDrive, switch to the folder that contains the Smartdrv.exe file, type **smartdrv** and then press ENTER. If you do not use SMARTDrive, you may notice that the portion of Windows XP Setup that copies files to the hard disk performs slowly.

4. At the command prompt, type *drive:* (where *drive* is the drive that contains the Windows XP CD-ROM), and then press ENTER.

5. Type **cd\i386**, and then press ENTER.

6. Type **winnt**, and then press ENTER.

   Windows XP Setup starts.

7. Type the path to the Windows XP installation files, and then press ENTER. For example, type **d:\i386**.

   Windows Setup copies files to the hard disk.

8. Remove any floppy disks from the computer, and then press ENTER.

   The computer restarts and Windows XP Setup resumes. Press ENTER to continue.

9. Follow the steps to select and format a partition in which to install Windows XP.

   If your hard disk contains only one partition, do not delete it from the list of existing partitions. Windows XP Setup has copied the installation files to this partition. You can later convert a FAT32-formatted partition to the NTFS file system. Setup copies the files necessary for Windows XP Setup, and then the computer restarts. If you chose to format the drive by using the NTFS file system, Windows checks the drive for errors and then restarts. Windows XP Setup resumes in graphical user interface (GUI) mode.

10. Follow the steps in the Windows Setup Wizard to complete the Windows XP installation.

How to Configure a Computer to Run Multiple Operating Systems

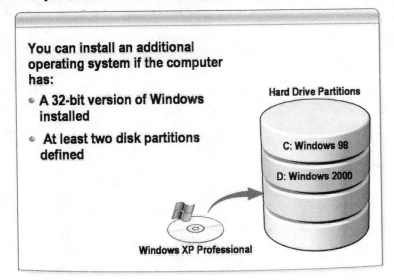

You can install an additional operating system if the computer has:

• A 32-bit version of Windows installed

• At least two disk partitions defined

Hard Drive Partitions

C: Windows 98

D: Windows 2000

Windows XP Professional

What is a multiboot configuration?

If a computer has the 32-bit version of Windows installed and at least two disk partitions are defined, you can install a clean copy of Windows XP without disturbing the existing Windows installation. At boot time, you choose the Windows version from a startup menu. Although this is typically called a *dual-boot system*, it is more accurate to call it a *multiboot configuration,* because you can theoretically install more than two copies of Windows NT, Windows 2000 Professional, and Windows XP.

Why have multiple operating systems?

The ability to choose an operating system at startup is valuable if a program or device will not work with Windows XP. For example, when you must use an older program or device, you can boot into the other Windows version. This capability is also useful for software developers who must test how their programs work under different operating systems. For experienced Windows users, installing a second copy of Windows XP in its own partition can be a useful way to test a program or device driver that is not certified as Windows XP–compatible without compromising the working system. If, after thorough testing, the program is determined safe to use, it can be added to Windows XP.

Requirements for a multiboot configuration

The requirements for running multiple operating systems include:

- The active partition must be formatted with a file system that is recognized by both operating systems because this partition is used to boot the system. For example, the active partition must be formatted with FAT when you have a dual-boot configuration with MS-DOS and Windows XP Professional. The active partition must be formatted with FAT32 when you have a dual-boot configuration with Windows 98 and Windows XP Professional.

- Windows XP Professional must be installed after the other operating system is installed. After the installation of the first operating system, Windows XP Professional can be installed on the active partition or on another primary or extended partition.

Selecting the operating system

After the new operating system is installed, it appears on the startup menu. The new operating system becomes the default menu option. It runs automatically if 30 seconds pass and you do not choose an operating system.

Additional reading

For more information on multiboot configurations, see Knowledge Base article 217210.

How to Repair an Installation

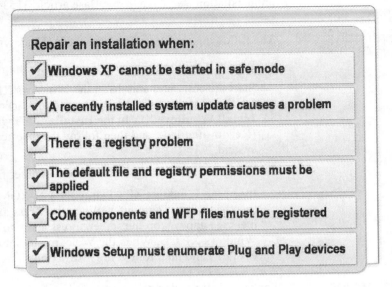

Repair an installation when:

✓ Windows XP cannot be started in safe mode

✓ A recently installed system update causes a problem

✓ There is a registry problem

✓ The default file and registry permissions must be applied

✓ COM components and WFP files must be registered

✓ Windows Setup must enumerate Plug and Play devices

Introduction

As a DST, there will be times when you will assist users in repairing an installation. The easiest way to repair an installation is to reinstall the operating system (perform an in-place upgrade). This section describes the circumstances in which a repair is required and the two methods for reinstalling a Windows XP installation.

Reasons to repair an installation

You may need to repair an installation for any of the following reasons:

- You cannot start Windows XP in safe mode. (*Safe mode* is a method of starting the operating system by using only the default settings necessary to start the computer.)

  Note   For additional information about how to start a Windows XP–based computer in safe mode, see Knowledge Base article 315222.

- A problem is caused by a recently installed system update (Windows Update, hotfix, Windows XP service pack, or Internet Explorer update), and you cannot solve the problem in any other way.
- There is a registry problem that cannot be solved by using other tools, such as System Restore or the recovery console.
- You must apply default file and registry permissions to the Windows XP installation.
- You must register Component Object Model (COM) components and Windows File Protection (WFP) files. (WFP prevents the replacement of protected system files, such as .sys, .dll, and .exe files.)
- You need Windows Setup to enumerate Plug and Play devices again, including the hardware abstraction layer (HAL).

Important   For information on the steps that you should take before you repair an installation, see Knowledge Base article 315341.

How to reinstall Windows XP

The following are two ways to reinstall Windows XP:

1. Reinstall Windows from within the operating system.

   Start the computer and insert the Windows XP CD into the CD-ROM or DVD-ROM drive. On the **Welcome to Microsoft Windows XP** page, click **Install Windows XP**. In the **Installation Type** box, click **Upgrade (Recommended)**, and then follow the instructions to reinstall the operating system.

2. Reinstall Windows by starting the computer from the startup CD.

   Insert the Windows XP CD into the CD-ROM or DVD-ROM drive, and then restart your computer. When the **Press any key to boot from CD** message appears on the screen, press a key to start the computer from the Windows XP CD. When the Welcome to Setup screen appears, press ENTER, and then follow the instructions.

Additional reading

For more information about repairing an installation, see Knowledge Base article 326676.

How to Troubleshoot an Attended Installation

Step	General troubleshooting process steps
1	Determine what has changed
2	Eliminate possible causes to determine probable causes
3	Identify a solution
4	Test the solution

Introduction

As a DST, your main objective in troubleshooting an attended installation is to help the user determine the cause of the installation problem. Remember that the troubleshooting process should be a logical process of elimination, whereby you eliminate in rapid order the possibilities that are *not* the issue. The pattern generally applied to the troubleshooting process is as follows:

1. Determine what has changed.
2. Eliminate possible causes to determine probable causes.
3. Identify a solution.
4. Test the solution.

General troubleshooting guidelines

A variety of problems can occur during an installation, and an equal number of solutions can be applied to each problem. However, the following guidelines can help you identify the problem:

1. Restart the computer.
2. Make sure any new hardware or software is properly installed. Unplug each new hardware devices, one at a time, to see if this resolves the error. If it does, go to step 3. Replace any hardware that proves faulty by this test. Also, try running any hardware diagnostic software supplied by the computer manufacturer. If this is a new installation of hardware or software, contact the manufacturer for any necessary Windows XP Professional updates or drivers.
3. Click **Start**, and then click **Help and Support**. Click **Get support, or find information in Windows XP newsgroups** (under **Ask for assistance**), and then click **Get help from Microsoft** in the left-hand column.
4. Click **Start**, click **Help and Support**, and then click **Fixing a problem** (under **Pick a Help topic**) for a list of Troubleshooters.
5. Check the Windows Catalog to verify that all the hardware and drivers are compatible with Windows XP Professional.

6. Disable or remove any newly installed hardware (RAM, adapters, hard disks, modems, and so on), including drivers and software.

7. If you have Internet access, visit the Microsoft Support site at http://support.microsoft.com.

8. Using a current version of antivirus software, check the computer for viruses. If you find a virus, perform the steps required to eliminate it from the computer. See the antivirus software instructions for these steps.

9. Verify that the hardware device drivers and the system BIOS are the latest available versions. The hardware manufacturer can help to determine the latest versions or help to obtain them.

10. Disable BIOS memory options such as caching or shadowing. If you need assistance, contact the hardware manufacturer.

11. Run any system diagnostic software supplied by the computer manufacturer, especially the memory check.

12. Verify that the computer has the latest service pack installed. For a list of service packs, go to the Windows Update Web site at http://v5.windowsupdate.microsoft.com

13. If you are unable to log on, restart the computer. When the list of available operating systems appears, press F8. On the **Advanced Options** screen, select **Last Known Good Configuration**, and then press ENTER.

Important   When you use last known good configuration, system setting, changes made after the last successful startup are lost. Last known good configuration is discussed later in this module.

Using installation log files to troubleshoot an attended installation

Windows XP generates log files during text-mode setup that can help you determine the cause of a failed installation. You will find the following files in the Windows directory in which you installed Windows:

- Setuplog.txt
- Setupapi.log

To troubleshoot a Windows XP installation, copy these two files to a floppy disk, take them to another computer, and then open the files using Notepad. These files may contain clues to help you identify the problem. For example, locate the last device that was installed by looking in the Setupapi.log file. Then, if the Setuplog.txt file indicates that a hardware device or driver is causing the problem, verify that the hardware is supported by that version of Windows.

GUI-mode setup includes log files that can help you troubleshoot a failed installation, such as:

- Setuperr.log. This file is created if errors occur during setup.
- Setupapt.log. This file records actions that are taken during setup.
- Setuplog.txt. This file describes tasks performed during setup.
- Setupapi.log and PNPlog.txt. These files list hardware and driver detection and installation issues.

Additional reading   For more information about troubleshooting attended installations, refer to articles 326676, 316400, and 310064 in the Microsoft Knowledge Base and http://www.microsoft.com/windowsxp/pro/using/howto/gettingstarted/guide /troubleshoot.asp.

Lesson: Troubleshooting an Upgrade

* What Is Upgrade Advisor?
* How to Uninstall an Upgrade
* How to Troubleshoot an Upgrade

Introduction

As a DST, you will receive many calls from users who want to upgrade to the latest operating system. When a user wants to upgrade to Windows XP, you must first determine if the computer is ready for the upgrade. This section describes how to use Upgrade Advisor to evaluate whether the hardware and software are ready for the update. This lesson also describes the specific tasks that users can perform before upgrading that will help them avoid common problems.

Lesson objectives

After completing this lesson, you will be able to:

- Explain the purpose and function of Upgrade Advisor.
- Uninstall an upgrade.
- Troubleshoot an upgrade.

What Is Upgrade Advisor?

Upgrade Advisor:

- Checks system hardware and software to verify system readiness for upgrade

- Prepares a report listing potential problems during the upgrade process

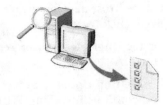

Introduction

Upgrade Advisor is a tool that checks system hardware and software to determine if it is ready for an upgrade to Windows XP. Before you can use Upgrade Advisor, you must first determine if the current version of Windows can be upgraded to Windows XP. If the version is eligible for upgrade, you can download Upgrade Advisor.

The Upgrade Advisor report

Upgrade Advisor produces a report that lists potential problems the user might encounter during the upgrade process, such as hardware and software incompatibilities. For example, Upgrade Advisor may advise the user to download a particular service pack. Upgrading from Windows 98 or Windows Millennium Edition to Windows XP sometimes requires uninstalling a particular application before upgrading to Windows XP, and then reinstalling the application after Windows XP Setup is complete.

How to run Upgrade Advisor

Windows XP Setup automatically runs Upgrade Advisor when upgrading from a previous version of the Windows operating system. However, you can also run Update Advisor manually without starting installation process.

To run Update Advisor manually:

- Insert the Windows XP CD into the CD-ROM or DVD-ROM drive. On the **Welcome to Microsoft Windows XP** page, click **Check System Compatibility**, and then click **Check My System Automatically**.

Note If the opening menu of the CD does not appear, at any command prompt, type *d*:**\i386\winnt32 -checkupgradeonly** where *d* is the correct drive letter.

To run Upgrade Advisor from the Microsoft Web site:

1. Log on to the domain as *ComputerName***Admin** with a password of **P@ssw0rd**.

2. Click **Start**, click **Run**, type **http://www.microsoft.com/windowsxp /home/howtobuy/upgrading/advisor.asp** and then click **OK**.

3. Click **Download the Upgrade Advisor**, and then click **Open**.

4. In **Microsoft Windows XP Upgrade Advisor**, click **Next**.

5. Click **I accept this agreement**, and then click **Next**.

6. On the **Download the latest files?** page, click **Next**.

7. On the **Most new hardware and software will work with Windows XP** page, click **Next**.

8. On the **Upgrade Advisor report issues in two main categories** page, click **Next**.

9. If a **Getting Updated Setup Files** window appears, select **Skip this step and continue installing Windows**, and then click **Next**.

10. Upgrade Advisor lists the results in the **Report System Compatibility** window. To view any incompatibilities, click **Details**. After you review the results (if any), click **Finish** to close this window, and then click **Finish** again to close Upgrade Advisor.

11. Close all windows.

Note   The Report System Compatibility window lists any incompatibilities between Windows XP and the installed hardware and software. In addition, if the user's computer requires updates that are available on the Windows Update Web site, Upgrade Advisor locates and installs the updates and reports its actions.

Additional reading   For more information about running Upgrade Advisor, see Knowledge Base article 307726.

How to Uninstall an Upgrade

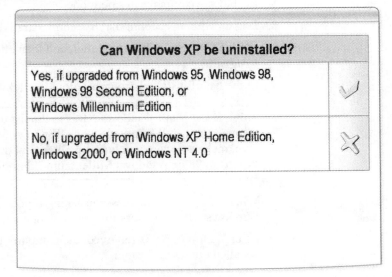

Can Windows XP be uninstalled?	
Yes, if upgraded from Windows 95, Windows 98, Windows 98 Second Edition, or Windows Millennium Edition	✓
No, if upgraded from Windows XP Home Edition, Windows 2000, or Windows NT 4.0	✗

Key points

Occasionally, users will upgrade the operating system on their computers only to find that they cannot use a necessary program or application in the new environment. They may want to uninstall the newer operating system and revert to the prior operating system.

Before you can assist a user in uninstalling Windows XP, you must consider the following factors:

- To successfully uninstall Windows XP, the user must have upgraded from Windows 95, Windows 98, Windows 98 Second Edition, or Windows Millennium Edition.

- If the user upgraded from Windows XP Home Edition, Windows 2000 Professional, or Windows NT 4.0, Windows XP cannot be uninstalled.

- If the user intends to remove Windows XP and return to Microsoft Windows 95, Windows NT, or Windows 2000 Professional, the user must:

  a. Reinstall Windows 95, Windows NT, or Windows 2000 Professional.

  b. Restart the computer in safe mode.

  c. Back up all of the critical data before reinstalling Windows 95, Microsoft Windows NT®, or Windows 2000 Professional.

Other factors for consideration include the amount of available free disk space and the potential impact of uninstalling the upgrade on programs already installed on the computer.

Procedure

To uninstall Windows XP:

1. Restart the computer in safe mode.

2. Log on with an account that has administrative credentials.

3. Click **Start**, click **Control Panel**, and then click **Add or Remove Programs**.

4. In the list of installed programs, double-click **Uninstall Windows XP**.

Note   If Uninstall Windows XP is in the list of installed programs, you must manually reinstall Windows 98 or Windows Millennium Edition. In this case, make sure that you back up all critical data before reinstalling Windows 98 or Windows Millennium Edition.

---

5. When you receive the message asking if you are sure you want to uninstall Windows XP and restore the previous operating system, click **Yes**.

6. After Windows XP is removed, the computer restarts to the previously installed operating system.

Additional reading

For more information about uninstalling an upgrade, see Knowledge Base article 303661.

How to Troubleshoot an Upgrade

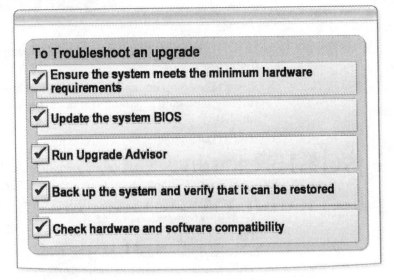

To Troubleshoot an upgrade

✓ Ensure the system meets the minimum hardware requirements

✓ Update the system BIOS

✓ Run Upgrade Advisor

✓ Back up the system and verify that it can be restored

✓ Check hardware and software compatibility

Introduction

When upgrading any operating system, the best advice is to avoid installation issues. This section lists the steps you can take to avoid problems when upgrading to Windows XP and then discusses how to troubleshoot some issues that can occur.

Preventing upgrade issues

Most upgrade-specific problems can be prevented by taking a few measures before starting the upgrade. Before upgrading any system, perform all of the following actions:

- Ensure that the system meets the minimum hardware requirements.
- Update the system BIOS.
- Check hardware and software compatibility.
- Run Upgrade Advisor.
- Back up the system and verify that the system can be restored.
- Turn off any power management and antivirus features in the computer's BIOS.
- Remove all antivirus software.
- Uncompress all hard disks.
- Run ScanDisk and ScanReg.
- Download available driver updates.
- Quit all running programs.

Troubleshooting a Setup program that stops responding

When upgrading to Windows XP, the computer may stop responding (hang) and a black screen may appear. This behavior is usually caused by either hardware or software that is incompatible with Windows XP. To work around this issue:

1. Wait 10 to 15 minutes to ensure that the computer does not continue the Setup procedure.

2. Restart the computer and ensure that the computer does not continue running the Setup program. If it does, restart until the Setup program finishes.

3. Restart the computer and cancel Setup.

4. Remove any antivirus programs, and then perform a clean boot.

5. If the upgrade stops again, there may be a hardware incompatibility issue and you may need to disable any unnecessary hardware and then restart the Setup program.

6. If the Startup program continues to stop responding, disable any unnecessary hardware, remove USB devices, network cards, and sound cards, and then restart the Setup program.

7. If the Startup program continues to stop responding, consider flashing the BIOS on the motherboard. Refer to the computer's manufacturer for information about how to do this.

8. If the BIOS does not resolve the issue, consider installing Windows XP with a standard PC HAL.

Troubleshooting file error messages

When upgrading to Windows XP, you may receive an error message stating that Windows cannot copy a particular file or a particular file is corrupt or missing. The following are some of the reasons this can occur:

- The Windows XP CD-ROM is scratched or dirty.

- The CD-ROM drive is not working correctly.

- You are using multiple CD-ROM drives.

- The computer has damaged or mismatched RAM or cache memory.

Lesson: Troubleshooting an Unattended Installation

- What Is an Unattended Installation?
- Methods for Performing an Unattended Installation
- Tools Used to Perform an Unattended Installation
- Disk Imaging in an Unattended Installation
- RIS in an Unattended Installation
- How to Troubleshoot an Unattended Installation

Introduction

Not every Windows XP installation is done manually. Large-scale deployments would be too costly and time-consuming if an administrator had to personally set up large numbers of computers. Such installations are therefore usually automated, using unattended or remote processes, such as Sysprep and Remote Installation Services (RIS). Because performing an unattended installation is a complex process that is typically performed by a network administrator, you should refer calls regarding this installation method to the appropriate support level. Understanding the basics of unattended installation will help you collect appropriate information so that you can identify the issue and escalate it as appropriate.

Lesson objectives

After completing this lesson, you will be able to:

- Explain the purpose and function of an unattended installation.
- Describe the methods for performing an unattended installation.
- Describe the tools used to perform an unattended installation.
- Describe the use of disk imaging in an unattended installation.
- Describe the use of RIS in an unattended installation.
- Troubleshoot an unattended installation.

What Is an Unattended Installation?

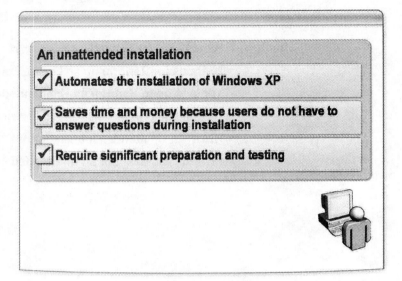

An unattended installation

- ✓ Automates the installation of Windows XP
- ✓ Saves time and money because users do not have to answer questions during installation
- ✓ Require significant preparation and testing

Introduction

An unattended installation is an automated method for installing Windows XP. Unattended installations are commonly used to perform bulk installations with minimal user intervention. It is the most flexible and versatile automated method of deploying the Windows XP Professional operating system. Unattended installations also speed up the deployment process, minimize user involvement during installation, and ensure consistency throughout an organization, which lowers support costs.

Advantages and disadvantages of unattended installations

Performing an unattended installation has the following advantages and disadvantages:

- Advantages. Unattended installations save time and money because users do not have to attend to each computer and answer questions during installation. Unattended installations can also be configured to enable users to provide input during the installation process. Also, unattended installations can be performed to upgrade many computers at once or to automate clean installations of the operating system.

- Disadvantages. Unattended installations require significant preparation and testing and may not be suitable for small deployments.

When an unattended installation is used

Unattended installations are typically used when:

- Upgrading a Windows operating system to Windows XP Professional.
- Performing automated installations on computers that have heterogeneous hardware configurations.
- Configuring a wide range of operating system settings during an automated installation without using batch files and scripts.
- Creating master installations for image-based and RIS installations.

Methods for Performing an Unattended Installation

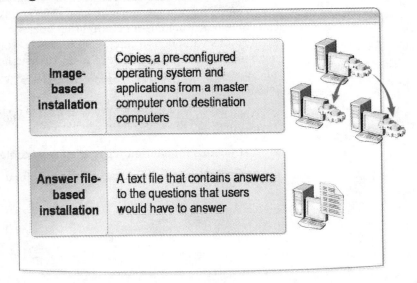

Image-based installation	Copies, a pre-configured operating system and applications from a master computer onto destination computers
Answer file-based installation	A text file that contains answers to the questions that users would have to answer

Introduction

Two methods are used to perform an unattended installation: Image-based installations and answer-file based installation. This section describes these two methods.

Image-based installation

The Image-based installation method copies, or clones, a preconfigured operating system and software applications from a master computer onto destination clients and servers.

Standardizing hardware and software—including application settings and directory structures—into a common, supportable corporate desktop on workstations across organizations has become a common practice. In some cases, the fastest way to deploy these standardized workstations involves duplication of a model workstation's hard disk to other computers within your organization.

1. The base operating system is installed on a clean, newly formatted system

2. Applications are installed

3. A standard corporate workstation "image" is created

4. The disk-image duplication process is used to deploy additional corporate desktop systems.

Answer file-based installation

To perform an unattended installation, you must first create an answer file. An *answer file* is a text file that contains answers to the questions that Windows Setup normally prompts the user for during an installation. An answer file also can contain instructions for configuring operating system settings and installing applications without user intervention. Before you can troubleshoot an unattended installation, you need to understand how Setup uses answer files. The answer file-based installation method uses a text file that contains setup instructions. These instructions include:

- Answers to the questions that Windows Setup normally presents during an installation.

- Instructions for configuring operating system settings.

- Instructions for installing applications without user intervention.

Tools Used to Perform an Unattended Installation

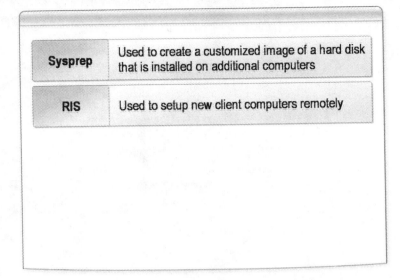

Sysprep	Used to create a customized image of a hard disk that is installed on additional computers
RIS	Used to setup new client computers remotely

Introduction	Windows XP includes tools that can be used to perform an unattended installation: Ssprep.exe and RIS. This section discusses these tools.
Sysprep	Windows XP include Sysprep, a program that allows an administrator to duplicate a customized image of a complete hard disk partition. After the image is created, the administrator can install this image on additional computers. Sysprep is useful for deploying a clean Windows XP Professional installation to hundreds of computers that require the same applications and desktop configurations. Sysprep uses disk imaging as the deployment method. As a DST, you could suggest that a user install a new image when the user has difficulties with another type of installation, or you might suggest an attended installation when the user is unable to successfully install an image
RIS	RIS enables an administrator to set up new client computers remotely without having to visit each client. The target clients must support remote booting. RIS can be used to perform a clean installation of Windows XP Professional on supported computers throughout an organization. The operating system can be simultaneously deployed on multiple clients from one or more remote locations.

Disk Imaging in an Unattended Installation

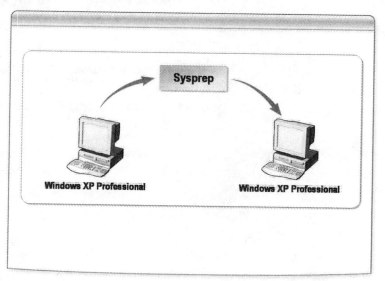

Introduction

Disk imaging involves first configuring a reference computer with Windows XP Professional, the appropriate desktop settings, and any applications users require. After this is done, an image is created of the reference computer's hard disk and transfer the image to other computers in the organization. This section describes the process of installing disk images.

Important To successfully duplicate a system image, the administrator must make sure that the computer hardware is compatible with the software contained in the image. Because a disk image has the foundation of the operating system preinstalled, and much of this information is hardware dependent, the image is suitable only for computers that have a hardware configuration very similar to the original machine. If the hardware configuration is not similar, Setup may fail or the resultant installation may experience problems accessing hardware components.

How disk imaging works

The following is the process that Sysprep uses to perform disk imaging:

1. Prepares the reference computer for disk imaging.

2. Creates a unique security identifier (SID) for each client computer which makes the process secure.

3. Detects Plug and Play devices and adjusts for systems with different devices.

4. Runs Setup Manager to select the screens displayed during Windows Welcome (Msoobe.exe) or during Min-Setup. These screens can be used to solicit user-specific information, such as user name or time zone selection.

Completing disk duplication

When you boot a duplicated system for the first time, the operating system executes a partial Windows setup process. This setup process detects and installs variations in hardware settings and user preferences.

Users complete the installation process in one of two ways, depending on the option selected by the administrator:

- Standard Disk Duplication
- Disk Duplication with Automated Mini Setup

Standard Disk Duplication

With Standard Disk Duplication, the setup process completes automatically when the user boots the computer for the first time. Setup performs the following tasks:

- Detects Plug and Play devices
- Runs the Windows Welcome portion of Windows Setup, which allows users to set up user accounts and to activate Windows
- Deletes the Sysprep folder and its contents
- Reboots the computer

Tip   If a user calls with a question about this process, focus troubleshooting efforts on these four tasks. Remember that the other installation processes were completed during the initial installation.

Disk Duplication using Automated Mini Setup

The process of duplicating a hard disk using Automated Mini Setup is very similar to the standard duplication process, except that during the boot process, it presents users with a series of Windows Setup dialog boxes. These dialog boxes allow users to specify additional settings, such as regional settings and the End-User License Agreement.

As with a regular unattended setup, administrators can create an answer file to automatically answer these questions for the user.

Tip   If a user calls with a question about the Automated Mini Setup process, focus troubleshooting efforts on the phases described previously, and if an answer file is in use, be sure to troubleshoot that file as well.

RIS in an Unattended Installation

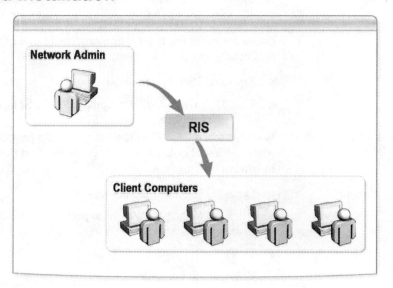

Introduction

This section covers only the client portion of RIS. It discusses how PXE-enabled computers can boot to the network to install Windows, as well as how to accomplish a RIS installation by creating a RIS-boot disk for non-PXE-enabled computers.

Important   Usually, a RIS-based setup issue is either an escalation issue or an issue for the user's IT department.

RIS on a PXE-enabled system

Computers equipped with a PXE DHCP-enabled boot read-only memory (ROM) network adapter can boot directly to a location on the network to access operating system installation files. If the BIOS was configured to boot from the network device previously, then when a PXE-enabled computer is first booted, the user can press F12 to perform a network boot. When booted in this fashion, the following occurs:

1. The PXE-enabled system broadcasts for a local DHCP server on the network.

2. The DHCP server responds with the IP address of a RIS server.

3. The PXE-enabled system accesses the RIS server, and the user is presented with a selection of applicable operating system images from which to install.

4. After an operating system is selected, the operating system installation proceeds automatically.

RIS on a non-PXE-enabled system

Computers that do not have PXE-enabled network adapters can still use the RIS system on the network for operating system installs, but they must boot with a RIS-boot disk that contains RIS server information for the network and a rudimentary set of common network card drivers to allow the client to connect to the network. The client computer must be configured to boot from the floppy device first.

The network administrator provides the RIS-boot disk. It is created on the RIS server by executing the Rbfg.exe utility from within the Remoteinstall\Admin folder of the server.

When the client computer is booted from the RIS-boot disk, the disk attempts to load the appropriate network card driver. It then emulates a PXE-enabled boot environment for the purposes of completing the RIS-based installation.

Additional reading

For more information on supported network adapter drivers, see Knowledge Base article 314836.

How to Troubleshoot an Unattended Installation

* Troubleshooting answer file issues
  * Local install – Command-line switch
  * Local install – CD-ROM
  * Network install
* Troubleshooting installation of a disk image
* Troubleshooting RIS installation issues

Introduction

Many unattended setup issues occur within a large corporate environment where the user is not a network administrator. Often, this type of call results in referring the user back to the organization's IT department for help.

If the caller is a network administrator, tier 1 support should attempt to address the general issue, collect information, and refer the caller to the appropriate support line, or to escalate the issue if the DST can positively identify the issue as a client issue.

The more challenging issues for the DST are those that involve a user at home, perhaps on a home network, attempting to run an unattended installation using an answer file.

Troubleshooting answer file issues

Unattended setup issues can be varied and obscure, whether the operating system is installed locally from the Windows CD or from a network share. The most important issue is to ensure that the user is accessing the unattended setup answer file appropriately, as follows:

- Local install – command-line switch

  Ensure that the answer file exists and is referenced properly in the **/unattend** switch at the command line.

- Local install – CD-ROM

  Ensure that:

  - The answer file has been copied to a disk and the disk is in the drive at boot time.

  - The answer file has been renamed Winnt.sif.

  - The Windows CD is in the CD-ROM drive at boot, and the BIOS is configured to boot from the CD drive.

- Network Install

  In this scenario, the user installs an unattended installation either by connecting to the network share on which the Windows source files are located and running the appropriate setup batch file, or the user boots with the appropriate setup disk. The network administrator should resolve both issues.

  In the former case, failure of the script to launch is highly unlikely. Other, more obscure issues might result in the unattended install, but the network connectivity issue is already resolved.

  In the latter case, the user must verify that the network connection is working and that the setup disk is capable of enabling the required network card for connectivity to the network share to occur. This situation is similar to troubleshooting non-PXE-enabled RIS-boot setup.

Troubleshooting installation of a disk image

Because using a disk image entails so many hardware-dependent and IT-dependent issues, most issues are the responsibility of the IT department that manages the images. Users should contact their network administrators to assist in resolving these types of issues.

Troubleshooting RIS installation issues

In the case of RIS-based installations, most issues should be referred to the user's network administrator because the entire back-end process is out of the user's control. However, you can check a few things regarding hardware configuration and network connectivity.

1. Find out whether the user's computer is PXE-enabled.

   a. Does the user have the option of booting to the network by pressing F12 at system start?

   b. Is the PXE-enabled network adapter set as the first boot option in the BIOS, if, in fact, it is an option?

   If the card is enabled and the user is booting to the network but the install fails, refer the user to his or her network administrator to resolve the issue or to open an incident report with the appropriate Windows server support line.

2. If the user's computer is not PXE-enabled:

   a. Does the user have the required RIS-boot disk?

   b. Does the user's computer have a network adapter model using a driver supported by the RIS-boot disk? (See Knowledge Base article 314836 for a list of supported drivers.)

   c. Is the user relatively certain that this specific computer on this specific network connection had connectivity in the past? Can the user test the network connection by plugging it into another computer already installed and running on the network?

   If these steps fail to resolve the issue, refer the user to his or her network administrator to resolve the issue or to open an incident report with the appropriate Windows server support line.

Lesson: Troubleshooting the Boot Process

- **What Is the Boot Process?**
- **How to Use the Last Known Good Configuration**
- **How to Use the Recovery Console to Resolve Startup Issues**
- **How to Configure Automated System Recovery**
- **How to Troubleshoot the Boot Process**

Introduction

The startup process for any operating system entails its own set of potential issues. This lesson describes how to use advanced boot options and the last known good configuration to troubleshoot startup issues.

Lesson objectives

After completing this lesson, you will be able to:

- Describe the boot process.
- Explain how to use the last known good configuration for troubleshooting.
- Use the Recovery Console to resolve startup issues.
- Configure Automated System Recovery (ASR).
- Troubleshoot the boot process.

What Is the Boot Process?

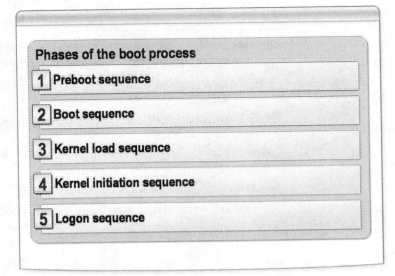

Phases of the boot process

1 Preboot sequence

2 Boot sequence

3 Kernel load sequence

4 Kernel initiation sequence

5 Logon sequence

Introduction

The Windows XP Professional boot process closely resembles that of Microsoft Windows NT and Microsoft Windows 2000, but significantly differs from Microsoft MS-DOS, Microsoft Windows 95, Microsoft Windows 98, and Microsoft Windows Millennium Edition. Before you can troubleshoot the boot process, you should understand the phases of the boot process and the files that required for the process.

Phases of the boot process

All computers running Windows XP Professional share the same startup process:

1. The preboot sequence

2. The boot sequence

    a. Initial boot loader phase

    b. Operating system selection phase

    c. Hardware detection phase

    d. Configuration selection phase

3. Kernel load sequence

4. Kernel initiation sequence

    a. Hardware key is created

    b. Clone control set is created

    c. Device drivers are loaded and initialized

    d. Services are started

5. Logon sequence

Note The preceding boot process applies to systems started or restarted after a normal shutdown, and does not apply to when a computer is brought out of hibernation or standby.

Files used during the boot process

For Windows XP Professional to start, the system and boot partitions must contain the files listed in the following table.

File name	Location	Boot sequence used
Ntldr.exe	System partition root directory	Preboot and boot
Boot.ini	System partition root directory	Boot
Bootsect.dos	System partition root directory	Boot (optional)
Ntdetect.com	System partition root directory	Boot
Ntoskrnl.exe	*Systemroot*\System32	Kernel load
Ntbootdd.sys	System partition root directory	Preboot (used only when using a small computer system interface [SCSI] controller)
Hal.dll	*Systemroot*\System32	Kernel load
System	*Systemroot*\System32\Config	Kernel initialization
Device Drivers *(*.sys)*	*Systemroot*\System32\Drivers	Kernel initialization

The string *systemroot* (typed as %systemroot%) is a placeholder for the folder name in the boot partition that contains the Windows XP Professional system files.

Ntbootdd.sys is the first SCSI driver file, renamed and copied to the system partition.

Additional reading

For more information on supported network interface card drivers, see Knowledge Base article 314836.

How to Use the Last Known Good Configuration

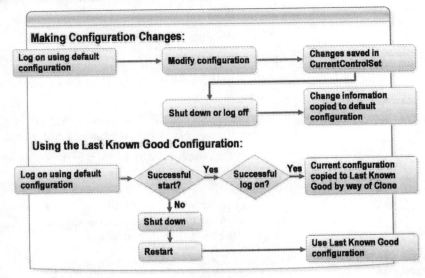

Introduction

Windows XP provides two configurations for starting a computer: the default configuration and the last known good configuration. You will usually use the default configuration, unless the default configuration is not operating correctly, in which case the last known good configuration is used.

Making configuration changes

You usually start a computer by using the default configuration. Each time you make a configuration change on a computer, the change is immediately stored in the **CurrentContolSet**. When the computer is shut down or restarted, those changes are copied to the default configuration, which is used the next time the computer is started. If you make a configuration change, such as adding a new device driver, and then encounter problems restarting the computer, it may be because the configuration changes damaged the default configuration. In this case, use the last known good configuration to safely restart the computer.

Using the Last Known Good configuration

During the kernel initiation sequence of the boot process, the kernel copies the information in the **CurrentControlSet** to the **CloneControlSet**. After a successful logon, the information in the Clone is copied to the last known good configuration.

If you encounter startup problems that you believe are related to operating system configuration changes, use the last known good configuration to start the computer by following these steps:

1. Shut down the computer without logging on.

2. Restart the computer.

3. When you are prompted to select the operating system from which to start, press F8.

4. On the **Windows XP Professional Advanced Options** menu, use the down arrow to select **Last Known Good Configuration**, and then press ENTER.

5. Select the operating system for which you want to use the last known good configuration, and then press ENTER.

The next time that you log on, the current configuration is copied to the default configuration, which ensures that the default configuration will start the computer the next time it is restarted.

When to use the last known good configuration

The following table describes a computer's default configuration that will require you to use the last known good configuration.

Problem	Solution
After installation of a new device driver, the operating system stops responding.	Use the **Last Known Good Configuration** option during startup, which starts the operating system by using the last known good configuration. The last known good configuration will not contain any reference to the new, and possibly defective, device driver. Note: LKG will *not* work if a driver *update* fails (as opposed to installing a new driver).
A critical device driver is accidentally disabled.	If a critical driver becomes disabled, use the **Last Known Good Configuration** option during startup. Some critical drivers are configured to keep users from accidentally disabling them. If these drivers are damaged, the computer automatically reverts to the last known good configuration the next time that it starts.

When not to use the last known good configuration

Do not use the last known good configuration in the following circumstances:

■ *When the problem is not related to operating system configuration changes.* The last known good configuration can help you solve only configuration problems.

■ *After logging on.* The system updates the last known good configuration with operating system configuration changes at logon.

■ *When startup failures are caused by hardware failures or missing or corrupted files.* The last known good configuration cannot help with these problems.

How to Use the Recovery Console to Resolve Startup Issues

Use the Recovery Console to start computer if Safe mode
and other startup options do not work

Recovery Console Tasks

- Start and stop services
- Reconfigure services
- Read and write data
- Repair system
- Format drives

Introduction

The Recovery Console feature in Windows XP Professional can be used to start the computer if safe mode and other startup options do not work.

Important   To use the Recovery Console, you must have the skills to locate and identify problem files by using basic commands. You must also know the administrator's password to use the Recovery Console.

You can accomplish the following tasks by using the Recovery Console:

- Start and stop services
- Reconfigure services that are preventing the computer from starting properly
- Format drives on a hard disk
- Read and write data on a local drive formatted with the FAT or NTFS file system
- Repair the system by copying a file from a floppy disk or compact disc
- Other administrative tasks

Using the Recovery Console

To use the Recovery Console to start the computer:

1. Start the Recovery Console from the **Operating System Selection** menu or from the operating system CD.

2. If the computer has a dual-boot or multiboot configuration, select the number representing the installation that you want to repair, and then press ENTER.

3. Enter the local administrator's password, and then press ENTER.

    After you enter the administrator's password, a command prompt is displayed. For information about the available commands, type **help**, and then press ENTER.

Important   The Recovery Console is a powerful tool that, if used improperly, can damage the operating system. Only advanced users and IT support professionals should use the Recovery Console, and only if advanced startup options do not solve the problem.

Common reasons to use the Recovery Console

You can use the Recovery Console to fix a variety of startup problems. Some of the most common startup problems and their Recovery Console solutions are defined in the following table.

Problem	Recovery Console solution
A service or device driver is starting but preventing the computer from starting properly.	Use the **disable** command to disable the service or driver, restart the computer without the service or driver functioning, and then determine the problem.
A missing file is preventing the computer from starting properly.	Use the **extract** command to repair the computer by uncompressing a compressed file and copying it from a disk or CD to the appropriate folder.
A missing file is preventing the computer from starting properly.	Use the **copy** command to repair the computer by copying an uncompressed file from a disk or CD to the appropriate folder.
The boot sector is damaged.	Use the **fixboot** command to write a new partition boot sector on the system partition.
The Master Boot Record is damaged.	Use the **fixmbr** command to repair the Master Boot Record on the partition boot sector.

How to Configure Automated System Recovery

- **Saves contents on the system drive to a backup medium, such as:**
  - Second physical disk
  - Network folder
  - Tape drive
- **Saves information about:**
  - Disk partitions
  - System files
  - Detected hardware
- **Does *not* back up or restore data on drives other than the system volume**

What is ASR?

Most people find out the hard way that Automated System Recovery (ASR) works only if a complete backup was prepared in advance. Creating an ASR backup set saves the complete contents of a system drive to the backup medium you select, such as a second physical disk, a network folder, or a tape drive. In addition, ASR saves information about the current arrangement of disk partitions, system files, and detected hardware on a floppy disk. The combination can quickly and effectively restore the system configuration; however, ASR does not back up or restore data on drives other than the system volume. For that task, use the Backup Utility in wizard mode, and choose the option to back up everything on the computer.

ASR is available only in Windows XP Professional.

Important Although the ASR feature is mentioned in the Windows XP Home Edition user interface, Automated System Recovery is not supported in Windows XP Home Edition. For more information, see Knowledge Base article 302700.

How to Troubleshoot the Boot Process

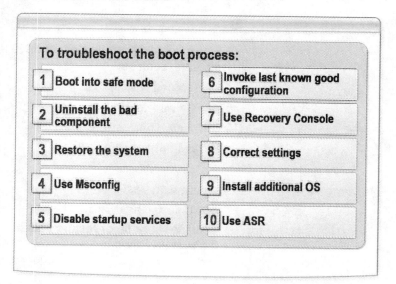

To troubleshoot the boot process:

1 Boot into safe mode	6 Invoke last known good configuration
2 Uninstall the bad component	7 Use Recovery Console
3 Restore the system	8 Correct settings
4 Use Msconfig	9 Install additional OS
5 Disable startup services	10 Use ASR

Introduction

To diagnose and correct a startup problem, you must understand what occurs during startup. The first step in isolating startup problems is to determine whether the problem occurs before, during, or after the operating system starts up.

Startup failures can be caused by a variety of problems, such as user error, application faults, hardware failures, or virus activity. If the condition is serious enough, you might need to reinstall the operating system or restore files from backup media.

In x86-based systems, startup failures that occur before the operating system loader (Ntldr) starts could indicate missing or deleted files or damage to the hard disk Master Boot Record (MBR), partition table, or boot sector. If a problem occurs during startup, the system might have incompatible software or drivers, incompatible or improperly configured hardware, or corrupted system files.

The startup process for Itanium-based computers is similar to that of x86-based computers.

Troubleshooting techniques

Although the following techniques are specifically related to troubleshooting the boot process, they can be useful in troubleshooting other system issues as well.

1. Attempt to boot into safe mode.

    a. If you can boot into safe mode, proceed to step 2.

    b. If you cannot boot into safe mode, proceed to step 7.

2. Attempt to uninstall or remove the component (or roll back the driver) that is suspected of causing the trouble, if applicable.

3. If the user has been systematically creating System Restore points, attempt to restore the system to a previous configuration.

4. Use Msconfig to troubleshoot startup options.

5. Temporarily disable suspect services that might be interfering with the boot process, if applicable. If the problem persists, more complex measures might be necessary and this can be a good time to escalate the issue.

6. Attempt to invoke the last known good configuration.

7. Use the Recovery Console to replace corrupted files or to perform other manual recovery operations.

8. Examine and correct the following:

    a. Boot.ini settings on x86-based systems

    b. Non-Volatile Random Access Memory (NVRAM) startup settings on Itanium-based systems

9. Install an additional instance of the operating system into a different folder, and use the Backup utility to restore operating system files from backup media, if available.

10. Use Automated System Recovery (ASR) (Windows XP Professional only) to reformat the system partition and restore operating system files from backup media.

Lab: Resolving Installation Issues

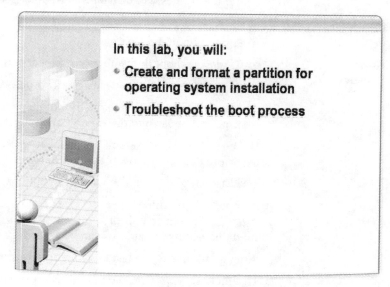

In this lab, you will:

• Create and format a partition for operating system installation

• Troubleshoot the boot process

Objectives

After completing this lab, you will be able to:

■ Create and format a partition for operating system installation.

■ Troubleshoot the boot process.

Prerequisites

Before working on this lab, you must have an understanding of how to use Microsoft Virtual PC.

Before You Begin

For each exercise in this lab, use a password of **P@ssw0rd**.

In Virtual PC, <right>ALT+DEL is the equivalent of CTRL+ALT+DEL.

Scenario

You are a DST for Northwind Traders, a company whose workers use Microsoft Windows XP Professional. Two users call with various Internet Explorer configuration and customization questions.

Estimated time to complete this lab: 30 minutes

Exercise 1
Creating and Formatting a Partition for an Operating System Installation

In this exercise, you will create and format a partition to prepare for a Windows XP Professional installation.

Scenario

A user calls and says that he has recently purchased Windows XP Professional and wants to install it. He is confused about how to prepare his computer for the installation. He is uncertain how to optimally partition his computer's hard disk for Windows XP, but he needs to assign file-level permissions.

Tasks	Guidance for completing the task
1. Boot the 2261_Lab08_Ex1 virtual machine using the Windows XP Professional evaluation CD ISO image.	▪ Use the Virtual PC console. ▪ If you are prompted to insert boot media, verify that you have configured Virtual PC to capture the C:\Program Files\Microsoft Learning\2261\drives\WinXPEval.iso image file.
2. Use the Windows XP Professional setup program to create a partition using 100 percent of the available disk space on the virtual machine.	▪ Abort the setup process after the Setup program has finished examining the disks and begins copying files.
3. Turn off the virtual machine and delete changes.	

Exercise 2
Troubleshooting the Boot Process

In this exercise, you will troubleshoot issues related to an unattended installation.

Scenario

In this exercise, you will troubleshoot a computer that will not start up. When the computer is turned on, the boot process fails but does not display an error message.

You have already escalated this issue to a systems engineer who determined that the boot failure is due to a corrupt Master Boot Record. She advises you to use the Recovery Console to fix the Master Boot Record.

Tasks	Guidance for completing the task
1. Start the 2261_Lab08_Ex02_Bonn virtual machine.	▪ Use the Virtual PC console. ▪ Verify no disc is in the CD-ROM drive.
2. Did the Bonn computer start successfully?	
3. Resolve the boot problem.	▪ Refer to the How to Use the Recovery Console to Resolve Startup Issues topic in this module. ▪ Successful resolution of this issue will result in successfully starting the 2261_Lab08_Ex02_Bonn computer.

Course Evaluation

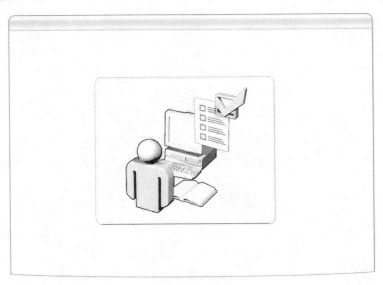

Your evaluation of this course will help Microsoft understand the quality of your learning experience.

To complete a course evaluation, go to http://www.CourseSurvey.com.

Microsoft will keep your evaluation strictly confidential and will use your responses to improve your future learning experience.

Notes